Desolation and Enlightenment

THE LEONARD HASTINGS SCHOFF MEMORIAL LECTURES

Desolation and Enlightenment

POLITICAL KNOWLEDGE AFTER TOTAL WAR, TOTALITARIANISM, AND THE HOLOCAUST

Ira Katznelson

COLUMBIA UNIVERSITY PRESS

NEW YORK

Columbia University Press
Publishers Since 1893
New York, Chichester, West Sussex

Copyright © 2003 Columbia University Press

Library of Congress Cataloging-in-Publication Data
Katznelson, Ira.
  Desolation and enlightenment : political knowledge after total war, totalitiarianism, and the Holocaust / Ira Katznelson.
     p. cm.
  Includes bibliographical references and index.
  ISBN 0–231–11194–0
  1. Political science—Philosophy. 2. Human behavior—Philosophy. 3. Political psychology. 4. Political sociology. 5. World politics—1945–1989. 6. War (Philosophy). 7. International relations—Philosophy. 8. Holocaust, Jewish (1939–1945). 9. Jews—Public opinion—History. I. Title.
JA71 .K35 2002
301'.01—dc21   200231579

Columbia University Press books are printed on permanent and durable acid-free paper
Printed in the United States of America

c 10 9 8 7 6 5 4 3 2 1

Illustration on p. viii:
El sueño de la razón produce monstruos.
(The Sleep of Reason Produces Monsters).
Los caprichos, plate 43.
Photo courtesy of Museo del Prado

For Emma,
who grows as she runs

UNIVERSITY SEMINARS

Leonard Hastings Schoff Memorial Lectures

The University Seminars at Columbia University sponsor an annual series of lectures, with the support of the Leonard Hastings Schoff and Suzanne Levick Schoff Memorial Fund. A member of the Columbia faculty is invited to deliver before a general audience three lectures on a topic of his or her choosing. Columbia University Press publishes the lectures.

DAVID CANNADINE
The Rise and Fall of Class in Britain
1993

CHARLES LARMORE
The Romantic Legacy
1994

SASKIA SASSEN
Sovereignty Transformed: States and the New Transnational Actors
1995

ROBERT POLLACK
The Faith of Biology and the Biology of Faith: Order, Meaning, and Free Will in Modern Medical Science
2000

CONTENTS

PREFACE AND ACKNOWLEDGMENTS

Originally intended by Goya for the frontispiece of his *Los caprichos, The Sleep of Reason Produces Monsters* is the most famous image in this series of etchings. "In sleep, the body is dark," Walter Benjamin explained to Gershom Scholem, "a spectral medium, in the middle of which life and death are located."[1] Goya portrays how, in sleep, demons can haunt reason. This is a book about reason and four decades of its sleep, with cruel and hideous monsters on the loose. It also is an injunctive book about history, social science, and liberal guardianship I offer in critical homage to the generation of my teachers who, in a climate of anxiety, sought to rouse reason and secure its wakefulness.

***

I wrote *Desolation and Enlightenment* before the shattering of lives and cityscapes on September 11, 2001. Some friends have urged me to rewrite sections to underscore its additional pertinence, counseling that the intellectual ef-

---

1. Cited in Jeremy Adler, "In the Absence of God: Isolation, Zionism and the Anguish of Gershom Scholem," *Times Literary Supplement,* January 4, 2002, p. 4. Adler draws on Scholem's diary report of conversations with Walter Benjamin in Switzerland late in the First World War after Scholem had successfully feigned insanity to avoid service in the German military.

forts I discuss by postwar scholars to map the origins of dark times and discern the character of the modern state resonate with themes familiar today. I have decided otherwise. Rather than rework the book to force this 'relevance,' I prefer to leave any such discovery to its readers.

I begin my acknowledgments with a statement of debt to George Steiner's *In Bluebeard's Castle* and to Lionel Trilling's essay, "Elements that are Wanted," concerned with the politics of T.S. Eliot. I read Steiner shortly after I had been invited to offer Columbia University's 1997–98 Leonard Hastings Schoff Memorial Lectures, the basis for this book. Steiner's fierce volume provided my initial impetus. I defined my subject—political knowledge after total war, totalitarianism, the holocaust—in part as an effort to determine why I had been disappointed by his customarily brilliant effort to understand the impact on the West's tradition of Enlightenment on what he called Europe's 1914–1945 "season in hell." Later, I came across Trilling's piece as I set out on my last round of revision. His writing reminded me that the boundaries between liberal and illiberal thought are not nearly as crisp as we might like and that the endowments of the liberal tradition depend on its capacity to engage with values and beliefs that are not easily compatible with its own temperament.

Bluebeard's Castle is based on the T.S. Eliot Memorial Lectures Steiner delivered at the University of Kent at Canterbury in March 1971. The subtitle he selected, *Some Notes Toward the Redefinition of Culture*, refers to *Notes Toward the Definition of Culture*, a powerful collection of essays Eliot had written mainly in 1945 and 1946. That volume, Steiner reproached, is "not an attractive book. One that is gray with the shock of recent barbarism, but a barbarism whose actual sources and forms the argument leaves fastidiously vague."[2] Confronting Eliot's refusal to visit the darkest places of twentieth-century European history, Steiner wrote that[3]

> an analysis of the idea and ideal of culture demands the fullest possible understanding of the phenomenology of mass murder as it took place in Europe. . . . The failure of Eliot's *Notes Toward the Definition of Culture* to face the issue, indeed to allude to it in anything but an oddly condescending footnote, is acutely disturbing.[4]

---

2. George Steiner, *In Bluebeard's Castle: Some Notes Towards the Re-definition of Culture* (London: Faber, 1971), p. 13.
3. Steiner, *Castle*, p. 34.
4. More than this silence offended Steiner. Just a month after delivering the Eliot Lectures, Steiner addressed a letter about "Eliot's anti-semitism" to the BBC weekly, *The Listener*:

Eliot's *Notes* had argued the West's cultural frailty and deterioration had been advanced not by fascism or war but by democracy, equality, secularization, the corrosion of aristocracy, and the erosion of piety, all of which he identified primarily with the Enlightenment. A preacher of ethical regeneration, Eliot also hearkened to the familiar trope of the Jew as the antithesis of an authentic Christian Europe, though only with a lone specific mention and without direct reference to the prior decades of European spoliation. Advancing the claim that the closer it comes to being a thoroughly homogeneous "really Christian society," the more the "culture of Europe" can warrant its status as "the highest culture the world has ever known," he asserted that cultural and demographic pluralism constitute a profound danger to advanced culture; hence he judged the United States to be a country unfortunately "swollen [by] that stream of mixed immigration."[5] In the footnote to which Steiner referred, Eliot avowed the status of Europe's Jews as permanent outsiders, asserting their (indirect) responsibility for the West's cultural decay while affirming their status as the Enlightenment incarnate.[6]

The obstinate puzzle is that Eliot's uglier touches tend to occur at the heart of very good poetry (which is *not* the case of Pound). One thinks of the notorious 'the Jew squats on the window-sill . . . . Spawned in some estaminet of Antwerp' in 'Gerontion'; of

The rats are underneath the piles.
The Jew is underneath the lot.

in 'Burbank with a Baedeker: Bleistein with a Cigar' of

Rachel *née* Raabinovitch
Tears at the grapes with murderous paws

in 'Sweeny among the Nightingales'.

The Listener, 29 April 1971; quoted in Christopher Ricks, *T.S. Eliot and Prejudice* (London: Faber and Faber, 1988, p. 29). Ricks finds Eliot's prose to be more ambiguous than Steiner avers.
5. Eliot, *Culture*, pp. 32, 44.
6. "Since the diaspora, and the scattering of Jews amongst peoples holding the Christian Faith," Eliot wrote, "it may have been unfortunate both for these peoples and for the Jews themselves, that the culture-contact between them has had to be within those neutral zones of culture in which religion could be ignored; and the effect may have been to strengthen the illusion that there can be culture without religion." Eliot, *Culture*, p. 70. On that page, he invoked the authority of "the Old Testament" to argue that "In certain historical conditions, a fierce exclusiveness may be a necessary condition for the preservation of a culture." Earlier, he had noted that "the actual religion of no European people has ever been purely Christian, or purely anything else. There are always bits and traces of more primitive faiths, more or less absorbed"; later, he observed, "If Christianity goes, the whole of our culture goes." pp.30, 126.

Not just Steiner's fiery rejoinder but his quite metaphysical explanation for the European crisis helped direct my attention to an alternative pathway mapped by a group of postwar thinkers in the United States who had turned to the social sciences and history in an effort to deepen and guard the tradition of Enlightenment. Seeking to come to terms with Europe's recent catastrophe and comprehend the character and capacities of the modern state at just the moment Eliot was composing his *Notes*, they provided a more appealing set of possibilities. I found myself drawn toward their work just as I was grappling with why I had been disappointed by Steiner's compound of Freudianism and literary critique.

Like Eliot, Steiner underscored the outsider status of Europe's Jews. Their religion's "summons to perfection," in the forms of Old Testament monotheism, primitive Christianity, and messianic Socialism, he argued, had been imposed "on the current and currency of Western life." This pressure had "built up in the social subconscious murderous resentments."[7] He thus understood[8]

> the genocide that took place in Europe and the Soviet Union during the period 1936–45 (Soviet anti-Semitism being perhaps the most paradoxical expression of the hatred which reality fells toward failed utopia), [to have been] far more than a political tactic, an eruption of lower middle-class malaise, or a product of declining capitalism. It was not a mere secular, socio-economic phenomenon. It enacted a suicidal impulse in Western civilization. It was an attempt to level the future—or, more precisely, to make history commensurate with the natural savageries, intellectual torpor, and material instincts of unextended man. Using theological metaphors ... one may say that the holocaust marks a second Fall. We can interpret it as a voluntary exit from the Garden and a programmatic attempt to burn the Garden behind us.

Revulsion against Jewish perfectionism, he claimed, combined with the elimination of religious markers had culminated in the death camps. "Hell [was] made immanent" as it was transferred "from below the earth to its surface."[9] Steiner implicated the Enlightenment in this outcome for having erased Christian doctrines of damnation, thus conducing a "loss of Hell." By sponsor-

---

7. Steiner, *Castle*, pp. 40, 41

8. Steiner, *Castle*, p. 42.

9. Steiner, *Castle*, p. 47. Steiner reprised the theme of the affront to the Christian world of Jewish perfectionism, which he associates with Moses, Jesus, and Marx, in a recent autobiographical work. Of this pressure on the imperfect existence of humankind, he wrote, "is loathing bred. From its smoulders and bursts into flame the impulse of relegation—the Jew must be banished, his voice gagged—and then of annihilation. ... I confess to finding no better explanation for the persistence of anti-Semitism more or less world-wide and after the Holocaust." George Steiner, *Errata: An Examined Life*. London: Weidenfeld and Nicholson, 1997, p. 61.

ing this divestiture, he claimed, the Enlightenment had "opened a vortex which the modern totalitarian state filled. To have neither Heaven nor Hell is to be intolerably deprived and alone in a world gone flat. Of the two," he concluded, "Hell proved easier to re-create."[10]

This account confronted Eliot's train of thought on his chosen anti-rational, romantic terrain, thus implicitly conceding far more than Steiner ever could have intended. His combination of psychoanalysis and theology offered a narrative of the Enlightenment summoning the demise of its own preferred values, as if ideas lacking agents can produce their own negation. More an instance of quixotic metaphor than persuasive analysis, this poetic chronicle had the unintended effect of wearing down the ground on which decent possibilities must stand in the face of experienced desolation.

Searching to secure such a foundation at a time the Enlightenment has come under renewed attack but has been defended in too-simple a way, I set out to explore the rational but not ingenuous strand of analytical history and social science written by scholars who had been my instructors either directly, as in the cases of Richard Hofstadter and David Truman, or at one remove. I soon decided to devote my lectures to this group, some refugee and some native, who had advanced a perspective during and following the Second World War sufficiently distinctive to be joined under the umbrella of the 'political studies enlightenment.' Refusing to stand in the space occupied both by Eliot and Steiner as interlocutors, these individuals had sought instead to renew and protect the Enlightenment's heritage by appropriating and transforming social science, history, and the study of public policy.

As I revised my text for the last time, I gathered sustenance from Lionel Trilling's elegant essay about T.S. Eliot's politics. Here, Trilling is characteristically more muted and more sympathetic to Eliot's traditionalist Anglo-Catholic impulses than Steiner's more censorious evaluation. Locating Eliot's 1939 lectures on *The Idea of a Christian Society*[11] in the nineteenth-century lineage of Coleridge, Newman, Carlyle, Ruskin, and Arnold, "the men who in the days of Reform, stood out, on something better than reasons of interest, against the philosophical assumptions of materialistic Liberalism," Trilling could not endorse Eliot's ideas but did "recommend to the attention of readers probably hostile to religion Mr. Eliot's religious politics."[12] What was so striking to Trilling

---

10. Steiner, *Castle*, p. 48.

11. T. S. Eliot, *The Idea of a Christian Society*. London: Faber and Faber, 1939. There were the Boutwood Lectures delivered at Corpus Christi College, Cambridge, in March 1939.

12. Lionel Trilling, "Elements that are Wanted," *Partisan Review*, September–October 1940; reprinted as "T. S. Eliot's Politics" in Lionel Trilling, *The Moral Obligation to be Intelligent: Selected Essays* [edited with an Introduction by Leon Wieseltier] (New York: Farrar, Straus, Giroux, 2000), p. 22.

was Eliot's inability to find deeply contrary bases to the undergirding philosophy of the period's liberal democracies and totalitarian regimes. To be sure, Eliot knew they were not the same, but he thought that the deep paganism underneath totalitarianism could not be opposed effectively by the liberalism of the 1930s, which he judged too thin and too exclusively negative for the task; hence he turned for positive sustenance to the Christian tradition.

Expressing deep skepticism about Eliot's triad of the Christian state, the Christian Community, and the Community of Christians, Trilling noted that prior Christian societies had not been insulated from the very doctrines Christianity now was said to be better-equipped to oppose than liberalism. Nonetheless, Trilling spoke of Eliot's writing "with respect because it suggests elements which a rational and naturalistic philosophy, to be adequate, must encompass." For if Eliot's supernaturalism provided no answers, neither, Trilling implied, did a liberalism lacking in "tragic presuppositions" or "the sense of complication and possibility, of surprise, intensification, variety, unfoldment, worth."[13]

This thickening of modern liberalism defined the project that animated the scholarship of the historians and social scientists whose writing I examine in this book. Like Trilling and Steiner, they were concerned to understand the requisite conditions for fashioning and sustaining a humane culture, especially a decent liberal democratic political culture, but their sanctioned apparatus was different. Putting faith in systematic social inquiry as an instrument of discernment and defense, these writers confronted the sources and character of their cheerless age. Aware of human depredation and haunted by recent catastrophes, the political studies enlightenment refused to abandon the liberal, secular, and pluralist values Eliot had renounced so definitively. Instead, by developing a characteristic history and social science, they fortified these purposes by opting for a particular kind of Enlightenment. Appreciative of analytical modernism's endowments and motivated by an understanding that how we come to know may, under some circumstances, explain how we can come to live, they produced a multifaceted program for epistemological and normative reconstruction.

In my lectures and now in this book, I have endeavored to critically appreciate this undertaking. Writing as a practicing social scientist concerned for the character and possibilities of my craft and as a historian interested in the lineage of ideas and the production of social knowledge, I have revisited the scholarship members of the political studies enlightenment produced after the Second

---

13. Trilling, "Eliot's Politics," pp. 32, 29–30. This formulation heralded themes he later was to take up in *The Liberal Imagination*'s effort "to recall liberalism to its first essential imagination of variousness and possibility, which implies the awareness of complexity and difficulty." Lionel Trilling, *The Liberal Imagination: Essays on Literature and Society* (New York: Harcourt Brace Jovanovich, 1979 [1950]), p. xii.

World War when the irreparable legacies of three decades of barbarism on an immense scale still were raw and the shock of disappointment in the West's high civilization was at its peak. In so doing, I have been determined to understand not just the achievements but the limits of their vision and to consider the bearing of the body of work they produced a half-century ago on today's fervent but thin controversies about social inquiry and the status of Enlightenment.

As it turns out, the three universities at which I have been employed—the University of Chicago, the New School for Social Research, and Columbia University—provided fortifying quarters for most of the scholars whose work I consider. Each institution, in its own way, has handed on its legacy in a living state. Thus I was especially pleased to have had the chance to deliver the Schoff Lectures under the patrimony of Columbia's University Seminars, an institution that has enriched the intellectual life of metropolitan New York and the wider culture for more than a half-century. Dean Aaron Warner, recently deceased at the start of his tenth decade, and his colleagues Jessie Strader and Anissa Bouziane, provided thoughtful counsel, administrative support, and unstinting encouragement as I worked to take advantage of the opportunity provided by Kenneth Jackson, Robert Belknap, and their colleagues on the Leonard Hastings Schoff Memorial Lectures Advisory Committee. I particularly appreciate Professor Jackson's encouragement. He urged me to accept the Committee's invitation and helped me think about the structure of my talks. I also wish to warmly thank Andreas Huyssen, Fritz Stern, and Lisa Anderson for their graceful introductions to the three public lectures.

For tough-minded comments and fertile suggestions, I am indebted to Tom Bernstein, Lewis Edinger, Andreas Huyssen, Andreas Kalyvas, Deborah Socolow Katznelson, Zachary Katznelson ("eliminate the big words," he counseled), Mark Kesselman (who convened a seminar to discuss the lectures), David Kettler, Kenneth Mischel, Andrew Nathan, Sayres Rudy, Rosalie Siegel, Michael Stanislawski, Mehmet Tabak, Kian Tajbakhsh, Nadia Urbinati, Mark von Hagen, and Harriet Zuckerman; and for his special generosity, to Robert K. Merton, whose attendance and approbation meant so much to me. Uri Ram and Oren Yiftachel at Ben Gurion University and Shlomo Avineri at the Hebrew University kindly proffered invitations that permitted me to test my ideas once again in public forums in May 2001 where, in a charged climate, I was pushed hard to clarify key aspects of my intellectual history. I am grateful, too, to my editors at Columbia University Press, co-sponsor of the Schoff Lectures. Kate Wittenberg provided intellectual partnership and steady patience while waiting too long for this short manuscript to leave my desk. Peter Dimock inherited the portfolio, shared in my passion for this project, and generously oversaw the production phase. Leslie Bialler's excellent copyediting clarified and elevated the book's prose. During the last phase of revision, Benjamin Fishman offered valuable research assistance.

Desolation and Enlightenment carries a dedication to my daughter Emma. In the age hierarchy of our family, it is her turn. So she will have to forgive me when I recall an event that took place some eighteen years ago, when she was just three years old. I stood before an audience at the University of Chicago, where I then taught, to deliver the kind of lecture one composes in advance, word by word. I turned to the penultimate page and confronted a blank sheet of paper. I improvised, then concluded. Arriving home, I asked my four children if any had seen a sheet from my talk. "Yes," Emma proudly beamed. "It made a great rocket ship." Quickly recognizing my consternation, she hastily added, "but I did put another piece back." So, dear Emma, these pages are for you.

New York City
March 2002

Desolation and Enlightenment

One

BEYOND THE COMMON MEASURE

At the University of Chicago celebration of the twenty-fifth anniversary of its Social Science Research Building in November 1955, Harold Lasswell concluded
his remarks by reflecting on the role of social scientists "in the social process,"
which he summarized as that of "reconstructing our institutions of enlightenment."[1] This was no mere turn of phrase. Lasswell, arguably the country's leading political scientist during the prior decade, had been a significant participant
in a many-shaped endeavor to recast political knowledge as a quest to renew and
protect the western tradition of Enlightenment.

During and especially after the Second World War, a learned array of scholars whose biography had placed them perilously close to Europe's abyss joined
others fortunate enough to have been protected by distance to defend liberality
and systematic thought while insisting the tradition of Enlightenment required
a new realism, a good deal of repair, and much fortification. Constituting a distinctive approach (though not a school, since they were not bound together
self-consciously[2]), these historians and social scientists understood that a simple reassertion of liberal modernism had become radically insufficient. "The

---

1. Harold D. Lasswell, "Impact of Psychoanalytic Thinking on the Social Sciences," in Leonard
D. White, ed., *The State of the Social Sciences* (Chicago: University of Chicago Press, 1956), p. 115.
2. The image of an extended family of the kind Peter Gay applies to the Enlightenment and the
notion of a 'generation-unit' advanced by Karl Mannheim together come reasonably close to the

tragic experiences of the 1930's and 1940's," the historian Fritz Stern observed in 1956,[3]

> have had a profoundly unsettling effect on historiography, and some of the basic presuppositions and categories of explanation of an earlier period no longer seem adequate today. The generous faith in rationality and the possibilities of human progress which underlay much of earlier historical thought seems discredited today, and yet the deepening of our historical experiences need not lead to its abandonment, but perhaps to a stronger sense of the precariousness of human freedom and to a still greater dedication to it.

Sharing this diagnosis and this commitment, the group I designate as the political studies enlightenment insisted on critical adjustments geared to shade the Enlightenment's philosophical anthropology, thicken its defenses against evil, deepen its capacity to reason, and restore full sight to an Enlightenment that, in the face of disaster and the loss of self-assurance, had become color-blind.[4] Confronting their period's dashed hopes for reason and knowledge, they asked not just whether the Enlightenment should define modernity, but which Enlightenment we should wish to have.

To this end, they drew on and advanced the resources of twentieth-century analytical history and social science. They adopted Tocqueville's famous statement of intent declaring that "a new science of politics is needed for a new world"[5] as their implicit motto. Affiliating disciplined study with normative purpose, they sought to secure a realistic version of Enlightenment and enlarge its span of sensibility as the best, perhaps the only, humane option on offer even after the disillusioning revelation that its ramparts had crumbled under pressure.

Their work is my subject. In the pages that follow, I reflect on their accomplishments, internal tensions, and limitations in a review of how members of

---

mark. So too does what Ludwig Fleck called a scientific thought collective whose members share questions, assumptions, and ways of working. Peter Gay, *The Enlightenment: A Comprehensive Anthology* (New York: Simon and Schuster, 1973); Karl Mannheim, "The Problem of Generations," in his *Essays on the Sociology of Culture* (London: Routledge and Kegan Paul, 1956); and Ludwig Fleck, *Genesis and Development of a Scientific Fact* (Chicago: University of Chicago Press, 1979). The text was first published in Switzerland in 1935.
3. Fritz Stern, "Introduction," in Fritz Stern, ed., *The Varieties of History* (Cleveland and New York: Meridian Books, 1956), p. 24.
4. I borrow this image from the treatment of achromatopia in Oliver Sacks, *The Island of the Colorblind* (New York: Knopf, 1997).
5. Alexis de Tocqueville, *Democracy in America* (New York: Knopf, 1945 [1835]), p. 7.

the political studies enlightenment sought to account for the sources of modern barbarism, assay the character of modern states, and guard against what one of their number, the political scientist David Truman, described as "morbific politics."[6] My consideration is not dispassionate.[7] Nor is it comprehensive. Judging the work of Hannah Arendt, Robert Dahl, Richard Hofstadter, Charles Lindblom, and Karl Polanyi, as well as Lasswell and Truman, to be representative of this intellectual tradition, I seek to understand sympathetically but not uncritically their quest for political studies that could repel anti-liberal predators and help guarantee battered but cherished values. These colleagues, I show, undertook two principal tasks. Treating evil as an analytical category, they sought, substantively, to discover the sources of desolation and probe the character of the modern state. They also set out to invent a realistic and proficient political science in an extended sense of the term that, at once, was institutional and historical, normative and behavioral.[8] They undertook both tasks in order to revise and thus secure the lineage of Enlightenment by returning it to the theme of desolation with which some of its founders had wrestled, thus rendering it less credulous and more capable.

This group of scholar-sentinels combined the deduction of politics from norms with its extrapolation from facts, affiliating engaged social criticism with disinterested social science to discover truth about how things work.[9] Social science furnished their pathway to ethics. Deeply grounded in the priority of knowledge over the priority of faith without displacing ethics, their realism insisted on taking humankind and its propensities as they are, rather than as they might or should be. They understood, moreover, that a sober, calm voice and patient investigation were required to approach a comprehension of the monstrous and proceed beyond testimony, victimhood, and personal memory to

6. David B. Truman, *The Governmental Process: Political Interests and Public Opinion* (New York: Knopf, 1951), p. 516.

7. "When I try to sum up what, above all else, I have learned from grappling with the sprawling prolixities of John Dewey's work, what I come up with is the succinct and chilling doctrine that thought is conduct and is to be morally judged as such. . . . [T]he reason thinking is serious is that it is a social act, and that one is therefore responsible for it as for any other social act. Perhaps even more so, for, in the long run, it is the most consequential of social acts." Clifford Geertz, *Available Light: Anthropological Reflections on Philosophical Topics* (Princeton: Princeton University Press, 2000), p. 21.

8. Even Arendt (in some ways, especially Arendt, I argue later in this book), who only rarely is thought to be a systematic social scientist or historian, let alone a political liberal, mobilized methodical instruments of political and historical analysis to pursue these objectives.

9. I borrow this distinction from Zygmunt Bauman, "No Way Back to Bliss: How to Cope with the Restless Chaos of Modernity," *Times Literary Supplement*, January 24, 1997.

4   ONE

understanding, research, and the protection of enlightened values.[10] After their
encounter with desolation without requital they treated analytical learning as a
pathway to knowledge about how humankind might secure the benefits of Enlightenment without staggering into unreason. In these ways, they sought to create a new knowledge base for a more capable political liberalism. Decades later,
we possess quite a stake in discerning the degree to which they succeeded.

I.

Enlightenment radicalism had sought to extirpate the Devil. "After 1650,"
Jonathan Israel observes, "tension between a thoroughgoing philosophical Naturalism, scorning belief in magic and the demonic, as part of a broader conceptual attack on authority, tradition, and Revelation, and, on the other side, both a
moderate and a more fundamentalist, conservative stance was everywhere evident in western and central Europe."[11] Inside the Enlightenment, many leading
figures, including Descartes and Boyle, sought a middle course that could ac-
commodate the demonic within a framework of scientific rationality. By contrast, other key thinkers, including Spinoza and Voltaire, who opposed reason to
magic, including ideas about diabolical spirits, ultimately were more successful.
Released from superstition, they insisted, humankind could be free to ascend
and progress.

Over time, this more radical and secular vision triumphed within the revolutionary impulse we call the Enlightenment. Its anti-absolutist politics, elaboration of concepts of toleration, consent, and representation (the core of political
liberalism), diffusion of Naturalism and materialism, assaults on traditional hierarchy, and extension of learning and the free flow of ideas based on systematic
reason and scientific inquiry pushed aside the ecclesiastical underpinnings for
systematic notions of evil, making it difficult for enlightened thinkers to address
the darker aspects of the human condition.

---

10. On testimony and memory, see Saul Friedländer, *When Memory Comes* (New York: Farrar,
Straus Giroux, 1979); Saul Friedländer, *Memory, History, and the Extermination of the Jews of Eu-
rope* (Bloomington: Indiana University Press, 1993); Dominick LaCapra, *History and Memory
After Auschwitz* (Ithaca: Cornell University Press, 1998); Barbie Zelizer, *Remembering to Forget:
Holocaust Memory Through the Camera's Eye* (Chicago: University of Chicago Press, 1998); and
Henry Greenspan, "Imagining Survivors: Testimony and the Rise of Holocaust Consciousness,"
in Hilene Flanzbaum, ed., *The Americanization of the Holocaust.* (Baltimore: Johns Hopkins
University Press, 1999).
11. Jonathan I. Israel, *Radical Enlightenment: Philosophy and the Making of Modernity,*
1650–1750 (Oxford: Oxford University Press, 2001), p. 376. Also see Stuart Clark, *Thinking with
Demons: The Idea of Witchcraft in Early Modern Europe* (Oxford: Clarendon Press, 1997).

The intellectual figures at the center of this book remained committed to the impulses, values, and achievements of the Enlightenment despite the West's long period of devastation from the start of the First World War to the conclusion of the Second. In holding tight to this tradition, they could not avoid the puzzle of how to grapple with the return of a secularized Devil without the categories, assets, or language of traditional religion. Could they make the demonic a constitutive feature of a realistic Enlightenment once again without sacrificing its central commitments and abilities?

It is their common commitment to this challenge, as well as their choice of history and social science as instruments, that binds together the figures and the scholarship I highlight: Polanyi's political economy of the breakdown of Europe's international and domestic institutions; Arendt's philosophical history of anti-Semitism, imperialism, and totalitarianism; Hofstadter's dour reading of American political development; Truman's pragmatist understanding of the ties between civil society and the modern American state; Lasswell's program for cross-disciplinary policy studies; and Dahl's and Lindblom's effort to marshal the technical details of policymaking to protective purposes.[12] Despite their internal diversity, this group shared an enterprise demarcated from other responses to Europe's catastrophes. Collectively, these members of the political studies enlightenment faced a task not unlike the one articulated by Madame de Staël after the Terror. In a "period which stands beyond the common measure," bereft of "a terminology," existing doctrines and words fail descriptively and analytically.[13]

It has become familiar these days to oppose the analysis of language based on notions that nothing is real unless signified to a materialism that understands nothing to be signified unless real.[14] By contrast, the political studies enlightenment refused such a choice. My subject, then, is how, via the pathway of

---

12. My personal feelings and professional convictions are bound up in this treatment, as is a history of personal acquaintance. Richard Hofstadter and David Truman were my undergraduate teachers at Columbia University. I experienced the power of Hannah Arendt's lectures at the New School for Social Research when I was a junior faculty member at Columbia, and her legacy provided a pervasive influence when I taught at the New School's Graduate Faculty. There, I co-taught twice with Charles Lindblom, once on Arendt and Polanyi, the second time on modern policy knowledge, and I count him as a friend.

13. Cited in Renee Winegarten, *Mme de Staël* (Leamington Spa: Berg, 1985), p. 99. Aristide Zolberg has suggested in an essay on France in 1789, 1848, and 1968 that there is a species of times he calls 'moments of madness,' when ordinary political structures and rules are suspended and everything seems possible; and he likens the mood of these times to a vast exultory party. The kind of moment de Staël is writing about, however, is quite different. These are times of disappointment and anomie, anxiety and loss of faith, when confusion and doubt overwhelm certainty. Aristide Zolberg, "Moments of Madness," *Politics and Society* 2 (Winter 1972).

14. "In much linguistic theory and a certain kind of semiotics," Raymond Williams observed in a discussion of the articulated and the lived, "we are in danger of reaching the point . . . in which

systematic social inquiry, they crafted a language of politics in the face of dark realities they could not elide.

Within this group, it was Arendt who most clearly reprised Staël's terminological theme and who addressed the absence of a theological language of evil. Writing in 1951, she pointed to the importance of linguistic invention to find means to say what ordinarily "is outside the realm of human speech." A search for analogies drawing on images of demons and perdition was compromised, she observed, because the "one thing that cannot be reproduced is what made the traditional conceptions of Hell tolerable to man: the Last Judgment, the idea of an absolute standard of justice combined with the infinite possibility of grace." It had become "evident that things which for thousands of years the human imagination had banished to a realm beyond human competence can be manufactured right here on earth, that Hell and Purgatory, and even a shadow of their perpetual duration, can be established by the most modern methods of destruction and therapy."[15] The Devil had returned, and a disoriented western consciousness now seemed sentenced to abiding sorrow and pain. Still, notwithstanding the reduction of nineteenth-century European civilization to ashes, Arendt insisted the task of fashioning an appropriate language of politics could not be abdicated. "In a secular society self-consciously lacking the tools to do so," one analyst of her writings put the point, "she sought to provide a rational vocabulary and explanation of this evil"[16] and devise means capable of giving humankind the chance to (re)build a decent politics and society.

These were the deepest pursuits she shared with the other members of the political studies enlightenment, all of whom utilized the systematic tools of social science to show how we might know, clarify what we do know, ask what knowledge is for, and defend valued standards of conduct.[17] Today, we possess a massive outpouring of work on totalitarianism, total war, and holocaust as defining a decisive breach in the history of the modern world. We hardly lack for ample accounts of the millions of citizen conscripts who turned into face-to-

---

the epistemological wholly absorbs the ontological: it is only in the ways of knowing that we exist at all. . . . [I]t is necessary to recall an absolutely founding presumption of materialism: namely that the natural world exists whether anyone signifies it or not." Raymond Williams, *Politics and Letters: Interviews with New Left Review* (London: New Left Books, 1979), p. 167.

15. Hannah Arendt, *The Origins of Totalitarianism* (London: George Allen and Unwin, 1951), pp. 446–447.

16. Steven E. Ascheim, "Hannah Arendt and the Discourse of Evil," *New German Critique*, no. 70 (Winter 1997): 139.

17. For treatments of the role of social critic, see Michael Walzer, *Interpretation and Social Criticism* (Cambridge: Harvard University Press, 1997); and Stephan Collini, "Speaking from Somewhere," *Times Literary Supplement*, April 15–21, 1998.

face killers,[18] the tens of thousands into active functionaries of genocide, the complicity of many others through a combination, at a cleansing distance, of active support and indifference, or of how degradation and moral corruption drew in some of the victims of Nazi ghettoes and extermination camps.[19] We know how stylized and 'civilized' nineteenth-century warfare was replaced by the demonization of enemies, the erosion of the distinction between combatants and noncombatants, and the normalization of barbarity.[20] Writing in the midst of transgressions to previously understood human limits at a time when trust in language and institutions had eroded, what stands out about the effort of the political studies enlightenment to apprehend their dark times is how they advanced beyond registering brutality or cataloging armies of the dead. Not unlike Hobbes, who also had searched for a new language of politics, they repudiated rhetoric as such in favor of advancing a science of politics and discovering an appropriate modernist syntax to repulse the recurrence of calamity.[21]

But a new language about what? My quest to understand, appreciate, and critique this effort begins, in this chapter, with the mirror image of the group's

---

18. Niall Ferguson argues that most conventional explanations in this respect are inadequate to explain the wanton disregard of life, including the soldiers' own. Niall Ferguson, "The Death Instinct: Why Men Fought," chapter 12 in Ferguson, *The Pity of War* (New York: Basic Books, 1998). Also see, Joanna Bourke, *An Intimate History of Killing: Face to Face Killing in Twentieth-Century Warfare* (London: Granta Books, 1999); Glenn Gray, *The Warriors: Reflections on Men in Battle* (New York: Harper and Row, 1977).

19. Christopher Browning, *Ordinary Men: Reserve Police Battalion 101 and the Final Solution in Poland* (New York: Harper Collins, 1992); Christopher Browning, *Nazi Policy, Jewish Workers, German Killers* (Cambridge: Cambridge University Press, 2001); Inga Clendinnnen, "Inside the Grey Zone: The Auschwitz *Sonderkommando*," and "The Men in the Green Tunics: The Order Police in Poland," and "The Auschwitz SS," in Clendinnen, *Reading the Holocaust* (Cambridge: Cambridge University Press, 1999); and Henry Friedlander, "The T4 Killers: Berlin, Lublin, San Sabba," in Michael Berenbaum and Abraham J. Peck, eds., *The Holocaust and History: The Known, the Unknown, the Disputed, and the Reexamined* (Bloomington: Indiana University Press, 1998). The vast majority, it should be said, were neither perpetrators nor victims, but bystanders, some of whom, with motives ranging from the altruistic to the pecuniary, acted at great risk to rescue Jews. For discussions, see Eva Fogelman, *Conscience and Courage: Rescuers of Jews During the Holocaust* (New York: Doubleday, 1994); Nechama Tec, *When Light Pierced the Darkness: Christian Rescue of Jews in Nazi-Occupied Poland* (New York: Oxford University Press, 1986); and Samuel P. Oliner and Pearl M. Oliner, *The Altruistic Personality: Rescuers of Jews in Nazi Europe* (New York: Free Press, 1988). On the cognitive sources of hate, see Aaron T. Beck, *Prisoners of Hate: The Cognitive Basis of Anger, Hostility, and Violence* (New York: Harper-Collins, 1999).

20. Eric Hobsbawm, "Barbarity: A User's Guide," *New Left Review*, no. 206 (July/August 1994).

21. Quentin Skinner, *Reason and Rhetoric in the Philosophy of Hobbes* (Cambridge: Cambridge University Press, 1996). They also refused to make successive linguistic formations, in the manner later advanced by Foucault, the causal motors of depredation. Michel Foucault, *Discipline and Punish: The Birth of the Prison* (New York: Pantheon Books, 1977).

linguistic quest, the invention of new words—'total war,' 'totalitarianism,' and 'holocaust'—that disclosed the deep insufficiency of early-twentieth-century social knowledge. These terms, especially the unexpected and harrowing reality they signified, motivated the political studies enlightenment and defined the subjects for their work. In grappling with this nomenclature and its challenge to settled meanings and practices, the political studies enlightenment undertook to address radical evil without losing the Enlightenment.

II.

By the early years of the twentieth century, the aspects of Enlightenment thought most engaged with desolation, magical or otherwise, largely had lapsed from consciousness. Just before the trauma of the First World War and Europe's subsequent festival of cruelty,[22] the disclosure and invention of knowledge were girded by a profound optimism that reason, which so often had been represented in the image of the light of a rising, ever-brighter, ever-warmer, sun, could shine on all aspects of human politics, morality, and political economy to realize the title of Pierre-Paul Prud'hon's painting of 1798 announcing that "Darkness Dissipates as Wisdom and Truth Descend to Earth." The positive standing of the Enlightenment as a knife of light able to scrape the darkness clean by "the exercise of a formal system of reasoning, with rules against which the veracity of the claims in question can be judged"[23] virtually was unquestioned in Anglo-American intellectual and academic life when, arguably, the greatest marker of such knowledge before the First World War, the massive Eleventh edition of the *Encyclopedia Britannica*, was published just four years before the assassination of Ferdinand in Sarajevo.[24] Taking a form long associated with Enlightenment thought and aspirations, these beautifully written and edited volumes deploying knowledge to push back against the forces of darkness appeared just as the modern university from which they drew most of their specialist authors was gaining ascendancy over other organizations devoted to the disclosure, invention, and circulation of knowledge.[25] Drawing on the body of

---

22. This is the title Jonathan Glover adopts for chapter six in his *Humanity: A Moral History of the Twentieth Century* (New Haven: Yale University Press, 2000).

23. Felipe Fernández-Armesto, *Truth: A History and a Guide for the Perplexed* (London: Black Swan, 1998), p. 86. For an extended consideration of truth in a philosophical and historical context, with an eye to current intellectual predicaments, see Richard Campbell, *Truth and Historicity* (Oxford: Clarendon Press, 1992).

24. *The Encyclopedia Britannica: Eleventh Edition* (New York: Encyclopedia Britannica, Inc., 1910).

25. For a discussion of the lineage of the encyclopedia as a genre, see Peter Burke, *A Social History of Knowledge* (Cambridge: Polity Press, 2000), pp. 171–173.

scholarship being produced in the university's new departments and disciplines, the *Encyclopedia* exulted in the endowments of systematic, professional, organized, disciplined ways of thinking—modes of thought which transcended the older forms of religion and moral philosophy—and it celebrated explicitly their capacity to tame barbarism and control the destiny of humankind.[26]

The genealogy and aspirations of the *Encyclopedia Britannica* attest to the seductive power and great accomplishments the creed of reason had, or seemed to have, achieved in Europe and North America during the Hundred Years Peace and the growth of nineteenth-century liberal civilization. Its editors rejoiced in the vast unfolding of human knowledge since the first edition had been issued by "a Society of Gentlemen in Scotland" in weekly numbers between 1768 and 1771. This inaugural offering and the second edition published in similar fashion between 1777 and 1784 had been compiled by just one or two men "still able to take the whole of human knowledge for their province." By the end of the eighteenth century, this way of working no longer was adequate. Beginning with the Third, all subsequent editions of the *Britannica* were written by many leading scholars as they grew to more than twenty large volumes. The twenty-eight books of the Eleventh edition were not mere elaborations of prior versions, however. This "entirely new and original . . . survey of the whole field of human thought and achievement, written by some 1500 eminent specialists drawn from nearly every country of the civilized world,[27] incorporating the results of research and the progress of events up to the middle of 1910," and aiming, in the words of its editors, "at achieving the high ambition of bringing all extant knowledge within the reach of every class of readers" was further distinguished by a shift in the venture's provenance. The *Encyclopedia*, previously published privately as a commercial venture, most recently by the *Times* newspapers of London, now was issued by a university, Cambridge, a sponsorship,

---

26. "For the European and American elites at the start of the century, . . . recent history had been one of almost unbroken progress. The phenomenal industrialization, urbanization, and growing prosperity of the previous century fueled a massive self-confidence about their position in the world and their ability (indeed their right) to rule it. There seemed little reason to believe that their optimism was misplaced or that this progress would not continue throughout the twentieth century. . . . Free trade, capitalism, the development of a rational science, continued technological improvement and the conquest of nature . . . the end of absolutism and the development of limited government, liberal institutions, partial democracy and the nation state—all seemed successful and unproblematic." Clive Ponting, *The Pimlico History of the Twentieth Century* (London: Pimlico, 1999), pp. 8–9.

27. This internationalization of knowledge was an aspect of a remarkable growth, under western hegemony, of global interdependence in commerce, communication, travel, and institutions of international cooperation as well as the development of a common high culture, punctuated by travel, amongst elites who crossed borders easily.

the editors noted, particularly well-equipped for the endeavor given the university's codification of knowledge based on Enlightenment principles and its democratization via "the complete abolition of the various tests which formally shut the gates of the English universities against a large part of the people."[28]

A new, more inclusive and meritocratic liberal system of knowledge production thus proudly feted its own accomplishments: its deep grounding in history, its use of statistics as illustrative "of substantial existing conditions and of real progress," its inclination toward the comparative method, and above all, its commitments to "the spirit of science" and to "the objective view." "While every individual article in an encyclopedia which aims at authoritative exposition must be informed by the spirit of history," the introduction stated, "it is no less essential that the spirit of science should move over the construction of the work as a whole." Further, the text continued, "the *Encyclopedia Britannica* itself has no side or party . . . giving fullest expression to this objective treatment of questions."[29] Here, epistemology was enclosed within its own circle, willfully ignoring the social milieus within which ideas are produced or the situations and standpoints of their authors. Written by scholars who were linked, as Jürgen Habermas later was to put it, by "a bond of naiveté,"[30] reason ran free. "Back then, before the Great War," the novelist Joseph Roth wrote in 1932, " . . . it was not yet a matter of indifference whether a person lived or died."[31] Back then, Arendt observed, if a tad too nostalgically, writing about the plight of Captain Dreyfus, "the doctrine of equality before the law was still so firmly emplanted in the conscience of the civilized world that a single miscarriage of justice could provoke public indignation from Moscow to New York. . . . The wrong done to a single Jewish officer in France was able to draw from the rest of the world a more vehement and united reaction than all the persecutions of German Jews a generation later."[32]

---

28. *Britannica*, vol. 1, p. ix.

29. *Britannica*, vol. 1, pp. xx, xxi.

30. Jürgen Habermas, "Historical Consciousness and Post-Traditional Identity: The Federal Republic's Orientation to the West," in Jürgen Habermas, *The New Conservatism: Cultural Criticism and the Historians' Debate* (Oxford: Polity Press, 1989), p. 251.

31. Joseph Roth, *The Radetzky March* (London: Penguin Books, 1995; original edition, Berlin, 1932), p. 112. Outside of Europe, the First World War had little impact. In the empires of the great powers (which, before the War, controlled about half the globe's population; that is, about 700 million people) especially the British, French, Belgian, Dutch, and German, brutality in war and administration was quite commonplace in a context of often quite continuous low-intensity warfare.

32. Arendt, *Origins*, p. 91.

The unanticipated cascade of events in the terrible period just ahead[33] soon placed in doubt the meliorist and progressive *Britannica* version of the Enlightenment and the liberal coordinates and assumptions of progress within which it was embedded (including a defanged aristocracy, the steady growth of a democratic order, the replacement of aristocratic absolutism and federalism with parliamentary centralism, and the supercession of religion by science), rendering them simple.[34] "By 1914," the historian Bernard Wishy observed in a Europe-centered formulation echoing the prewar tendency to censor out the excluded and the nonrational from the program of reason, "men knew what [liberal-humanism] meant and they called its components Civilization. Reasonableness, kindness, decency, privacy, tolerance, freedom, and, where possible, love—these were the great virtues, firmly associated with the best aspects of the life of the middle classes on the eve of the First World War. But no one," he continued, "who went through that war could still find the criteria of rationalistic liberalism adequate for understanding life."[35] The Great War left some ten million dead and introduced mechanized, mass killing on a heretofore unknown scale. France alone, just in the first four months of the war in 1914, suffered 300,000 war dead, with twice that number wounded, out of a total military age male population of 10 million. By 1918, the country had 630,000 war widows and 750,000 war orphans who had been 'adopted' by the state in the aftermath of the killing or wounding of fully 60 percent of its 8 million men under arms. Two million Germans died in the war, or 13 percent of the male cohort born between 1870 and 1899; one and a half million Tsarist soldiers perished. Serbia lost

---

33. "In the 1900's," Eric Hobsbawm observes, "war drew visibly nearer, in the 1910s its imminence could and was in some ways taken for granted. And yet its outbreak was not really *expected*." Eric Hobsbawm, *The Age of Empire: 1875–1914* (New York: Pantheon, 1987), p. 304.

34. The year this edition of the *Britannica* was published, Norman Angell's *The Great Illusion* (a reissue of his *Europe's Optical Illusion* published the year before, in 1909), became a global bestseller. Angell, a British Liberal journalist, argued that under modern industrial conditions, the key nations of the world, including Germany, France, Britain, and the United States, were quickly losing their capacity for aggression and appetite for war in favor of the advantages of peace. The potential devastation of war, given the build-up in armaments, he believed, for aggressors as well as targets, would constitute both geopolitical and economic suicide. Increases in territory no longer would bring about increases in wealth or trade. War had become futile. Cooperation would, in consequence, supplant struggle. More generally, humankind had made enormous civilizational progress, and more, especially in the international dimension, now would follow. It was, in short, an illusion that war would benefit capital. Norman Angell, *The Great Illusion: A Study of the Relation of Military Power in Nations to their Economic and Social Advantage* (London: G.P. Putnam's Sons, 1910).

35. Bernard W. Wishy, "Is There a Revolt Against Reason?," *Political Science Quarterly* 71 (June 1956): 244–245.

15 percent of its total prewar population of five million. Hundreds of thousands of the five million wounded in the war were marked for life by missing limbs, eyes, and facial injuries so severe they came to holiday in segregated rural establishments.[36] "The days before and the days after the first World War," Arendt observed,[37]

> are separated not like the end of an old and the beginning of a new period, but like the day before and after an explosion. Yet this figure of speech is as inaccurate as are all the others, because the quiet of sorrow which settles down after a catastrophe has never come to pass. The first explosion seems to have touched off a chain reaction in which we have been caught ever since and which nobody seems able to stop.

Now, in the crucible of war, liberal knowledge itself was called into question. Who, any longer, "can still believe that *tout comprendre c'est tout pardonner?* . . . Knowledge and learning now do not always inspire happiness or rational action, as men once believed they would, but often oppression and slaughter."[38]

And still, one plausible reading of the war experience in its immediate aftermath suggested the triumph of Enlightenment liberalism. Dynastic absolutist empires had collapsed, and with them the old order of aristocratic privilege. Militaristic nationalism had been defeated and new forms of pacific nationalism had been fashioned at Versailles, initiated under the leadership of the globe's leading liberal democracy, that seemed to project a new, more just, peaceful order.[39]

Such hopes soon were dashed. In quick order, the carnage of global warfare was followed by a twenty-year period of recurrent civil wars; "by migrations of groups who, unlike their happier predecessors in the religious wars, were welcomed nowhere and could be assimilated nowhere";[40] by the crowding and collapse of liberal constitutional regimes which lacked a broad and deep social base and which were challenged by a wide array of strident "new anti-liberal mass movements" which "rose form below to challenge the trusteeship of the educated middle class, to paralyze its political system, and to undermine its confi-

---

36. John Keegan, *The First World War* (London: Hutchinson, 1998), pp. 3, 6, 7. The wartime killings were followed by the remarkable influenza epidemic, killing some 2 million Europeans, which began late in 1918.
37. Arendt, *Origins*, p. 267.
38. Wishy, "Revolt," p.245.
39. Howard, *Invention*, pp. 61–63.
40. Arendt, *Origins*, p. 267.

dence in the rational structure of history";[41] by Bolshevism's Russian triumph (and its new mechanisms of control,[42] including labor camps[43] and invasive secret police that bifurcated the Left into camps of one-eyed supporters and disillusioned socialists who found it hard to sustain an effective politics); by fascism's efflorescence, arguably the one fresh ideological invention of the *fin-de-siècle*; and by the reassertion of traditional right-wing, Christian-nationalist authoritarianism—all in the context of what Hajo Holborn characterized as "the revolutionary event of the twentieth century," the collapse of the geopolitical system of Europe that had been created in 1815, crashed in the First World War, and irrevocably destroyed in the Second "since the statesmen at the Peace Conference of

---

41. Carl E. Schorske, "Politics in a New Key: Schörner," in Leonard Krieger and Fritz Stern, eds., *The Responsibility of Power: Historical Essays in Honor of Hajo Holborn* (London: Macmillan, 1968), p. 235. Support for liberal regimes was both disproportionately middle class and Jewish, often both. Writing about Austria, and the buffeting liberal hopes had received from a variety of movements and social classes, Schorske notes that "By the end of the century even the Jews, to whom Austro-liberalism had offered emancipation, opportunity, and assimilation to modernity, began to turn their backs on their benefactors. The failure of liberalism left the Jew a victim, and the most persuasive answer to victimization was the flight to a national home that Zionism proffered. Where other nationalists threatened the Austrian state with disruption, the Zionists threatened secession." Schorske, "Politics," pp. 234–235.

42. These included not only formal instruments but the self-policing of civil society. In 1934, *Pravda* famously published a poem by thirteen-year old Pronya Kolibin, the recipient of a cash prize for having denounced his mother for having stolen grain, partly to feed him, from a collective farm. A year later, Sergei Eisenstein directed a film, *Bezhin Lug*, celebrating the denunciation of his father and grandfather by Pavel Morozov. This kind of theme became quite popular and more generalized to include films in which an airman killed his best friend who was a traitor (*Aerograd*) and a wife was killed by her husband, a 'hidden enemy' of the state (*Partiinyi Bilet*). These are discussed in Martin Gilbert, *A History of the Twentieth Century: Volume Two: 1933–1951* (New York: Morrow, 1998), pp. 66–67; and Sheila Fitzpatrick, "Signals from Below: Soviet Letters of Denunciation of the 1930's," in Sheila Fitzpatrick and Robert Gellately, eds., *Accusatory Practices: Denunciation in Modern European History, 1789–1989* (Chicago: University of Chicago Press, 1997).

43. The White Sea–Baltic canal mobilized 300,000 slave laborers of whom some 200,000 died during the construction.. This massive public works project achieved a mythical status as part of the Soviet *hubris* to be able to remake human beings. Based on a visit made by Maxim Gorky and other literary luminaries to the construction site, a collective book, *The White Sea Canal*, based on interviews with convicts and camp managers "described the process by whereby convicts were remade into good Soviet citizens. This was clearly a propaganda project: the visit could not have occurred except as the result of a high-level political decision, the book was dedicated to the Seventeenth Party Congress, and it was swiftly translated into English and achieved wide circulation via the Left Book Club and other 'fellow-travelling' outlets." Sheila Fitzpatrick, *Everyday Stalinism—Ordinary Life in Extraordinary Times: Soviet Russia in the 1930's* (New York: Oxford University Press, 1999), p. 76.

Paris and in the interwar period failed to revive it on a stable foundation."[44] The program geared to 'make the world safe for democracy,' installing democratic polities in Germany, post-imperial Austria, and the new countries created at Versailles, was undertaken, as Fritz Stern has observed, in circumstances marked by "a kind of economic, political, and cultural illiteracy" about "the preconditions for democracy and . . . the connections between economic and social conditions and democratic politics." Discussion "about the problems of transition to democracy," moreover, of the kind that dominate political discourse today, "were almost entirely absent in Europe in the years after 1918."[45]

The expectation that, somehow, after monarchy, empire, and the old regime, liberal democracy would consolidate quickly and securely was bitterly disappointed. One after another, representative legislative assemblies were dissolved or rendered inconsequential in Europe in the interwar period, primarily by successful challenges from the Right which installed one-party command in, among other countries, Portugal, Spain, Hungary, the Baltic states, Poland, and Romania.[46] As the Spanish Civil War dramatized, the space between revolution and reaction was crushed. Of the continent's twenty-six parliamentary democracies after Versailles, only twelve had survived by 1938 as an age of dictators flourished. The democracies created in the Paris peace settlement soon were dislodged by various anti-liberal models;[47] even the surviving democracies experienced mass movements seeking to supplant liberal democracy by alternative regime models. In Britain, with the creation of the National Government of 1931, "the two-party system was suspended and no precipitation was shown to restore it."[48] Seven additional liberal political orders collapsed into dictatorship during the first two years of the Second World War, leaving only Finland, Great Britain, Ireland, Sweden, and Switzerland as functioning European democracies at the end of 1940. "It is now often conveniently forgotten," Arendt noted,

---

44. Hajo Holborn, "The Collapse of the European Political System, 1914–1945," *World Politics* 1 (July 1949): 443. Also see Hajo Holborn, "Origins and Political Character of Nazi Ideology," *Political Science Quarterly* 79 (December 1964).

45. Fritz Stern, "The New Democracies in Crisis in Interwar Europe," in Axel Hadenius, ed., *Democracy's Victory and Crisis* (Cambridge: Cambridge University Press, 1997), p. 17.

46. See Stephen J. Lee, *The European Dictatorships, 1918–1945* (London: Methuen, 1987); David Clay Large, *Between Two Fires: Europe's Path in the 1930's* (New York: Norton, 1990); George L. Mosse, *The Fascist Revolution: Toward a General Theory of Fascism* (New York: Howard Fertig, 1999); and Stanley G. Payne, *Fascism in Spain 1923–1977* (Madison: University of Wisconsin Press, 1999).

47. France, of course, being a leading instance. See the excellent overview by Julian Jackson, *France: The Dark Years, 1940–1944* (Oxford: Oxford University Press, 2001).

48. Karl Polanyi, *The Great Transformation: The Political and Economic Origins of Our Time* (New York: Rinehart & Company, 1944), p. 228.

"that at the moment of the outbreak of the second World War, the majority of European countries had already adopted some form of dictatorship and discarded the party system, and that this revolutionary change in government had been effected in most countries without revolutionary upheaval."[49] Likewise, the broadly liberal, internationally oriented, parliamentary consensus in Japan of the 1920s was replaced by authoritarianism, economic nationalism, and imperial conquest; and in Latin America, the main locus of independent constitutional regimes outside Europe and North America, virtually all such governments failed to endure the crisis of the 1930s.[50] Liberalism collapsed, surrounded by often broad and deep hatred of parliamentary democracy and its abstractions of representation and law as constituting sham protectors of plutocracy and bourgeois domination against the collective interests of the people and the nation.

The period was marked, further, by an intensification of colonial violence and plunder as the colonized began to stir (their rebelliousness was resisted successfully; by the start of the Second World War no nonwhite colony yet had been granted independence), by a wrenching reorganization of international relations and missed chances to rebuild a coherent European order after Versailles, superseded first by German hegemony and then by an Atlantic and Russian great-power system, both of which left Europe deeply divided,[51] by death on a vast scale in Russia (some 10 million died between 1929 and 1933, the period of forced collectivization, and another 2 million during the purge period of

---

49. Arendt, *Origins*, p. 263.

50. In this period, Eric Hobsbawm correctly reminds us, the threat to liberal states came from the Right rather than the Left. He writes:

> Soviet Russia (from 1922: the USSR) was isolated and neither able nor, after the rise of Stalin, willing to extend communism. Social revolution uner Leninist (or any) leadership ceased to spread after the initial post-war wave had ebbed. The (Marxist) social-democratic movements had turned into state-sustaining rather than subversive forces, and their commitment to democracy was unquestioned. In most countries' labour movements communists were minorities, and where they were strong, in most cases they were, or had been, or were about to be, suppressed. The fear of social revolution, and the communists' role in it, was realistic enough, as the second wave of revolution during and after the Second World War proved, but in the twenty years of liberal retreat not a single regime could be reasonably called liberal-democratic had been overthrown from the left. The danger came exclusively from the Right. And the Right represented not merely a threat to constitutional and representative government, but an ideological threat to liberal civilization as such, and a potentially world-wide *movement*, for which the label 'fascism' is both insufficient and not wholly irrelevant.

Eric Hobsbawm, *The Age of Extremes: A History of the World, 1914–1991* (New York: Pantheon Books, 1994), p. 112.

51. Hajo Holborn, *The Political Collapse of Europe* (New York: Knopf, 1951).

1937 and 1938 as Stalin's version of Revolution conduced death and repression on an unprecedented scale in peacetime[52]), and by the nearly complete breakdown not just of western but western-dominated global capitalism in the Great Depression, spreading economic misery and putting enormous strain on civil societies and political systems everywhere.[53] At its depth, in 1932 and 1933, the United States had nearly 12 million unemployed, about a quarter of its wage labor force, and had lost just over half the national income it had possessed in 1929. Malnutrition became common; savings and property were lost; medical care was put off; no public safety net proved adequate; humiliation and distress multiplied.[54]

Then, cataclysm intensified. What Marshall Foch had called a "twenty-year truce" expired. A more terrible global war killing some 50 million, more than half out of uniform, proved vastly more destructive than the first. John Maynard Keynes' foretelling in 1919 was confirmed: "vengeance, I dare predict, will not limp. Nothing can then delay for very long that final civil war between the forces of Reaction and the despairing convulsions of Revolution, before which the horrors of the late German war will fade into nothing."[55] Well ahead of the atomic explosions of 1945, permanently heightening the prospect of human annihilation, the technology of death had intensified remarkably. The major combatants now deployed weapons which had been used only at the margins of the First World War; the full range of tanks, submarines, and especially aircraft with the capacity to devastate whole cities. Military engagements became more deadly, especially when exchanges were uneven. Suffering grew exponentially. By the end of 1941, the Red Army had lost 2,663,000 soldiers, twenty for every German killed. By war's end, we now know that at least 28 million civilians and Soviet sol-

---

52. Catherine Merridale, *Night of Stone: Death and Memory in Modern Russia* (London: Granta, 2000), chapter 1; also see J. Arch Getty and Oleg V. Naumov, *The Road to Terror: Stalin and the Self-destruction of the Bolsheviks, 1932–1939* (New Haven: Yale University Press, 1999). This, of course, in the name of freedom. At the Seventeenth Communist Party Congress in 1934, Karl Radek observed that "All we have gone through in the last years has shown how, having destroyed the freedom of the press and all other bourgeois freedoms, the working class under the Party's leadership has erected such freedoms for the creative activity of the masses of workers and peasants that the world has not seen before." Cited in Piers Brendon, *The Dark Valley: A Panorama of the 1930s* (New York: Knopf, 2000), p. 254.

53. These developments were punctuated by moments of optimism, such as that in 1922 when the Washington agreements of February outlawed poison gas and submarine attacks on merchant ships or, in economic terms, between 1925 and 1929 when the United States prospered and Europe rebounded from its wartime and postwar losses.

54. Curiously, President Hoover utilized the term 'Depression' in order to avoid using 'Panic.' Brendon, *Dark Valley*, p. 80.

55. John Maynard Keynes, *The Economic Consequences of the Peace* (London: Macmillan, 1919), p. 268.

diers had died, perhaps as many as 38 to 40 million.[56] More generally, limits which traditionally had distinguished civilians from combatants eroded (no fewer than 30 million civilians died under the impact of the war between 1939 and 1945). Deliberate disruptions to civilian life punctuated by displacement and atrocity became commonplace. At the extremity of cruelty, instantiating killing without barriers, the ruthless, premeditated, ideologically driven annihilation of Europe's Jews, and the willful organized murder of Gypsies and other categories of cast out people, mocked the very concept of codes of conduct.

In retrospect, the bloodbath of the First World War had been relatively benign, having been contained largely as a rural conflagration, leaving Europe's major cities and cultural heritage intact, and, with the exceptions of Belgium and Serbia, the continent's populations largely in place. For a brief moment, after 1918, it was possible to conceive of the war as a terrible but contained "interruption of normality" to "the rational and liberal civilisation of the European enlightenment."[57] The next quarter-century gave lie to this conceit. As Gerhard Weinberg observes, the Second World War differed from the First in goals and intentions. To be sure, the costly and destructive methods of the Great War "ended up completely transforming the prewar world and doing so in ways that none of the belligerents had anticipated." In the Second War, however, intentionality was married to means from the start. Now "the *intent* was . . . a total reordering of the globe. . . . a struggle not only for control for territory and resources but about who would live and control the resources of the globe and which peoples would vanish entirely because they were believed inferior or undesirable by the victors."[58] It was in the midst of the butchery that the Hungarian émigré Karl Polanyi gravely observed without the slightest hyperbole at the start of *The Great Transformation*, the book he published in 1944 to understand what his subtitle labeled the "political and economic origins of our time," that "Nineteenth century civilization has collapsed. . . . a torrent of events is pouring down on mankind."[59]

III.

So radical was the shift to the human condition in Europe and North America during this extended fanatical era that 'total war,' 'totalitarianism,' and 'holocaust,'

---

56. Merridale, *Night of Stone*, chapter 1.
57. Keegan, *War*, pp. 7, 8.
58. Gerhard L. Weinberg, *A World at Arms: A Global History of World War II* (Cambridge: Cambridge University Press), pp. 1–2.
59. Polanyi, *Transformation*, pp. 3, 4. In consequence, "the very possibility of freedom is in question." (p. 257).

the keywords with an apocalyptic edge which came into usage before and after
the Second World War to name the developments that haunted the political
studies enlightenment, cannot be found in the prewar edition of the *Britannica*.
They were yet to be imagined or conjured. Nor do they appear in the remarkable three-volume postwar supplement whose entry on physics was penned by
Albert Einstein and the one on the Russian Revolution by Trotsky, or for that
matter, in the twelve volumes of *The Cambridge Modern History* published between 1902 and 1910, conceived by Lord Acton as the expression of the best historical science the period had to offer.[60]

'Total war,' as a designation, dates from 1921 when Giulio Douhet, the Italian
supporter of air power (and of Mussolini) and a prophet of strategic bombing who
believed that in future war from the air could most effectively decimate civilian
areas, wrote that "The prevailing forms of social organization have given war a
character of national totality—that is, the entire population and all the resources
of the nation are sucked into the maws of war. And since society is now definitely
evolving along this line, it is within the power of human foresight to see now that
future wars will be total in character and scope."[61] This perspective was taken up
by other interwar military theorists, including Billy Mitchell in the United States
and Lord Trenchard in Britain, who, like Douhet, believed it could be possible to
force an enemy to sue for peace by directing massive air attacks to destroy its industrial capacity and transport links and demoralize its densely concentrated,
hence vulnerable, urban populations. By 1930, "Die total Mobilmachtung," the
term deployed in 1930 by Ernst Jünger in *Krieg und Krieger*, had entered into
wider discourse. With the spread of conflict to peoples and nations from mon-
archs and limited professional armies, civil society and economic production, he
observed, now had been subordinated to unprecedented military requirements.[62]

---

60. Cambridge: Cambridge University Press, 1902–1910.

61. Cited in Mark E. Neely, Jr., "Was the Civil War a Total War?," In Stig Förster and Jörg Na-
gler, eds., *On the Road to Total War: The American Civil War and the German Wars of Unifica-
tion, 1861–1871* (Cambridge: Cambridge University Press for the German Historical Institute,
Washington, D.C.), 1997, p. 33. Total war rested on the economic achievements of nineteenth-
century industrial capitalism, which offered vastly amplified resources for military production
and mobilization and on a new orientation to military strategy which stressed speedy mobilization based on pre-existing strategic plans. Together, Holborn has written about the late ninetenth
century, capitalist economics and strategic innovation produced a militarization that "laid the
groundwork for treating the national societies as independent, isolated entities. In the contracting
geographical condition of the age of modern capitalism the national states, for reasons of defense,
grew more like medieval cities. The walls, gates, and moats were not visible, as yet, but their blueprints were under way. In retrospect we can easily discern the beginnings of social organization
for total war." Holborn, *Political Collapse*, p. 65.

62. Ernst Jünger, *Krieg und Krieger* (Berlin: Junker und Dunnhaupt, 1930).

Until the second decade of the twentieth century, Gilbert Murray observed in the Hibbert Lectures of 1937, wars were. with few exceptions, limited "in the numbers engaged, in geographical extent, and in what one might call penetration below the surface. The armies," he explained, "destroyed everything in their path, but the path was narrow, and towns a little way out of the path were hardly affected."[63] After the appalling slaughter at the Somme, Verdun, Passchendale, and the other set stalemate locations of trench warfare, total war by air (initiated by the bombing of German cities by the French in 1914) which could directly attack enemy industrial and population centers seemed more efficient, even more humane.[64] With the mobilization of all the human and productive resources of the countries at war, there was no longer a barrier to legitimate military targeting. "The problem," a legal scholar observed,[65]

> is not the prohibition of aerial warfare, but its regulation in such a manner as to spare, so far as is practicable, unoffending non-combatants, private property and public institutions from indiscriminate destruction, and to insure that the wars of the future will not degenerate into struggles of reciprocal reprisals and barbarism, in which no distinction will be made between combatants and non-combatants or between public property and private property.

By the close of the Second World War, the combatants routinely were utilizing heavy, four-engined, long-range bombers designed to destroy industrial infrastructure, urban housing, and kill civilians. Whereas 5 percent of total deaths

---

63. Gilbert Murray, *Liberality and Civilization: Lectures Given at the Invitation of the Hibbert Trustees in the Universities of Bristol, Glasgow, and Birmingham in October and November 1937* (London: George Allen and Unwin, 1938), p. 59.

64. For discussions, see John Keegan, *The First World War* (New York: Knopf, 1999), chapter 1; Sven Lindqvist, *A History of Bombing* (London: Granta, 2001). Lindqvist notes that bombing was first thought of in conjunction with the imperialist ventures of the European powers in Africa in the late nineteenth century. Libya was the site of the first bomb dropped from a plane, mistakenly hitting Italian troops camped outside Tripoli. Patrick Wright, "Dropping their Eggs," *London Review of Books* 23 (August 2001): 11. Wright further observes that the technique was tested on colonial targets by the Spanish in Morocco, the French in Syria, and the British in Egypt and India before and in the early stages of the First World War. During the First World War, the English mathematician F. W. Lanchester invented the idea of deterrence through air power. F. W. Lanchester, *Aircraft in Warfare: The Dawn of the Fourth Arm* (London: Constable and Company, 1916).

65. James W. Garner, "Proposed Rules for the Regulation of Aerial Warfare," *American Journal of International Law* 18 (January 1924): 66.

had been civilian in the First World War, aerial bombardment, including terror bombing, raised this proportion to 65 percent in the Second.[66]

Further, by the 1940s, building on the experience of the 1910s, the meaning of 'total war' had been extended beyond the effort by air to destroy the resources of the enemy—an undertaking that included tremendous pre-nuclear air raids killing between 50,000 and 100,000 people in single nights of bombing in Dresden, Hamburg, and Tokyo[67]—to refer to the full mobilization at home of the whole economy and civil society to pursue the war effort. Although popular enthusiasm for the First World War had not played a role in its outbreak, the remarkable and unexpected eagerness of millions to go to war and support the decisions of political leaders to wage it across ideological and class lines heralded more than the integrative powers of nationalism or the legitimization of conscripted military service into a professional army facing astonishing risks, but the willingness to support unprecedented levels of financial and industrial mobilization of the whole society. Backed by the full resources of the relevant population pool for military deployment and deeply felt national and ideological feeling supporting elite decisions, the pursuit of credit by the state through domestic and foreign borrowing and the raising of levels of taxation to unprecedented heights through the use of such new instruments as the income tax were advanced as wartime budgets spiraled upwards, well beyond any prior expectations. Following a period of rapid depletion of high explosive shells and other armaments and the insufficient supply of modern rifles, field guns, grenades, and other implements of war for the new massive armies deployed across the Continent during the initial period of the First World War, the combatant countries moved quickly to combine state planning with industrial expertise to quickly secure raw materials, convert industry to wartime purposes, and accelerate the manufacture of weapons on an astonishing scale. Old producers were joined by new ones as virtually the entire private economy and the network of transport were disciplined and directed by the purposes of war. Traditional debates about state collectivism and liberal capitalism or the character of civilian

---

66. For discussions, see Mark Connelly, *Reaching for the Stars: A New History of Bomber Command in World War Two* (London: I. B, Tauris, 2000); Sven Lindqvist, *A History of Bombing* (London: Granta Books, 2001); and the review of both books by Joanna Bourke, "Women and Children First," *Times Library Supplement*, June 8, 2001, p. 28. Also see Tami Davis Biddle, *Rhetoric and Reality in Air Warfare: The Evolution of British and American Ideas about Strategic Bombing, 1914–1945* (Princeton: Princeton University Press, 2002).

67. In this respect, the destructive force of the Allies far outstripped that of the Axis powers. 74,000 tons of bombs were dropped on Britain, killing some 51,000. By contrast, the 2 million tons dropped by the Allies killed 900,000 in Japan, 600,000 in Germany, and 62,000 in Italy. Ponting, *Twentieth Century*, p. 281.

control over the military did not entirely disappear, but they were recast in the fundamentally new and intensified context of total war.[68]

Such a system of organization became more pressing and present during the Second World War as "the extent of destruction was very much greater, and spread over vastly larger areas."[69] Immense efforts now were mounted to accelerate the production of faster airplanes, heavier tanks, and more powerful ammunition in support of innovations in land fighting, naval warfare, and especially strategic bombing and rocket campaigns guided by new technologies like radar that were not only directed against military personnel but also given an independent role to strike the home territories of the enemy in order to destroy both the means and the will to make war. The frightful, instantaneous, near-complete eradication of Hiroshima and Nagasaki introduced a further, qualitatively distinctive intensification to the idea of total war. Thus, by 1945 'total war' had secured not just the "three distinct traits" identified by the émigré sociologist, Hans Speier: "(1) a particularly close interdependence between the armed forces and the productive forces of the nation, which necessitates large scale governmental planning; (2) the extension of siege warfare involving the nation as a whole in both offensive and defensive actions; and (3) a general vilification of the enemy nation,"[70] but also the ultimate destructive capacity of nuclear weaponry. In the postwar years, a contemporary wrote, "the term total war" with this quadruple-meaning, unknown only three decades earlier, "has become . . . definitely accepted as a part of the everyday vocabulary."[71]

'Totalitarianism,' sharing the same root word, came to be closely identified with the notion of total war.[72] Ernst Jünger, an accomplished war memoirist

---

68. See the excellent discussions of these themes in Hew Strachan, *The First World War. Volume I: To Arms* (Oxford: Oxford University Press, 2001), chapters 2, 10, and 11.

69. Weinberg, *A World at Arms*, p. 3.

70. Hans Speier, "Class Structure and Total War," in Hans Speier, *Social Order and the Risks of War: Papers in Political Sociology* (Cambridge: MIT Press, 1952), p. 254.

71. Neely, Jr., "Civil War," p. 35. Also see, for a discussion of the transformation of warfare, David Kaiser, *Politics and War: European Conflict from Philip II to Hitler* (London: I. B. Tauris, 1990); and, on the democratization of war, Geoff Eley, "War and the Twentieth-Century State," *Daedalus* 124 (Spring 1995). In retrospect, we can see an awful harbinger of total war at the gathering of the Hague Convention of nations in 1907. In 1899, at the first Hague Peace Conference, dropping of bombs from balloons "or other kinds of aerial vessels" had been proscribed by international agreement Though limits on targeting were enacted, this restriction was not renewed. A giant step had been taken.

72. One of the more visible international evocations of fascism was an explicit demonstration of the role of air power on the basis of the theories of General Douhet in the spectacular cross-Atlantic air journeys led by the Italian Fascist Minister of Aviation, Italo Balbo, for whom Balbo Avenue was named in Chicago following his July 1933 landing near Navy Pier with an armada of 24 Savoia Marchetti flying boats escorted by 43 American fighters spelling out the word 'Italia.'

and novelist who had flirted with Nazism in the 1920s only to practice the political detachment of an 'inner emigration' during the Third Reich, who had characterized the mobilization of populations during the First World War by the
words *total* and *Totalität*, and who had advocated a total mobilization of workers and the military based on mechanization, will, and hierarchical organization to overcome the decadence of liberal society, also elaborated a concept of
the totalitarian state. Likewise, Carl Schmitt, the conservative jurist and scholar
best known for his distinction between friend and enemy and his collaboration
with the Third Reich, grounded his notion of a "qualitatively total" state representing the triumph of an executive-centered state over society (as opposed to a
"qualitatively total" society via an extension of welfarism where the society dom-
inates the state) in Jünger's ideas about total war.[73] Extending this linkage, and
anticipating Harold Lasswell's 1941 dystopia called "The Garrison State,"[74] General Erich Ludendorff's *Der totale Krieg*, published in 1935 was the first book to
utilize the term in its title. (He had been in charge, virtually as a dictator, of the
war effort in Germany in 1917 and 1918; in the 1920s, as a deep racial anti-Semite
and *völkish* radical nationalist he offered his prestige and collaboration to Hitler
and his paramilitary movement.[75]) Ludendorff argued that modern war required totalitarian direction by specialists in violence under the auspices of state
and party, thus fusing military and political command, with domestic affairs
subsumed to the requirements of war and international relations.[76] Indeed,
John Keegan observes, totalitarianism, the "new word for a system that rejected
the liberalism and constitutionalism which had inspired European politics
since the eclipse of monarchy in 1789," represented "the political continuation
of war by other means. It uniformed and militarised its mass electoral following,
while depriving voters generally of their electoral rights, exciting their lowest political instincts, and marginalising and menacing all internal opposition."[77]

The term 'totalitarianism' was invented, of course, well before it was mus-
tered for Cold War purposes, since it first was coined by leading anti-fascist journalists in Italy in the early 1920s—in 1923, for example, Giovanni Amendola,
writing in *Il Mondo*, used the phrase *systema totalitaria* first to refer to the
regime's refusal to allow the opposition to organize and present its electoral list
and then, more broadly, to announce that the most "salient characteristic of the

---

73. Carl Schmitt, *Der Hüter der Verfassung* (Tübingen: Mohr, 1931).

74. Harold D. Lasswell, "The Garrison State," *American Journal of Sociology* 46 (January 1941).

75. See Ian Kershaw, *Hitler, 1889–1836: Hubris* (New York: Norton, 1998), pp. 194–195, 262–269.

76. This was how the émigré scholar, Emil Lederer, described trends in 1939. See his "Domestic
Policy and Foreign Relations," in Hans Speier and Alfred Kahler, *War in Our Time* (New York:
Norton, 1939).

77. Keegan, *War*, pp. 8–9.

fascist movement . . . remains its 'totalitarian spirit'."[78] By 1925, fascism's theorists, notably Giovanni Gentile, and practitioners, including Mussolini, distinguished fascism's dynamism and absorption of civil society into the state from more slack liberal regimes.[79] "Now liberalism is preparing to close the doors to its temples," Mussolini claimed, "deserted by the peoples who feel that the agnosticism it professed in the sphere of economics and the indifferentism of which it has given proof in the sphere of politics and morals, would lead the world to ruin in the future as they have done in the past." Hence, he concluded, "this explains why all the political experiments of our day are anti-liberal."[80] Writing under Mussolini's name for the *Encyclopedia Italiana* in 1932, Gentile announced that "the fascist concept of the state is all-embracing; outside of it no human or spiritual values can exist, much less have value. Thus understood, fascism is totalitarian." When Mussolini visited the Vatican in February 1932 on the third anniversary of the signing of the Lateran accord, Pius XI announced that "during these times of crisis and great misery," there could be useful collaboration between what he called "Fascist totalitarianism" and "Catholic totalitarianism." Soon, in its early days in power, Nazism took up this formulation.[81] In the fall of 1933, Goebbels declared that "our party has always aspired to a totalitarian state," and Hitler entreated the annual Lawyer's conference meeting in Berlin "to guard the authority of this totalitarian state."[82]

---

78. Abbott Gleason, *Totalitarianism: The Inner Story of the Cold War* (New York: Oxford University Press, 1995), p. 14. Abbott's history of the term can be read profitably alongside the 'genealogy of totalitarianism' in Jeffrey C. Isaac, *Arendt, Camus, and Modern Rebellion* (New Haven: Yale University Press, 1992), pp. 37–45.

79. Notwithstanding, there were vast differences between Mussolini's fascism and Nazism, a point regularly made by Nazi political leaders and theorists. Certainly, considered in comparison with Nazism, especially after 1938, and Bolshevism, especially after 1930, the term, in Mussolini's hands, appears "unrealistic and bombastic." Bernard Crick, "On Rereading *The Origins of Totalitarianism,*" *Social Research* 44 (Spring 1997): 107; also see Arendt, *Origins*, pp. 308–9, 419–420. It also might be noted that fascist thought was distinct from earlier Italian elitist thought. I thank Nadia Urbinati for this translated citation from Noberto Bobbio: "In the two major . . . creators of the doctrine of fascism, the philosopher Gentile and the jurist Rocco, the theory of elites had no part, not even a peripheral one. . . . The actual followers of the political class have not been fascist writers, but anti-fascist and democratic writers." Noberto Bobbio, *Saggi sulla Scienza Politica in Italia*. Bari: Laterza, 1969, pp. 247–248.

80. Benito Mussolini, *Fascism: Doctrine and Institutions* (Rome: Ardita, 1935; first published in Italian in 1932), p. 10. For discussions, see Dante Germino, "Italian Fascism in the History of Political Thought," *Midwest Journal of Political Science* 8 (May 1964); and Gilbert Allardyce, "What Fascism is Not: Thoughts on the Deflation of a Concept," *American Historical Review* 84 (April 1979).

81. Brendon, *Dark Valley*, p. 148.

82. Both are cited in Franz L. Neumann, *Behemoth: The Structure and Practice of National Socialism* (New York: Knopf, 1951), p. 47. A central theme in this work in a key tension between the glorification of the state as totalitarian and the impulses of the Nazi party to create a movement-

If much in the politics of the West after the eclipse of monarchy by the American and French Revolutions had been inspired by a combination of constitutionalism, liberalism, and democracy, totalitarianism superseded the first two in the name of a particular version of radical democracy, rejecting the limits liberal constitutionalism had placed on the extension of politics and the reach of the state by making what Hitler called a "comprehensive claim to power destroying all liberal forms of autonomy" emphasizing, in Nazi theorist Roland Friesler's words, that "fundamental rights which create free spheres for individuals untouchable by the state are irreconcilable with the totalitarian principle of the new state," and turning the broadly common nationalization of patriotism characteristic of the nineteenth century into a fighting creed.[83] Under the direction of mass parties, totalitarian regimes harnessed mammoth states unchecked by liberal rights and institutions to pursue various projects designed to create new civilizations based on diverse images, including racial purity and socialist utopia.[84] It was this double-meaning of the one-party state respecting no traditional political perimeters and which penetrated and repressed civil society in unprecedented ways that convoked and justified the extension of the term from Nazism to Stalinism during the 1930s as a wide array of thinkers "saw with unwelcome horror that there were astonishing similarities between the style, structure of thought, and the key institutions of the Nazis and the Russian Communists."[85] This list of the shared features of totalitarian polities is quite

centered polity that created a kind of societal totalitarianism. Also see Hajo Holborn, "Origins and Character of Nazi Ideology," *Political Science Quarterly* 79 (December 1964).

83. See Maurizio Viroli, *For Love of Country: An Essay on Patriotism and Nationalism* (Oxford: Clarendon Press, 1995).

84. Such large goals were to be established both by shattering traditional civil society, generalized surveillance and repression, mass mobilization by instruments of the new media, and planning on unprecedented scales. For discussions, see Emile Lederer, *State of the Masses: The Threat of the Classless Society* (New York: Norton, 1940); Gerhard Jacoby, *Racial State: the German Nationalities Policy in the Protectorate of Bohemia-Moravia* (New York: Institute of Jewish Affairs, 1944); Michael Burleigh and Wolfgang Wippermann, *The Racial State: Germany, 1933–1935* (Cambridge: Cambridge University Press, 1991); and Stephen Kotkin, *Magnetic Mountain: Stalinism as a Civilization* (Berkeley: University of California Press, 1995).

85. Crick, "Rereading," pp.107–108. Even at the time, however, the many scholars and journalists who came to use the term recognized the differences in spite of the similarities not only between German Nazism and Russian Bolshevism, but between these and Italian Fascism, yet they came to think, rightly, that 'totalitarianism' was apt as a cover term for a form of rule not covered by more traditional terms like dictatorship. See, Halévy, *Era*, pp. 278–285; Robert M. MacIver, *Leviathan and the People* (Oxford: Oxford University Press, 1940); Leonard Schapiro, *Totalitarianism* (New York: Praeger, 1972); Hans Buchheim, *Totalitarian Rule: Its Nature and Characteristics* (Middletown: Wesleyan University Press, 1968); Carl J. Friedrich and Zbigniew Brzezinski, *Totalitarian Dictatorship and Autocracy* (Cambridge: Harvard University Press, 1956); Carl J. Friedrich, ed., *Totalitarianism: Proceedings of a Conference Held at the American Academy of Arts*

long: the primacy of political will; veneration of violence as means to overcome traditional barriers to appropriate patterns of state building, economic develop-ment, and military capacity; a fundamental and proud aversion to the liberal political tradition; the transcendence of law; the corruption of language and his-torical truth; a stress on the integral unity of the movement state led by a deeply ideological political party; an unremitting identification and exclusion of 'out-siders'; and a consciousness of mobilization led by a 'legitimate' dictator. Older words like dictatorship, tyranny, and despotism seemed well short of descriptive or conceptual marks. Noting the shared characteristics of the new type of regime, Paul Tillich, the German émigré Protestant theologian, wrote in 1934 soon after arriving in the United States that "in Russia the totalitarian state has been more effectively realized than even in Germany."[86] This theme also was taken up on the Left, as in the acknowledgment by the Austro-Marxist Otto Bauer in 1936 that in the Soviet Union "the dictatorship of the proletariat had assumed the specific form of a monopolistic, totalitarian dictatorship of the Communist Party."[87] By the end of that decade, the liberal-totalitarian antin-omy had begun to be applied widely and urgently by liberalism's defenders, es-pecially by refugee intellectuals who had experienced Nazism directly, rather more than by totalitarianism's advocates.[88]

---

and Sciences, March 1953 (Cambridge: Harvard University Press, 1954); Les K. Adler and Thomas G. Paterson, "Red Fascism: The Merger of Nazi Germany and Soviet Russia in the American Image of Totalitarianism," *The American Historical Review* 75 (April 1970); Richard Bessell, ed., *Fascist Italy and Nazi Germany: Comparisons and Contrasts* (Cambridge: Cam-bridge University Press, 1996); Ian Kershaw and Moshe Lewin, eds., *Stalinism and Nazism: Dictatorships in Comparison* (Cambridge: Cambridge University Press, 1997); Simon Tormey, *Making Sense of Tyranny: Interpretations of Totalitarianism* (Manchester: University of Man-chester Press, 1995); Michael Curtis, *Totalitarianism* (New Brunswick: Transaction Books, 1979); and Ellen Frankel Paul, ed. *Totalitarianism at the Crossroads* (New Brunswick: Transac-tion Books, 1990).

86. Paul Tillich, "The Totalitarian State and the Claims of the Church," *Social Research* 2 (No-vember 1934): 410.

87. Cited in François Furet, *The Passing of an Illusion: The Idea of Communism in the Twentieth Century* (Chicago: University of Chicago Press, 1999), p. 159.

88. The Russian purge trials and the Nazi-Soviet pact proved key turning points in confirm-ing a widespread, though not uniform, pattern of disillusionment about Stalin's USSR. For a useful discussion, see Adler and Paterson, "Red Fascism." This moment was marked by the pub-lication of Frank Borkenau, *The Totalitarian Enemy*, London: Faber and Faber, 1940); George Orwell's review of Borkenau, which can be found in Orwell, *The Collected Essays, Journalism, and Letters*. Volume Two (New York: Harcourt, Brace and World, 1968, pp. 24–26); Ignazio Silone, *The School for Dictators* (London: Cape, 1939); Arthur Koestler, *Arrival and Depar-ture* (New York: Macmillan, 1943); and by the symposium on the 'totalitarian state' convened by the American Philosophical Society in 1940, edited by Carlton Hayes: "Symposium on the Totalitarian State," *Proceedings of the American Philosophical Society*, 82 (February 1940).

'Holocaust,' as the most common label for the planned annihilation of Europe's Jews as a central ideological goal aiming at a total erasure and succeeding in murdering most—an act for which we can find no meaning except for Nazi meaning[89]—would have to wait for some two decades of representational incoherence to pass for what Winston Churchill had called "a crime without a name" to secure one, eventually besting 'Shoah,' 'Churban,' 'Final Solution,' 'Judeocide,' 'War Against the Jews,' 'Judenvernichtung' (annihilation of the Jews), and 'Auschwitz,' among other alternatives.[90] "Even though it implies a

---

Raphael Lemkin, *Axis Rule in Occupied Europe: Laws of Occupation, Analysis of Government, Proposals for Redress* (Washington: Carnegie Endowment for International Peace, 1944). Also see, Schapiro, *Totalitarianism*, pp. 13–13; Gleason, *Totalitarianism*, pp. 13–30; Mazower, *Dark Continent: Europe's Twentieth Century* (London: Allen Lane, the Penguin Press, 1998), pp. 34, 32. For a discussion of how totalitarianism had its effects on the conduct of constitutional democracies, see David Vincent, *The Culture of Secrecy: Britain, 1832–1998* (New York: Oxford University Press, 1998); and Mary Sperling McAuliffe, *Crisis on the Left: Cold War Politics and American Liberals, 1947–1954* (Amherst: University of Massachusetts Press, 1978).

89. A point made by Yehuda Bauer, "A Past that Will Not Go Away," in Berenbaum and Peck, eds., *Holocaust and History*, p. 15. This system of meaning, in which the Jew was 'parasite,' 'evil,' 'vampire,' and 'filth,' to note only some of Hitler's appellations, was metaphysical, not simply racial or political, though it was these as well.

90. Cited in Martin Gilbert, "'That Most Horrible Crime': Churchill's Prophetic, Passionate, and Persistent Response to the Holocaust," *Times Literary Supplement*, June 7, 1996, p. 3. On the issue of naming, see Peter Haidu, "The Dialectic of Unspeakability: Language, Silence, and the Narratives of Desubjectification," in Saul Friedländer, ed., *Probing the Limits of Representation: Nazism and the 'Final Solution'* (Cambridge: Harvard University Press, 1992). The inability to find a name was matched by the inability of scholars to find a voice; for the first two decades after the Second War, there hardly was a scholarly debate about its comprehensibility, character, causes, and meaning. For an excellent compilation of papers published as the result of a conference convened by the United States Holocaust Memorial Museum indicating how the Holocaust has entered into mainstream historiography, see Berenbaum and Peck, eds., *Holocaust and History*.

The first reference to Nazism using the term 'holocaust' I can find came at the start of the regime when Eustace Wareing, the Berlin correspondent of London's *Daily Telegraph*, reported on the May 10, 1933 burning of more than 20,000 'un-German' books by Jews, who were the primary target, as well as pacifists, Marxists, and other undesirables at a bonfire outside Berlin's Kroll Opera House as the culmination of a month-long campaign by the National Socialist Student Association against what they saw as the fouling of German intellectual life. Using 'holocaust' literally as eradication by fire, Wareing wrote, "As the Opera House Square in which the holocaust was accomplished was reserved for the students and their friends, the only part of the ceremony visible to the wider public was the torchlight procession by which the condemned volumes were escorted to the bonfire." Cited in Gilbert, *History*, p. 5. On more recent usages, the literature, of course, is vast; see Saul Friedländer, *Memory, History, and the Extermination of the Jews of Europe* (Bloomington: Indiana University Press, 1993); Henry Greenspan, "Imagining Survivors: Testimony and the Rise of Holocaust Consciousness," in Hilene Flanzbaum, ed., *The Americanization of the Holocaust* (Baltimore: Johns Hopkins University Press, 1999); and Zelizer, *Remembering*.

particular (a Jewish) perspective and is a misnomer according to its original religious meaning," the historian of anti-Semitism Gavin Langmuir has observed,
"nonetheless, precisely because of its ambiguous religious overtones, the word
suggests a cosmic or overarching perspective that could embrace all the structures, events, agents, and casualties involved in the killing."[91] It also implies a
rupture more specific in time and place than the more general term 'genocide,'
itself first named in 1944 in Raphael Lemkin's examination of *Axis Rule in Occupied Europe* to denote a phenomenon that moved persecution and discrimination to a new level of directed, deliberate killing of target populations. The
Nazi's planned and organized liquidation of Jews, as Saul Friedländer has put
the point, inscribed "the most radical form of genocide encountered in history:
the willful, systematic, industrially organized, largely successful attempt to totally exterminate an entire human group."[92] And it seemed, as the war continued, to trump all other objectives, including the most productive use of their
labor or the successful pursuit of the military encounter. Hidden yet known, the
product of planning and improvisation, this project was deeply consistent with
Nazi ideological appeals, its warped historical and causal analyses of Germany's
plight, its larger policies of racial purity and medicalized murder, and its systematic practices of Jewish extrusion from the society, economy, and polity into
which they had entered after achieving emancipation in 1870–1871. Though
"the killing of 6 million European Jews was part of a wider Nazi project,"[93] and
although the globe has witnessed a good many other instances of mass killing
and genocide on an extraordinary scale, the temporal elongation and compre-
hensiveness of the eliminationist program together with the enormity and
meticulousness of its execution and continental scope marked by the quest to
extirpate and murder Jews even in places in which the Nazis "had no connection, and which Germans had neither settled nor had any desire to settle, trans-
porting them hundreds of thousands of miles to their deaths in extermination

91. Gavin I. Langmuir, "Continuities, Discontinuities and Contingencies of the Holocaust," in
Jonathan Frankel, ed., *The Fate of the European Jews, 1939–1945: Continuity or Contingency?*
[*Studies in Contemporary Jewry* 13 (1997)] (New York: Oxford University Press, 1997), p. 9. Greek
in origins, referring to a burnt offering to the Lord, 'holocaust' carries with it an often unexamined implication of sacrifice, albeit with unclarity about purpose, embedded in a larger eschatology.
92. With the compliance of the leaders of Germany's large corporations, it also transformed Jews
into uncompensated factors of production as slave laborers before their deaths. Lemkin was a
Polish-Jewish lawyer; Saul Friedländer, "Introduction," in Friedländer, ed., *Limits of Representation*, p. 3. Also see, Mark Mazower, *Dark Continent*, pp. 161–162, and Michael André Bernstein,
"The Lasting Injury," *Times Literary Supplement*, March 7, 1997.
93. Richard Vinen, *A History in Fragments: Europe in the Twentieth Century* (Cambridge: Da
Capo Press, 2000), p. 199.

camps in Poland," singles out this enterprise of desolation as the ultimate concentrated negation of the promise of Enlightenment.[94]

To be sure, the *Britannica's* contributors in 1910 had a good deal to say about
anti-Semitism and what they called "anti-Jewish excesses," including post-1881
pogroms in Russia, the Ukraine, Poland, and other locations in East Europe,
but even after the Armenian massacre, the beastly and irreducible events to
come still were well beyond the horizon of the encyclopedia's editors and contributors, or, for that matter, any one else's.[95]

Of all the developments from the outbreak of the First World War to the
close of the Second, it was the Jewish nightmare that arguably made unrevised
reaffirmations of Enlightenment impossible. The inclusion of Jews into western
modernity on terms the American and French Revolutions first had propelled
now had proved compatible with persecution and liquidation on a vast scale.
Among the various offspring of Enlightenment, German liberalism and social
democracy, Austrian modernism, and French Republicanism all had failed to
stem horrors' tide.

The pogrom mounted against Germany's Jews on November 9 and 10, 1938,
best known as *Kristallnacht* for the shattered glass that covered a large swath of
the German landscape, decisively crushed the emancipatory promise of "common ground between the German and Jewish *Bildungbürger* which had once
seemed so certain,"[96] a faith that had flourished in the climate of parliamentary
democracy in the Weimar years, which we retrospectively remember for its failures while repressing its achievements.[97] As Goebbels gleefully observed the

---

94. Of course, the relevant literature is so immense as to make extended citation virtually impossible. The chapters on Nazis and Jews in Michael Burleigh's recent synthesis provide an excellent
point of access. Michael Burleigh, *The Third Reich: A New History* (London: Macmillan, 2000),
chapters 4 and 8.

95. Still, the concluding paragraph of the entry on "Anti-Semitism" is chilling: "Though anti-
Semitism has been unmasked and discredited, it is to be feared that its history is not yet at an end.
While there remains in Russia and Rumania over six million of Jews who are being systematically
degraded, and who periodically overflow the western frontier, there must continue to be a Jewish
question in Europe; and while there are weak governments, and ignorant and superstitious elements in the enfranchised classes of the countries affected, that question will seek to play a role in
politics." *Britannica*, vol. 1, p. 145.

96. George Mosse, *German Jews Beyond Judaism* (Cincinnati: Hebrew Union Press, 1985), p. 14.

97. Hans Mommsen, *The Rise and Fall of Weimar Democracy* (Chapel Hill: University of North
Carolina Press, 1996), pp. vii-xi. Germany's Jews, moreover, crafted a complex culture in
Weimar's crucible by fashioning a Jewish sphere "as a cultural realm compatible with participa-
tion in the larger non-Jewish society and culture." Michael Brenner, *The Renaissance of Jewish
Culture in Weimar Germany* (New Haven: Yale University Press, 1996), p. 2. For an overview, see
Peter Gay, *Weimar Culture: The Outsider as Insider* (London: Martin Secker & Warburg, 1969).

height of the thuggery by members of the Gestapo, the Nazi Automobile Corps, and the German Labor Front that murdered more than 100 Jews, sent 26,000 to concentration camps, and destroyed hundreds of synagogues and some 7,500 Jewish shops, he jotted in his diary, "As I am driven to the hotel, windowpanes shatter [they are being smashed]. Bravo! Bravo! The synagogues burn like big old cabins. German property is not endangered."[98] Many women's memoirs, Marion Kaplan's history of ordinary life for Jews under the Nazis observes, speak less of the glass or the fire than of how the air filled with floating feathers, ripped from pillows and blankets by brutal invaders of their private space. The "broken glass in public and strewn feathers in private spelled the end of Jewish security in Germany,"[99] bringing to a close a half-decade of expectation that the curse of radical anti-Semitism eventually would pass, and, more generally, ending the sense many Jews had had that the exit from the ghetto proffered by enlightened emancipation would be accompanied by entry tickets into modern western politics and society.[100]

Instead, over and over and over there were moments like *Kristallnacht* or *Jeudi Noir*, July 16, 1942, when 4,500 French police in Paris rounded up some

---

98. Cited in Saul Friedländer, *Nazi Germany and the Jews, Volume I: The Years of Persecution, 1933–1939* (New York: HarperCollins, 1997), p. 272. Ninety synagogues were set ablaze in Germany, of which 76 were destroyed. A further 102 synagogues, both large and small, were torched in Vienna.

99. Marion A. Kaplan, *Between Dignity and Despair: Jewish Life in Nazi Germany* (New York: Oxford University Press, 1998), p. 125. *Kristallnacht*, of course, only marked a moment, albeit a particularly dramatic one, in the course of Jewish extirpation. Writing about the months that preceded it, Peter Gay's memoir remarks how "portents proliferated and at unprecedented speed. In June, Munich's largest synagogue was torched. In July, Jewish physicians were forbidden to treat gentile patients and deprived of their status as doctors. . . . In August, the forced sale of synagogues in various German cities at ludicrously low prices went forward. In September, it was the Jewish lawyers' turn: like Jewish physicians, they were stripped of their gentile clients and their professional title. . . . Then in early October the passports of German Jews were differentiated from those of 'real' Germans by a red *J* stamped on the front page." His text includes a particularly unsentimental, hence poignant, account of November 9 and 10 from the perspective of a boy, interpreting the events, as Peter Loewenberg has, as a spectacle of degradation. By later standards, *Kristallnacht* was tame—synagogues burnt and desecrated, thousands of businesses and homes ravaged, 26,000 sent to concentration (not death) camps, about 100 Jews killed—but what it confirmed was the destructive fury possible when civil society racism and state power mediated by a totalitarian party combined. Peter Gay, *My German Question: Growing Up in Nazi Berlin* (New Haven: Yale University Press, 1998), pp. 123, 133–137); Peter Loewenberg, "The Kristallnacht as a Public Degradation Ritual," *Leo Baeck Institute Yearbook*, XXXII (1987).

100. Pierre Birnbaum and Ira Katznelson, eds., *Paths of Emancipation: Jews, States, and Citizenship* (Princeton: Princeton University Press, 1995); Zygmunt Bauman, "Exit Visas and Entry Tickets: Paradoxes of Jewish Assimilation," *Telos*, no. 77 (Fall 1988).

27,000 stateless and immigrant Jews. The historian Annie Kriegel recalled this day after she had sat for the *baccalauréat* at the age of fifteen, (also the day after her mother, having heard rumors, had counseled her not to return home) wearing the yellow star:[101]

> I nevertheless went on my way until, at the crossing of the rue de Turenne and the rue de Bretagne, I heard screams rising to the heavens: not cries and squawks such as you hear in noisy and excited crowds, but screams like you used to hear in hospital delivery rooms. All the human pain that both life and death provide.

The shock of disappointment proved profound. Those who had experienced forced extrusion from citizenship were stunned by the failure of enlightened, liberal culture to confront the Nazi persecution of the Jews either inside, or outside, Germany and by the pervasiveness of cool unconcern. They observed that "nothing in the next-door world of Dachau impinged on the great winter cycle of Beethoven chamber music played in Munich. No canvases came off the museum walls as the butchers strolled reverently past, guide-books in hand."[102] The main reason for her own emigration, Hannah Arendt later remarked, was the indifferent behavior, or, as in the case of Benno von Wiese, not to speak of Heidegger, the unpressured support for the new order by her Aryan acquaintances; "Our friends Nazified (*gleichschalteten*) themselves! The problem . . . after all, was not what our enemies did, but what our friends did."[103] Heidegger was more than complicit; he was electrified by the rise of Nazism.[104] The basic norms of western civilization were turned upside down. We know now, after decades of controversy, that the terror constellation of Gestapo and camps was widely known among Germans and its bloody practices elicited a good deal of consent and participation.[105]

---

101. Annie Kriegel, *Réflexion sur des questions juives* (Paris: Hachette, 1984), p. 18; cited in Susan Zuccotti, *The Holocaust, the French, and the Jews* (New York: Basic Books, 1993), p. 104. For a striking account of postwar failures to take the measure of the ferocity and relentlessness of Vichy's anti-Semitic measures, see Pierre Birnbaum, "Sorry Afterthoughts on *Anti-Semite and Jew*," *October*, no. 87 (Winter 1999).

102. George Steiner, *In Bluebeard's Castle: Some Notes Towards the Re-definition of Culture* (London: Faber, 1971), p. 54.

103. Friedländer, *Nazi Germany*, p. 55; Kaplan, *Dignity*, p. 43.

104. Rüdiger Safranski, *Martin Heidegger: Between Good and Evil* (Cambridge: Harvard University Press, 1998), pp. 248–263.

105. An overview is presented in Robert Gellately, *Backing Hitler: Consent and Coercion in Nazi Germany* (New York: Oxford University Press, 2001).

Academic, intellectual, legal, and medical elites, in particular, proved ready to collude with National Socialist ideology and practices. Within the country, the only public protest against Nazi racial policies and the deportation of the Jews came in February 1943 when hundreds, perhaps more than a thousand, gentile women demonstrated against the detainment of their Jewish husbands and relatives, many of whom, in fact, soon were released by the regime.[106]

Even where resistance to Nazi savageness against the Jews might have been expected to be easier and more robust, opposition and hindrance were meager. As part of the broader pattern of appeasement by liberal regimes, the more the German state sought to expel the country's Jews, the more other governments resisted their entry. In Britain, "when faced with the danger of an emigration *en masse*, Anthony Eden asked, in the manner of a pedlar spreading his hands, what he was meant to do with a million Jews."[107] At the Evian Conference of July 6–14, 1938, called by President Roosevelt to decide how to apportion the new refugees, the representatives of the thirty-two countries on hand reiterated policies of closed doors, pleaded their inability to absorb the Jews (the United States declined to liberalize its small quota), and, in fear of accelerating the demand, declined to condemn Germany's anti-Jewish practices and policies. "Nobody Wants Them," the headline of the Nazi newspaper *Völkischer*

---

106. Kaplan, *Dignity*, p. 193; Richard Bessel, "Snatched from the Jaws," *Times Literary Supplement*, May 16, 1997. "One of the most depressing and troubling lessons of the Holocaust is that the German intelligentsia and academic elite played a major role in the electoral successes of the Nazi party and in the establishment of a rule of terror, violence, and finally mass murder. The legal profession was deeply complicit in passing and enforcing racial legislation that facilitated the Holocaust. The medical profession organized and legitimized the murder of the physically and mentally handicapped, the horrifying medical 'experiments' in the concentration camps, the selections at the killing centers. The leaders of the notorious Einsatzgruppen, the murder squads of the SS, as well as many of the most active and extreme members of the Reich Main Security Office—charged with organizing the Final Solution—were holders of doctorates from Germany's most prestigious universities. The Third Reich's school system was filled with Nazi teachers who taught eugenics, racism, and antisemitism to millions of children. Anthropologists, geographers, historians, biologists, as well as professors of literature, writers, journalists, artists, filmmakers, radio announcers, actors, and so forth were all involved in this venture of transforming Germany into a genocidal society." Omer Bartov, *Mirrors of Destruction: War, Genocide, and Modern Identity* (New York: Oxford University Press, 2000), pp. 184–185. Also see Max Weinreich, *Hitler's Professors: The Part of Scholarship in Germany's Crimes Against the Jewish People* (New York: Yiddish Scientific Institute, 1946). In addition to Martin Heidegger and Carl Schmitt, amongst the most distinguished ardent supporters of the regime were the biologist Erwin Baur, the jurist Victor Bruns, and the literary historian Hans Naumann.

107. Frederic Raphael, "On Not Keeping One's Voice Down," *Times Literary Supplement*, May 6, 1994, p. 7.

32   ONE

Beobachter boasted accurately.[108] Reflecting on this history, Arendt observed that[109]

Even the Nazis started their extermination of Jews by first depriving them of all legal status (the status of second-class citizenship) and cutting them off from the world of the living by herding them into ghettos and concentration camps; and before they set the gas chambers into motion they had carefully tested the ground and found out to their satisfaction that no country would claim these people. The point is that a condition of complete rightslessness was created before the right to live was challenged.

During the War, the Allies knew quite a lot about the unfolding of the mass murder of the Jews but treated it, in effect, as a sideshow, only in part because there was not much they could hope to accomplish.[110] Even after the allied victory, even in the globe's most assuredly liberal and rich country, and even after the scope of the Jewish disaster had become manifest, America's Congress, in 1948, passed a highly restrictive Displaced Person Act.[111]

---

108. Götz Aly and Susanne Heim, "Forced Emigration, War, Deportation, and Holocaust," in Frankel, ed., *Fate*, pp. 58–59; Friedländer, *Nazi*, pp. 248–50. Arendt noted the "great shock the European world suffered through the arrival of the refugees was the realization that it was impossible to get rid of them or transform them into nationals of the country of refuge. . . . The only practical substitute for a nonexistent homeland was an internment camp. Indeed, as early as the thirties this was the only 'country' the world had to offer the stateless." Arendt, *Origins*, pp. 281–284. On Allied knowledge of the Holocaust, see Richard Breitman, *Official Secrets: What the Nazis Planned, What the British and Americans Knew* (London: Allen Lane, 1998).
109. Arendt, *Origins*, p. 296.
110. Omer Bartov mordantly observes that "had Hitler killed Jews within internationally sanctioned borders, they would not have tried to thwart him." Bartov, *Mirrors of Destruction*, p. 167. For discussions, see Richard Breitman, *Official Secrets: What the Nazis Planned, What the British and Americans Knew* (New York: Hill and Wang, 1998); and Louise London, *Whitehall and the Jews 1933–1948* (Cambridge: Cambridge University Press, 2000).
111. Leonard Dinnerstein, "Anti-Semitism in the 80th Congress: The Displaced Person Act of 1948," *Capital Studies* 6 (Fall 1978). For a discussion of restrictions on postwar refugees in Ireland, set in the context of earlier anti-Semitic, often pro-Nazi, orientations, see Dermot Keogh, *Jews in 20th Century Ireland: Refugees, Anti-Semitism, and the Holocaust*. (Cork: University of Cork Press, 1998). As Omer Bartov has observed, "What facilitated the genocide of the Jews was a combination of circumstances that made escape and rescue increasingly difficult, and the made the work of perpetrators astonishingly easy. . . . for most of the war, Germany's enemies did not make the genocide of the Jews a major focus of their military, diplomatic, or propaganda efforts—indeed, they feared that doing so would enhance anti-Semitism among their own populations, or would be detrimental to their wartime and postwar policies." Omer Bartov, "The Anti-Hero as Hero," *The New Republic*, August 13, 2001, p. 33. Of course, the abandonment of the Jews was not complete or uniform. For one important, and morally complex, instance, see Tzvetan Todorov,

IV.

This closing of the gate was emblematic of just how much a world deeply threatening to the Enlightenment and to liberal values and politics had been born within the scope of one generation. Not just the travail of the Jews, of course, but the long European crisis of rancor, illiberalism, and suffering administered to the family of Enlightenment—a trauma of glass and fire, feathers and screams.[112] In Europe, Habermas has noted, "something happened that up to now nobody considered as even possible."[113] For those of us who live in a world of unprecedented quotidian comfort, the triptych of total war, totalitarianism, and holocaust can seem unreal, quite fantastic. Even survivors found it hard to attend the immensity of what just had happened. Writing in 1946, Primo Levi remarked, "Today, at this very moment as I sit writing at a table, I myself am not convinced that these things really happened."[114]

This was more than a crisis of ideas, institutions, or behavior. The twentieth-century compound of totalitarianism, holocaust, and total war obviously and profoundly challenged the tradition of Enlightenment, displacing inquiry to the question of whether its program of daring to know in a free, critical, unprejudiced spirit—"the making of rational men," as Karl Leonhard Reinhold had put the point in 1784, "out of men who are capable of rationality"—in fact had, or could have, forged a pathway to human maturity as its progenitors had hoped and expected.[115] Less than two centuries after Diderot and other contributors to

---

The Fragility of Goodness: Why Bulgaria's Jews Survived the Holocaust (Princeton: Princeton University Press, 2001) and Michael Bar-Zohar, *Beyond Hitler's Grasp: The Heroic Rescue of Bulgaria's Jews* (London: Adams Media Corporation, 2001).

112. The period's statistics, as George Steiner notes, "mock the imagination. We cannot take in the figures. Conservative estimates put at circa 75 *million* the total of men, women and children gunned, bombed, gassed, starved to death, slaughtered between deportations, slave-labour, and famines." George Steiner, *Errata: An Examined Life* (London: Phoenix, 1997), p. 105. This is a low estimate. Eric Hobsbawm cites Zbigniew Brzezinski's estimate of 187 million deaths between 1919 and 1990, "calculating this corresponds to something like 9 percent of the world's population in 1914." Hobsbawm, "Barbarism," p.47.

113. Jürgen Habermas, "Eine Art Schadensabwicklung," *Die Zeit*, July 11, 1986; cited in Saul Friedländer, *Memory, History and the Extermination of the Jews of Europe* (Bloomington: Indiana University Press, 1993), p. 49. "To most intelligent men and women of the nineteenth century," George Steiner observes, "a prediction that torture and massacre were soon to be endemic again in 'civilized' Europe would have seemed a nightmarish joke." Steiner, *Bluebeard's Castle*, p. 43.

114. Primo Levi, *If This is a Man and the Truce* (London: Abacus, 1987), p. 108.

115. Karl Leonhard Reinhold, "Thoughts on Enlightenment," in James Schmidt, ed., *What is Enlightenment? Eighteenth-Century Answers and Twentieth-Century Questions* (Berkeley: University of California Press, 1996), p. 65. When Frederick the Great's personal physician, J. K. W. Möhsen, "proposed that it be determined precisely: What is enlightenment?" as the task to "first

his and d'Alembert's great *Encyclopédie* (published in seventeen volumes of text containing 72,000 articles between 1751 and 1772, collecting "all the knowledge scattered over the face of the earth") confidently had professed that torture and other instances of depraved and savage conduct were human atavisms about to be tamed by toleration and a decline in religious passion, and German, French, English, and Scottish Enlightenment thinkers had invented a peaceful "international order in which war plays no part,"[116] devastation in the heartland of Europe insulted their expectations[117] and posed powerful questions about both the capacities and culpabilities of this tradition.

Among other outcomes produced by this disturbance to the intellect, one result was an uncertainty so fresh and so intense that the elements of language and knowledge for a newly enlightened world that had been confidently deployed by the editors and contributors to the *Britannica* now were out of alignment. Ordinarily, crises are characterized as "situations in which agents cannot anticipate the outcome of a decision and cannot assign probabilities to the outcome."[118] Indeed, some of the most challenging current work on cognition, linking psychology to economics, has taught us that people decide differently under conditions of acute risk. When these occur, both the magnitude and duration of uncertainty is much in question, so that doubt and irresolution are produced—so much so that standard stories grounded in rational choice taking the form of expected utility theory do not travel well to conditions of such significant uncertainty where it is difficult to measure or predict the actual degree of

---

attack and root out those prejudices and errors that are most pernicious," he also had thought it urgent to know why, in spite of improving education and some four decades of a climate of freedom in Prussia, "the enlightenment of our public has as yet not advanced very far." J. K.W. Möhsen, "What is to Be Done Toward the Enlightenment of the Citizenry?," Berlin Wednesday Society, December 17, 1783, in Schmidt, ed., *Enlightenment?*, pp. 49–50.

116. Michael Howard, *The Invention of Peace: Reflections on War and International Order* (London: Profile Books, 2000), p. 2.

117. For an overview of European literary treatments of otherness and barbarians from the fifteenth century to the recent past, see Claude Rawson, *God, Gulliver, and Genocide: Barbarism and the European Imagination* (Oxford: Oxford University Press, 2001).

118. Jens Beckert, "What is Sociological about Economic Sociology? Uncertainty and the Embeddedness of Economic Action," *Theory and Society* 25 (November 1996): 804. I am indebted to Mark Blyth for the distinction between the quality of uncertainty as heightened risk and uncertainty in which, as the economic Frank Knight once put it, probabilities cannot be assigned to outcomes because "it is impossible to form a group of instances because the situation dealt with *is in a high degree unique*." Frank Knight, *Risk, Uncertainty, and Profit* (Boston: Houghton Mifflin, 1921), p. 229; quoted in Beckert, p. 807. For a discussion of Knightian uncertainty, I have profited from Blyth's unpublished paper, "Uncertain Interests: Economic Ideas and Exogenous Institutional Change," 2001.

risk.[119] Recently, too, more effort has been made to recognize that "uncertainty is ubiquitous, consequential, and ineradicable in political life," since politics is characterized both by "a puzzling lack of sureness" and an "absence of strict determination." In this view, even in normal times, politics happens on a ground where "outcomes are neither predetermined (with probability 1) nor impossible (with probability 0), but lie somewhere in between. *Where* in between, and *how* and *why* are classic puzzles of politics."[120]

Desolation in the West had produced a qualitatively intensified state of affairs taking disbelief and uncertainty a good way beyond even such situations of flux and complexity, or the ever-present and defining features of 'normal' political uncertainty. By the close of the Second World War, it had become exceptionally difficult, perhaps impossible, to assess interests, identities, or even the broad contours of existing possibilities because the multidimensional configuration of uncertainty had produced an uncommonly severe and concentrated degree of uniqueness. It was difficult, some might say impossible, to discern parallel or homologous sets of events that could be considered as points of reference. Total war, totalitarianism, and holocaust literally had made the world precariously unstable and had rendered the world of political thought and ideas dizzying.

Curiously, most scholars in the humanities and social sciences turned away, taking refuge in small and manageable questions. It is possible to read the large majority of articles the leading learned journals in sociology, political science, and history published during the decade following the close of the Second World War without discerning that the Devil had returned. By contrast, two intellectually powerful responses—by rejectionists for whom the Enlightenment had done worse than fail miserably, and by reconstructionists who saw no decent option to its revivification—wrestled painfully with their period's unanticipated horrors.

In circumstances where the very extent of the era's spoliation made it difficult to take stock, recognize what just had transpired, or discover desolation's contours, a skepticism so thoroughgoing as to constitute a rejection of the Enlightenment beckoned. Humanism and reason, the rejectionists observed, had not contained the onslaught. Even worse was the likelihood that the Enlightenment

---

119. See their work, and that developed by co-authors to fashion an alternative 'prospect theory' concerned with choices undertaken by decisionmakers under risk usefully collected in Daniel Kahneman and Amos Tversky, eds., *Choices, Values, and Frames* (New York: Cambridge University Press, 2000).

120. Claudio Cioffi-Revilla, *Politics and Uncertainty: Theory, Models and Applications* (New York: Cambridge University Press, 1998), pp. 3, 5.

had produced its own ruination.[121] More than a failure at defense, in this reading the Enlightenment was a cause. Working within the traditions of hermeneutics and German historical philosophy, the anti-modernist émigré political theorist Leo Strauss, for example, famously thus judged the price of Enlightenment, especially its validation of intellectual and cultural pluralism, to have been far too high. Modernity's emergency, "primarily the crisis of modern political philosophy," was grounded in how the Enlightenment had conduced humanity's loss of "faith in reason's ability to validate its highest aims." As a result, "modern man no longer knows what he wants" and "no longer believes that he can know what is good and bad, what is right and wrong."[122] Turning their backs on the Enlightenment, Strauss and his American acolytes sought refuge from the uncertainties of modern reason in the more steady, homogeneous, and predictable epistemological and normative ideals of Greek antiquity.

Strauss was not alone in his skepticism, even scorn. Members of the Frankfurt School, whose expanded Marxism Strauss abhorred and who shadowed the themes and writings of the scholars I attend, reached not dissimilar, if more ambivalent, conclusions. Faced "with the actual reversion of enlightened civilization to barbarism," Max Horkheimer and Theodor Adorno reluctantly concluded in their *Dialectic of Enlightenment*, written in California during the most uncertain period of the Second World War, it was the "Enlightenment itself," that "already contains the seed of the regression apparent everywhere today," arguing that the modes of domination the Enlightenment had sustained were more harmful than the superstitions it had overcome since they are underpinned by the force of reason and the appearance of rationality. The hegemony of reason had advanced facts over ideas and had substituted the dogmas of "rational, scientific truth" for those of religion and tradition. To be sure,

---

121. The Enlightenment's "emplotment in an intellectual trajectory . . . seemed to lead inexorably to a catastrophe that philosophy confronts as its own ruin." Anson Rabinbach, *In the Shadow of Catastrophe: German Intellectuals between Apocalypse and Enlightenment* (Berkeley: University of California Press, 1997), p. 16.

122. Leo Strauss, "Three Waves of Modernity," in Hiail Gildin, ed., *Political Philosophy*. Indianapolis: Liberty Press, 1975, pp. 82, 81. These themes are not limited to the Straussian tradition, of course. Leszek Kolakowski, for example, has also contended that Enlightenment skepticism "threatens our ability to make the distinction between good and evil altogether," leaving human beings "conceptually defenseless in the face of totalitarian doctrines, ideologies, and institutions." In contrast to Strauss, Kolakowski has counseled a more robust role for religion and spirituality in human affairs. Leszek Kolakowski, "The Idolatry of Politics," *Atlantic Community Quarterly* 24 (Fall 1986): 223–224. Also see Kolakowski, *Freedom, Fame, Lying and Betrayal: Essays on Everyday Life* (London: Penguin Books, 1999). A useful, sympathetic consideration of Strauss in the American context and academy is provided by Kenneth L. Deutsch and John A. Murley, eds., *Leo Strauss, the Straussians, and the American Regime* (Boulder: Rowman and Littlefield, 1999).

Horkheimer and Adorno were "wholly convinced" that "social freedom is inseparable from enlightened thought," and they understood, as the book's opening sentence averred, that "in the most general sense of progressive thought, the Enlightenment has always aimed at liberating men from fear and establishing their sovereignty." Notwithstanding, the force of their argument, especially in the first part on "The Concept of Enlightenment," professed to show how "Enlightenment is totalitarian" and why its "universal mediation" had been so baneful: "Its untruth does not consist in what its romantic enemies have always reproached it for: analytical method, return to elements, dissolution through reflective thought; but instead in the fact that for enlightenment the process is always decided from the start." By mathematicizing knowledge, they argued, enlightened reason had converted into wrongful commensurability "even that which cannot be made to agree, indissolubility and irrationality." By demythologizing myth, moreover, the Enlightenment had itself given way to myth, making a commodity of thought. The result was "the self-destruction of the Enlightenment," whose paradoxical character "ultimately degenerates into a swindle, and becomes the myth of the twentieth century; and its irrationality turns it into an instrument of rational administration by the wholly enlightened as they steer society toward barbarism."[123]

Lecturing to the American Philosophical Association after the Second World War, in 1946, Horkeimer challenged "Philosophy, almost synonymous with

---

123. Max Horkheimer and Theodor W. Adorno, *Dialectic of Enlightenment* (New York: Herder and Herder, 1972), pp. vxi-xvii, xiii, 3, 6, 12, 24, xiii, 20. This text, of course, is difficult, allusive, and contradictory. Jürgen Habermas has attributed a tension in the text between a Nietzschean strain, which he identifies with Adorno, and a contrary impulse to seek to rescue the Enlightenment by clarity about the costs of its objectification and control of nature, which he attributes to Horkheimer. Rabinbach identifies the same opposing elements but thinks the former to be the work of Horkheimer, the latter the perspective of Adorno. Either way, even where this text seeks to advance Enlightenment values, its account of the tradition's immanent defects grounded in its understanding of its flawed impulses is so thoroughgoing that it is difficult to see how the book's effort to philosophically outwit myth and to create the 'possibility of escape' through enlightenment sensitized to the power of mimesis," as Rabinbach summarizes the project, persuasively could accomplish this goal. At minimum, it is clear that *Dialectic* arguably can be located within the tradition of Enlightenment while it deeply undermines it. Jürgen Habermas, *The Philosophical Discourse of Modernity: Twelve Lectures* (Cambridge: MIT Press, pp. 117–121); Rabinbach, *Shadow*, pp. 166–171. *Dialectic*, of course, remains a difficult book, one that is not entirely consistent and does not easily hang together. When Horkheimer and Adorno first circulated a mimeographed version to colleagues in December 1944, Herbert Marcuse wrote to say, that "there are too many passages which I don't understand, and too many ideas which I cannot follow up beyond the condensed and abbreviated form in which you gave them." Cited in James Schmidt, "Language, Mythology, and Enlightenment: Notes on Horkheimer and Adorno's *Dialectic of Enlightenment*," *Social Research* 65 (Winter 1998): 810.

Reason, . . . to show how the catastrophe came about" by coming to grips with how enlightenment reason had turned against itself by emptying its cupboard of ethics and metaphysics, thus denuding reason of substance, rendering it merely technical and open to exploitation. Reason thus had liquidated itself.[124] Herbert Marcuse, in a particular application of this perspective, contended in his essay, "The Struggle Against Liberalism in the Totalitarian View of the State," that totalitarianism was not the negation of liberalism but an expression of their shared underlying Enlightenment basis, a theme famously taken up in the early 1950s by Jacob Talmon and quite recently in Zygmunt Bauman's reflections on the holocaust as the quintessential expression of modernity's quest for reason and order.[125] From this angle of vision, the rupture with times past convened by modern, secular reason had produced, against its intentions, what Hegel had called "the coldest and meanest of all deaths . . . convening "a fury of destruction."[126]

"The intent of *Dialectic of Enlightenment*," a thoughtful analyst concluded, "was to offer a critique of enlightenment as relentless and unforgiving as that mounted by the enlightenment's fiercest critics and yet, somehow, remain loyal to the enlightenment's hopes."[127] The "totalizing critique" was so thorough, complete, and pessimistic, however, and so rooted in the genetic torque of enlightenment thought, that it became nearly impossible to discern this loyalty. Whatever the value of autonomous reason, its transformation into instrumental reason had created a closed circle without escape, except via some kind of

---

124. Max Horkheimer, "Reason Against Itself: Some Remarks on Enlightenment," in Schmidt, *Enlightenment*, p. 360.

125. Herbert Marcuse, "The Struggle Against Liberalism in the Totalitarian View of the State," in Marcuse, *Negations* (Boston: Beacon Press, 1958); Jacob Talmon, *The Origins of Totalitarian Democracy* (London: Secker and Warburg, 1952); and Zygmunt Bauman, *Modernity and the Holocaust* (Cambridge: Polity Press, 1989). This theme was not unique to the Frankfurt School. Isaiah Berlin, for example, who assuredly did not share the Frankfurt School's anti-science, anti-positivism, anti-technology, anti-Enlightenment orientation, assessed Voltaire as an incipient totalitarian for his quest for perfection advanced by reason. Isaiah Berlin, *The Crooked Timber of Humanity: Chapters in the History of Ideas* (New York: Knopf, 1991). In June 1942, Marcuse wrote on "The New German Mentality" for the Office of War Information. There, he argued that Nazi Germany, in a syncretism of the modern and anti-modern, combined efficient rationalization with myth-making and paganism, hardly core Enlightenment values. For a discussion, see Jeffrey Herf, "One-Dimensional Man," *The New Republic*, February 1, 1999, pp. 39–40. Also see Douglas Kellner, ed., *Technology, War, and Fascism: Collected Papers of Herbert Marcuse, Volume One* (Boston: Routledge, 1998).

126. G.W.F. Hegel, *Phenomenology of Spirit* (Oxford: Oxford University Press, 1977), p. 359; cited in Schmidt, *Enlightenment*, p. 21.

127. James Schmidt, "Language, Mythology, and Enlightenment," p.835.

utopian leap. "The critique of Enlightenment," Seyla Benhabib thus perceives, "is cursed by the same burden as Enlightenment itself."[128]

It was precisely this enclosure and the charge that the Enlightenment somehow had inspired the deepest negation of its articulated values that the reconstructionists of the political studies enlightenment declined decisively. In part their resistance was empirical. Nazi Germany, they argued, had repudiated the values of Enlightenment, not confirmed them. More profoundly, they believed the faultfinders had produced a critique that was too heavy, too dark and oppressive, leaving virtually no room to breathe or maneuver. Just as they knew there could be no simple return to the icon of western modernity as manifestly superior, advanced, and steadily progressing with culture banishing barbarism, so they recoiled from the idea that Enlightenment is a mere fantasy or, worse, the main source of radical evil. Placing themselves in-between innocent approbation, as if nothing had happened, and the blunt idea that over-investments in reason had produced the calamities of the twentieth century, they sought to craft a space at once realistic about human capacities, structures, and processes but not so pessimistic as to be disabled by the traps of prophetic gloom and penitential immobilism.[129] This, of course, is an exquisite balance, hard to discern and difficult to sustain.[130]

For these supporters of the lineage of Enlightenment, a pressing task was the reduction of such heightened uncertainty by making sense of the disoriented political field. This quest posed profound analytical, conceptual, and moral challenges, not just a set of empirical puzzles.[131] The permanent availability and presence of a secularized purgatory implied that evil no longer could be confronted in the separate and specialized world of theology. Much as the eighteenth-century Enlightenment thinkers (and, such seventeenth-century precursors as Grotius, Pufendorf, and Locke) had produced political ideas that transcended the particularity of their experiences of massive change, deep

---

128. Seyla Benhabib, "The Critique of Instrumental Reason," in Slavoj Zizek, ed., *Mapping Ideology* (London: Verso, 1994), p.78.

129. The phrase is deployed by T. S. Eliot in his *Notes Toward the Definition of Culture* (New York: Harcourt Brace, 1949).

130. So, too is a balance between sufficient remembrance so as not to forget and a remembrance so encompassing as either to paralyze or conduce bitterness and revenge. For a nuanced discussion, see Zelizer, *Remembering*. On this subject, I also have been informed by Andreas Huyssen, "The Culture of Memory: Media, Politics, Amnesia," unpublished manuscript, January 1999. Also see Peter Novick, *The Holocaust in American Life* (Boston: Houghton Mifflin, 1999), and the tough-minded review by Tony Judt, "The Morbid Truth," *New Republic*, July 19 and 26, 1999, pp. 36–40.

131. For a call to social scientists to think harder about conceptual problems for ongoing research about fundamental questions, see James Johnson, "How Conceptual Problems Migrate: Rational-Choice, Interpretation, and the Hazards of Pluralism," *Annual Review of Political Science* 5 (2002).

conflict, and pervasive bloodshed, the post–Second World War generation sought to turn their sacked epoch into a time for the invention of political knowledge in light of the discovery, as Arendt wrote to Karl Jaspers, that "evil has proved to be more radical than expected." They thus sought to discover resources within the Enlightenment to recognize complexity and danger without quitting expectations for a less cruel world.[132]

Their Enlightenment was not one of ahistorical, superficial, or innocent reason in which its *philosophes* had offered humankind scientific reason as a secularized religion that could confer grace but a much less simple or one-sided tradition containing large doses of skepticism, reckonings with the dark side of the human condition, and a realistic quest to confront fanaticism. To be sure, writing in the late eighteenth century after decades of effort by compatriots in Europe to develop what ultimately became the dominant vision of western modernity, Reinhold, together with Immanuel Kant, Gothold Lessing, and Moses Mendelssohn, among others, had responded to the question, "What is Enlightenment?" in a tone of confidence that knowledge freed from superstition and unshackled from arbitrary rule could combat a wide array of baneful circumstances, including poverty, crime, disease, civil disorder, and tyranny. Extracting large zones of human conduct from religious control, they sought to make reason autonomous from revelation, placing faith in education, the extension of knowledge, and systematic empirical inquiry in the natural and biological sciences.[133] But this coupling of reason and civilization had not been their only

---

132. Hans Jonas, "The Outcry of Mute Things," *New School Commentator*, 4 (May 1993); Hannah Arendt and Karl Jaspers, *Correspondence, 1926–1969* (New York: Harcourt, Brace, and Company, 1992), p. 166. Because the radical evil they confronted lacked compensatory justification, it required political theory and political science without solace. See Norman Jacobson, *Pride and Solace: The Functions and Limits of Political Theory* (Berkeley: University of California Press, 1978).

133. Of course, the Enlightenment was complex, multifaceted, and contradictory and the population thought to eligible to enter its ken was limited. The relevant literature is immense. Still germane are Ernst Cassirer, *Die Philosophie der Aufklärung* (Tubingen: Mohr, 1932); Paul Hazard, *European Thought in the Eighteenth Century, from Montesquieu to Lessing* (New Haven: Yale University Press, 1954); Jean Ehrard, *L'idée de nature en France dans la première moitié de XVIIIe siècle* (Paris: Chambery, 1963); Peter Gay, *The Enlightenment: An Interpretation* (two volumes) (New York: Knopf, 1967, 1969), and C.B.A. Behrens, *Society, Government and the Enlightenment: The Experiences of Eighteenth Century France and Prussia* (London: Thames and Hudson, 1985). More recent works include Michel Vovelle, *Enlightenment Portraits* (Chicago: University of Chicago Press, 1997); Emmanuel Chukwudi Eze, *Race and the Enlightenment: A Reader* (Oxford: Blackwell, 1997); Mary Seidman Trouille, *Sexual Politics in the Enlightenment* (Albany: SUNY Press, 1997); Daniel Roche, *France in the Enlightenment* (Cambridge: Harvard University Press, 2000); Dorinda Outram, *The Enlightenment* (Cambridge: Cambridge University Press, 1995); Roy Porter, *The Creation of the Modern World: The Untold Story of the British Enlightenment* (New York: Norton, 2000); and William Clark, Jan Golinski, and Simon Schaffer, eds., *The Sciences in Enlightened Europe* (Chicago: University of Chicago Press, 1999).

theme. Reprising Voltaire's attack on optimism in his reaction to the Lisbon earthquake of November 1, 1755, which killed at least some 30,000 (some thought 70,000) in just six minutes in Europe's fourth largest city, including his "Poème sur le désastre de Lisbonne" and his assault on Pangloss in *Candide* four years later for thinking the earthquake to have been a necessary event with a coherent rationale rather than being an instance of unmitigated and inexplicable evil, their writing also contains a brooding and largely forgotten recognition of danger and disorder, which adjudges how the supercession of faith or the denial of local cultures, practices, and norms can threaten to rend the social fabric and unleash irrationality.[134] Concerned with the clash between enlightenment and culture, Mendelssohn wrote in this vein to caution that[135]

The more noble a thing is in its perfection, says a Hebrew writer, the more ghastly it is in its decay. A rotted piece of wood is not as ugly as a decayed flower; and this is not as disgusting as a decomposed animal; and this, again, is not as gruesome as a man in his decay. So it is also with culture and enlightenment. The more noble in their bloom, the more hideous in their decay and destruction.

Likewise, Kant worried about demagogic uses of reason, whose "new prejudices will serve, like the old, as the leading strings of the thoughtless masses."[136]

The individuals who composed the political studies enlightenment in the United States after the Second World War defended the legacy of reason with just such utterly realistic understanding. Shedding illusion and writing within *this* particular version of Enlightenment, they cautioned, as Arendt put it, that "to turn our backs on the destructive forces of the century is of little avail."[137] For these reconstructionists, it was important to recapture the tradition's dark and realistic strains that had been present at its founding yet overlooked in the

---

134. For an appreciation of this element in Enlightenment thought, see Lester G. Crocker, "Interpreting the Enlightenment: A Political Approach," *Journal of the History of Ideas*, 46 (April-June 1985). We can see this aspect of Enlightenment thought represented by the biting visual representations of Goya's *Los Caprichos*, executed in 1798–1800 and *Los Desastres de la Guerra*, accomplished between 1810 and 1820. For discussions, see Alfonso E. Pérez Sánchez and Julián Gállego, *Goya: The Complete Etchings and Lithographs*. Munich: Prestel, 1995); F. D. Klingender, *Goya in the Democratic Tradition* (London: Sidgwick and Jackson, Ltd., 1948); and Janis A. Tomlinson, *Goya in the Twilight of Enlightenment* (New Haven: Yale University Press, 1992). Goya's imagery plays a pivotal role in Ilie, *Minerva*.

135. Moses Mendelssohn, "On the Question: What is Enlightenment?," in Schmidt, *Enlightenment*, p. 56.

136. Immanuel Kant, "An Answer to the Question: What is Enlightenment?," in Schmidt, *Enlightenment*, p. 59.

137. Arendt, *Origins*, p. ix.

pages of the *Britannica*. Its virtually unbounded expectation of progress and per-
fectibility defined a credulous and thin doctrine that had exposed the Enlightenment to predators. These shortcomings, they believed, could be remedied by
putting analytical history and social science to work to better comprehend what
had happened and to defend against recurrences. For reasons of sociological realism and limited normative options, the political studies enlightenment thus
refused either to break with the Enlightenment or disproportionately expose its
deficiencies. Rather, in recapturing it from caricatures authored both by its
friends and its enemies, they worked to extend, revivify, and fortify the Enlightenment tradition by probing issues of origins, state, and policy.

Not uncritical fealty but loyalty came first as they sought to rediscover a less
abstract, buoyant, or unitary Enlightenment. Far from innocent, sharing an appreciation for the dark side of modernity, and looking to history, institutions,
and the tools of modern social science, the political studies enlightenment
spurned both naked rejection or a critique so strong as to constitute its equiva-
lent, understanding how much more bereft humanity would become if it were
to succumb to the dispossession and forfeit of the Enlightenment. However diverse their background—émigré or native, Jew or Christian, idealist philosopher or materialist empiricist—the members of the political studies enlightenment sought to deploy a constellation of historical understanding, normative
commitment, and systematic analysis to wrestle with their period's new demons.
They proceeded by entwining desolation with Enlightenment in order to rouse
the liberal imagination and to situate it realistically to produce means with
which to advance a decent politics.

As realists, they knew that the Enlightenment's break with encrusted traditional privileges and myths had made the world potentially better but vastly
more dangerous. By widening the scope of human possibility, the Enlightenment neither was singular nor determinative, they believed, but plural and contingent.[138] What mattered at least as much as first principles were the discovery
and utilization of the precise terms of political knowledge and institutional creativity that best could canalize the Enlightenment's protean force in desirable
directions.

These were tasks of conceptual, empirical, and linguistic invention situated
inside the dominion of death's omnipresence and the shattering of traditional
frames of reference defined by the nomenclature of total war, totalitarianism,
and holocaust. Like Strauss and the Frankfurt School, in short, the political
studies enlightenment grappled with their time's disorienting combination of
desolation and enlightenment but came to rather different conclusions based

---

138. For a discussion along these lines, see James Schmidt, ":Liberalism and Enlightenment in
Eighteenth-Century Germany," *Critical Review* 13, nos.1–2 (1999).

on different emphases. Though they recognized that Hitler's and Stalin's focus on planned rationality had dressed their regimes in Enlightenment clothing, even claiming at times to be its saviors, they thought the various totalitarian projects, despite their mimetic qualities, represented the negation of Enlightenment far more than its authentic culmination. Totalitarianism, mounted on the torque of impersonal laws of struggle between races and classes, was Enlightenment humanism's antipode, Arendt and her colleagues fiercely believed. When the scientific, medical, and academic communities participated in advancing Nazi anti-Semitism, for example, this, they held, was the result of the corruption of these professions, not an expression of their essential character. "The subterranean stream of Western history," Arendt wrote, "has finally come to the surface and usurped the dignity of our tradition."[139]

Thinking the repudiation of enlightened inquiry and values inconceivably dangerous in the face of this challenge, the political studies enlightenment scholars drew on the full array of philosophical, historical, and social scientific resources the Enlightenment offered to affect a revision, fearing the price of abandonment in the face of their epoch's remarkable aggregate of suffering. Their writing had many limitations, some grave, I will not shy from addressing. Notwithstanding, we possess a stake in understanding how this postwar group shielded and renovated the Enlightenment to sustain its best promises. The arc of their project and the scope of its attainment thus beckon us into the pages of their work and into the vocation of their studies.

V.

As historians of ideas, we have forgotten the basic unity and qualities of this enterprise geared to dominate unreason by appropriate political knowledge. As citizens, in consequence, we have lost an important asset. Though our times are different, of course, we continue to be marked directly and indirectly by the legacies of holocaust, totalitarianism, and total war. After these transgressions, our trust in institutions, language, values, even fellow humans, never can be restored as before.[140] Yet, just a half-century on, our quest for political knowledge has repressed the smell of fear. My purpose in writing is to recall scholarship to the tasks, subjects, and means deployed by the postwar generation while refusing the too-simple choices proffered by current critics and defender of Enlightenment. I do so, I underscore, not to celebrate their work as in a museum.

139. Arendt, *Origins*, p. ix. Arendt gave *Dialectic of Enlightenment* the back of her hand. There is no reference to this text in *Origins*.
140. For a discussion in these terms, see Bernstein, "Lasting Injury."

Rather, by subjecting the political studies enlightenment to an appreciative critique, we might fortify our own capacities at a time stamped by its own large measure of desolation and radical evil.

The substantive heart of this effort was a quest both to understand the origins of dark times and comprehend the modern state. Chapter two's title, "The Origins of Dark Times," is a contraction, of course, of Hannah Arendt's *The Origins of Totalitarianism* and her *Men in Dark Times*. It also alludes to the subtitle, *Political and Economic Origins of Our Time*, Karl Polanyi adopted for *The Great Transformation*.[141] As two amongst a larger number of scholars seeking to specify sources for the murderous scissions dividing the present from the past in the heart of enlightened Europe, they produced the most considerable and durable books we possess written during and just after the Second World War by students of politics in the United States who endeavored to grapple with the issue of beginnings. A seemly future, they believed, required understanding not only why what had happened had occurred, but why these developments had not been inevitable. This section of *Desolation and Enlightenment* thus seeks to understand the elements that distinguished the specific type of text penned by Arendt and Polanyi both from their close first cousins, other texts by fellow refugee and indigenous American scholars who were concerned to understand the era's deep illiberal impulses, and from more ordinary efforts to place the period's events and institutions in a familiar causal grid.

The difference in their effort two centuries after Samuel Johnson had sought "to inquire what were the sources of . . . the evil that we suffer,"[142] I argue, lies in Arendt's and Polanyi's understanding of historical rupture and in their complex treatment of causation. They characterized 'the burden of our times' (Arendt's title for *The Origins of Totalitarianism* when it first was published in Britain) in terms of a break with the past so deep and fundamental that it demanded fresh categories of analysis, even experimentation with epistemology. "We can no longer afford to take that which was good in the past and simply call it our heritage," Arendt put the point, or "discard the bad and simply think of it as a dead load which by itself time will bury in oblivion."[143] The study of origins, they believed, must be integral to the quest for a new political science of protection and defense under thoroughly changed circumstances. Writing *The Great Transformation* in Vermont during wartime, between 1940 and 1943, Polanyi declaimed that "the dividing line" separating liberalism from fascism and bolshe-

141. Arendt, *Origins*; Hannah Arendt, *Men in Dark Times* (London: Penguin Books, 1973); Polanyi, *Transformation*.

142. Samuel Johnson, *Rasselas: The Prince of Abyssinia* (London: R. and J. Dosley; and W. Johnston, 1759), p. xxix.

143. Arendt, *Origins*, p. ix.

vism is freedom and the institutional basis on which it might be upheld.[144] Similarly scandalized by depredation inside what had been thought to be Europe's humane and rational civilization, Arendt cautioned, "Anti-Semitism (not merely the hatred of Jews), imperialism (not merely conquest), totalitarianism (not merely dictatorship)—one after the other, one more brutally than the other— have demonstrated that human dignity needs a new guarantee which can be found only in a new political principle."[145] My reading of these texts seeks to show how their entwining of a temporality of beginnings, a configurative approach to the elements of large-scale change, and a fine-grained, local approach to causation permitted their authors to retain the ideals of the age of reason in the midst of catastrophe and to craft barriers against recurrences.

Chapter 3, "A Seminar on the State," regards how members of the political studies enlightenment sought to identify the institutional, normative, and policy requisites for healthy liberal polities. I take my title from an actual seminar founded just as the Second World War was about to end by a multidisciplinary array of colleagues at Columbia University. Concerned initially with the braiding of modernity and bureaucracy, it soon extended its scope to a wide range of political subjects. The Seminar's membership in its first decade included Gabriel Almond (visiting from Princeton) and Robert Merton, Karl Wittfogel and Daniel Bell, David Truman and C. Wright Mills, Richard Hofstadter and William Leuchtenburg, all of whom we still read with great profit.

Like Arendt and Polanyi, the scholars who shared in the seminar's project (irrespective of whether they attended its meetings) were keen to understand the origins of their time, an aim they pursued by engaging with the modern sovereign state. They took this tack against the tide of prewar wisdom, which had come to regard the state as a concept and as an object of analysis as hopelessly old-fashioned and merely legalistic, insufficient to advance a systematic and modern behavioral science of politics. Resisting this diminished importance, these students of politics recognized they could not credibly avoid dealing with the state as a site of mobilized coercion or as an instrument for public purpose. Nor could they fail to grapple with the nature and meaning of the liberal state in America, the last great constitutional democracy left standing in the interwar period. Here, I primarily explore how the political scientist David Truman and the historian Richard Hofstadter pursued these tasks.

I also assay the founding moment of policy studies. During and after the Second World War, an overlapping but distinctive community of scholars concentrated less on what the liberal state is than on what it does; that is on its public policies. Focusing both on process and content, Harold Lasswell, Robert Dahl,

---

144. Polanyi, *Transformation*, p. 258..
145. Arendt, *Origins*, p. ix.

and Charles Lindblom, among others, fashioned modern, cross-disciplinary policy studies. They were persuaded that technical advances could, indeed must, be harnessed to the moral and political purpose of guarding liberal democracy. Guided by experience and anxiety, they sought to learn how to pilot governmental action to prevent harm as well as to do good.[146]

The name I assign to the last chapter is "The New Objectivity." Writing as the Weimar Republic was in a state of advanced decay, Karl Mannheim devoted his *Ideology and Utopia* to the discovery by intellectuals working as historically informed social scientists of standards for practice and judgment that could take into account modernity's heterogeneous social order and often incommensurable values, interests, ideas, and ways of life.[147] I close the volume by examining how the philosophically encoded histories, empirically realistic audits of states and political behavior, and practical-minded analyses of public policy composed by the political studies enlightenment advanced Mannheim's project in just the epistemological space he defined located between an aseptic objectivity and a foundationless relativism. One of my goals is to show how, in promoting this program and navigating this location, these scholars produced a coherent alternative to the choices offered today both by stern critics and fierce defenders of the Enlightenment.

Yet for all their analytical and normative achievements, the work written by the postwar generation also was marked by uncomfortable biases and glaring omissions. Beleaguered by desolation and fear, they celebrated America's post–New Deal regime in ways that frequently ignored deep inequalities based not just on class or gender, but on race and the diversity of cultures, and they tilted rather more in the direction of liberalism with a strong elitist slope than toward democracy (a leaning that later helped bring about the New Left which inclined the other way). Further, as some members of the political studies enlightenment later shed their fears, their appreciation for America's liberal regime transposed into uncritical celebration, especially in the context of the Cold War. We do well to remember these dispositions, less to revisit familiar critical impulses demonstrating how 'totalitarianism' can mask differences between types of regime, how interest group pluralism hides structured inequities, or how academic policy studies have been designed and deployed for uglier purposes than to revivify the tasks of remedy and guardianship pursued by the political studies enlightenment in their stunning and realistic social science. Even if their sensibilities and ours differ, at times radically, their central tasks hardly have been exhausted.

---

146. I am aware, of course, that my determination to focus on these scholars and subjects, and my decision to join them under a common label, muffles others.
147. Karl Mannheim, *Ideology and Utopia* (London: Routledge, 1936 [1929]).

Two

THE ORIGINS OF DARK TIMES

We continue to be inundated by efforts to comprehend the character and sources of the decades of desolation that spanned the twentieth century's two world wars. On my desk, as I write, sit a 'black book' chronicling 'crimes, terror, and repression' under Communism; a synoptic treatment of that ideology's appeal by one of France's leading intellectuals; a haunting reconsideration of death and memory in Russia; a revisionist account of the role of the German army in killing civilians early in the First World War; a controversial memoir of the geography of killing and escape in the holocaust; a magisterial history of the Third Reich; the second volume of a notable biography of Hitler; an empirical assessment of support for his regime by ordinary Germans; two volumes of incisive essays grappling with the genocide of the Jews; a detailed history of a concentration camp and the construction of its remembrance; an elegiac fable of memory haunted by ghosts; and a complex reconstruction of aggressive fictional fantasies of extirpation, and barbarism in the European literary imagination, directed at conquered savages, the poor, the Irish, and the Jews. Each has been published in the past three years.[1]

---

1. Stéphanie Courtois, et.al., *The Black Book of Communism: Crimes, Terror, Repression* (Cambridge: Harvard University Press, 1999); François Furet, *The Passing of an Illusion: The Idea of Communism in the Twentieth Century* (Chicago: University of Chicago Press, 1999); Catherine Merridale, *Night of Stone: Death and Memory in Russia* (London: Granta Books, 2000); John

To their side, lie two other books written more than a half-century ago by newcomers to the United States from Austria (via England) and Germany (via France). Making a rather small pile by comparison, they remain touchstones for the journeys of investigation and understanding undertaken by all the others. None of these, from the limited to the encompassing, whether written close to or at a distance from the events they assay, has quite replicated the intellectual bravura, the moral and analytical appeal, or the ability to impose clarity without losing complexity achieved by *The Great Transformation*, published at the height at the Second World War, and *The Origins of Totalitarianism*, a product of postwar reflection.[2]

Three decades after the outbreak of the First World War, members of the political studies enlightenment confronted an exquisite dilemma with respect to the status of contemporary history. With the *Britannica*'s linear, cumulative search for order and certainty having been shattered by the manifest end of progress, and with its codification of knowledge having been disqualified as a realistic guide to investigations of the origins of desolation, various options beckoned. Scholars could declare the recent past inaccessible to coherent explanation ("I feel more than ever," a leading historian of the First World War has written, "that the war is a mystery and will remain so"[3]); bracket it as exceptional, thus leaving it unmastered; return to eternal verities, casting either the Enlightenment or modernity more generally in the role of villain; undermine the tradition of liberality and reason from the direction of radical uncertainty (of

---

Horne and Alan Kramer, *German Atrocities, 1914: A History of Denial* (New Haven: Yale University Press, 2002); Salomon Isacovici, *Man of Ashes*. (Lincoln: University of Nebraska Press, 1999); Michael Burleigh, *The Third Reich: A New History* (London: Macmillan, 2000); Ian Kershaw, *Hitler 1936–1945: Nemesis* (New York: Norton, 2000); Robert Gellately, *Backing Hitler: Consent and Coercion in Nazi Germany* (New York: Oxford University Press, 2001); Omer Bartov, *Mirrors of Destruction: War, Genocide, and Modern Identity* (New York: Oxford University Press, 2000); István Deák, *Essay's on Hitler's Europe*. (Lincoln: University of Nebraska Press, 2001); Harold Marcuse, *Legacies of Dachau: The Uses and Abuses of a Concentration Camp, 1933–2001* (New York: Cambridge University Press, 2001); W. G. Sebald, *Austerlitz* (New York: Random House, 2001); Claude Rawson, *God, Gulliver, and Genocide: Barbarism and the European Imagination, 1492–1945* (New York: Oxford University Press, 2001).

2. Karl Polanyi, *The Great Transformation: Political and Economic Origins of Our Time* (New York: Rinehart and Company, 1944); Hannah Arendt, *The Origins of Totalitarianism* (New York: Harcourt Brace and World, 1951). It was quite common during the decade in which they wrote to lament the absence of genuinely historical accounts of the prior decades. See, as an example, Oron James Hale, "The Dignity of History in Times of War," *The Journal of Modern History*, 15 (March 1943).

3. John Keegan, letter to the editor, *Times Literary Supplement*, July 27, 1001, p. 15. In a rejoinder, Michael Howard remonstrates that "It is the job of the historian to explain why. . . . the peoples of Europe believed, rightly or wrongly, that they were fighting for 'great issues'." Letter to the editor, *Times Literary Supplement*, August 3, 2001, p. 15.

the kind already embraced by Neils Bohr and Werner Heisenberg in physics[4] that later found expression in a postmodernist insistence on the inconsonant status of people and events and the irreconcilable quality of human idioms), albeit at the potential cost of leaving humankind defenseless against barbarism; or reinvigorate the Enlightenment and reinforce its doctrinal and institutional ramparts against unreason by rendering as precisely as possible the constellation of sources for recent disasters. Rejecting mute incomprehension, Karl Polanyi and Hannah Arendt sought to understand the origins of dark times not as a means to overcome humankind's cruelty and potential for harm, for this they knew to be impossible, nor was it to devise an ideal state and its rules, the traditional task of political philosophy, but to learn how to live with the now-widened spectrum of ugly possibility by first discerning how the collapse of the best elements in the western tradition could have been conceivable.[5]

In subject matter, orientation, and analytical decisionmaking, these books advanced the first basic project the political studies enlightenment undertook: understanding the derivation and development of the twentieth century's triptych of radical evil. More than a half-century since the close of the period Élie Halévy called "The Era of Tyrannies" and Eric Hobsbawm labeled the 'Age of Catastrophe,'[6] we have yet to resolve any of the great debates concerned with the status of 1914–1945 in the matrix of modernity; among others, questions of provenance, cause, scope, units of analysis, comparison, uniqueness, representation, and meaning. Though we know more factually, of course, than Polanyi and Arendt, any attempt to make sense of the momentous developments spanning the past

---

4. For Heisenberg the uncertainty principle of quantum mechanics stipulated that two observables could not both be precisely known at the same time; thus as one achieves greater certainty of definition, the other becomes increasingly uncertain. More broadly, it is impossible, this principle stipulates, to determine all the dynamic variables simultaneously.

5. Indeed, a core feature of their efforts was a refusal to treat evil as a metaphysical or theological category outside the ken of the historian and social scientist. If, as George Kateb once wrote, "evil is the deliberate infliction (or sponsorship or knowing allowance) for *almost* any reason whatever, of suffering of great intensity," and if political evil is the infliction of such harm by governments of modern states," then it is critical to understand the origins of such efforts and of their sponsors. George Kateb, *The Inner Ocean: Individualism and Democratic Culture* (Ithaca: Cornell University Press, 1992): 200, 205. See the discussion of Kateb in William E. Connolly, "Evil and the Imagination of Wholeness," in Austin Sarat and Dana R. Villa, eds., *Liberal Modernism and Democratic Individuality: George Kateb and the Practice of Politics* (Princeton: Princeton University Press, 1996). The distinction between the tasks of political philosophy and the search for origins I draw from Vittorio Hösle, "Morality and Politics: Reflections on Machiavelli's *Prince*," *Politics, Culture, and Society* 3 (Fall 1989): 59.

6. Élie Halévy, *The Era of Tyrannies* (New York: Doubleday, 1965); "Age of Catastrophe" is Eric Hobsbawm's name for the period 1914–1945 in *The Age of Extremes: A History of the World, 1914–1991* (New York: Pantheon Books, 1994).

century's two world wars still must begin with his *Transformation* and her *Origins*.

Some fifteen years after the publication of *Origins*, Arendt singled out Bertold Brecht's "Children's Crusade 1939" as "the only German poem of the last war that will last." It is, she observed, "a ballad written in the bitter sad tone of folk songs . . . telling the story of fifty-five war orphans and a dog in Poland who set out for '*ein Land, wo Frieden war*' — 'a country where peace was' — and didn't know the way."[7] Like Brecht (whom she admired fiercely despite his romance with Stalinism), she and Polanyi sought to find the way. Each deployed a distinctive voice; not by writing poetry (though aspects of their writing surely are poetic) but as scholars who sought to reconstruct past times analytically. The search for the sources of their period's 'dark times' thus implied more than terrible times and demanded more than probes appropriate to 'ordinary' crises, however deep or profound. Taking the phrase from Brecht's "Die Nachgeborenen," which begins, "Truly, I live in dark times!," Arendt embraced his sense that such moments sever the tie the Enlightenment had sought to establish between unfolding wisdom secured by rational inquiry and estimations of the just and the good. "Dark times," she cautioned, "are as such not identical with the monstrosities of this century which indeed are of a horrible novelty."[8]

The clash between disorienting desolation and simple political knowledge had become so great that a new approach had to be crafted to confront a profound challenge[9] similar to the radical newness Tocqueville had discerned on his visit to America. In such states of affairs, Arendt counseled, there must be a quest for comprehension in terms appropriate to the object of analysis.[10] She stipulated that "darkness has come" at those historical moments when existing conceptions of human experience in the public realm no longer "can throw light on the affairs of men by providing a space of appearances in which they can show in deed and word, for better and worse, who they are and what they can do." Unless there is a breakthrough in human understanding, truths "degrade . . . to meaningless triviality."[11] Likewise, Polanyi announced the ambition to make sense of the sources causing the "social transformation of planetary

---

7. Hannah Arendt, *Men in Dark Times* (New York: Harcourt, Brace, and World, 1968), p. 210.

8. Arendt, *Dark Times*, p. ix.

9. David Luban, "Explaining Dark Times: Hannah Arendt's Theory of Theory," in Lewis P. Hinchman and Sandra K. Hinchman, eds., *Hannah Arendt: Critical Essays.* (Albany State University of New York Press, 1994).

10. Arendt, *Origins*, p. viii.

11. In such circumstances, she held that Heidegger's "sarcastic, perverse-sounding statement, *Das Licht der Öffentlichkeit verdunkelt alles* ('The very light of the public obscures everything') went to the very heart of the matter and actually was no more than the most succinct summing-up of existing conditions." Arendt, *Dark Times*: viii, ix.

range . . . being topped by wars of an unprecedented type in which a score of states [have] crashed, and the contours of new empires are emerging out of a sea of blood." Inquiry, he insisted, must seek to "account for the suddenness of the cataclysm" and adjust its "aim to the extreme singularity of the subject matter."[12] Left unfathomable, both believed, these developments would bequeath a legacy of vulnerability to an even darker, more brutal, future. The problem of origins thus had to come first.[13] Otherwise, "all efforts to escape from the grimness of the present," Arendt concluded in her preface to the first edition of *The Origins of Totalitarianism*, " . . . or into the anticipated oblivion of a better future, are vain."[14]

In part because they were so radically different than more conventional studies, the books Polanyi and Arendt wrote to pursue these goals proved difficult for the traditional disciplines of history and social science to assimilate, then and now. Although widely read and debated, neither work has been incorporated into any disciplinary canon with the exception of a limited site in political theory in the case of *Origins* and a small zone of political economy in the instance of *Transformation*. When they burst on the scene with uncommon intellectual force, each was greeted with icy reserve within the mainstream disciplines, and, over the years, often dismissed as unsystematic, inconsistent, and empirically flawed. The economics profession swiftly swatted Polanyi's heretical skepticism about free markets. The reviewer in *The Economic Review* dismissed the book as merely "sociological . . . full of vague generalizations"; in the *Journal of Political Economy* he was reproached for an "arbitrary use of terms and exaggerated interpretations of events." Historians, as the assessor in *The American Historical Review* put it, focused on "the rather long itemized list of distortions of fact," and recoiled from its conceptual and model-building approach to the past. These traits so offended the contributor to *The Journal of Modern History* that he dismissively observed that "although [Polanyi] draws liberally upon 'history' to explain origins and to show effects, . . . the method which [he] employs in the development of his thesis is that of the institutional sociologist rather than of the historian."[15]

---

12. Arendt, *Origins*, p. 4; Polanyi, *Transformation*, p. 4.
13. The issues bundled in the word 'origins' include matters of descriptive inference—identifying objects of analysis and providing a scheme of periodization—and of causal inference, entailing simplified but powerful analytical models of history and its sequencing. In identifying a particular moment as the time of origins, two sets of causal problems are raised: the sources of this constituting moment and the mechanisms governing its subsequent effects.
14. Polanyi, *Transformation*, p. 4; Arendt, *Origins*, p. ix.
15. The reviews of *The Great Transformation*, respectively, are by George H. Hildebrand, Jr., *The American Economic Review* 36 (June 1946): 404; Witt Bowden, *The Journal of Political Economy* 53 (June 1945): 283; J. H. Hexter, *The American Historical Review* 50 (April 1945): 502; and Shephard B. Clough, *The Journal of Modern History* 16 (December 1944): 3.

Likewise, when *Origins* first appeared, the reviewer in *The American Economic Review* announced "the reader . . . will not find a consistent theory either of the meaning of 'totalitarianism' or of the causes for the growth of totalitarian societies in the recent past." Historians tended to be especially harsh. In *The American Historical Review* the book was upbraided for "a persistent tendency for overstatement" and "a general neglect of economic forces. . . . the work as a whole conveys an impression of miscarriage," and in *The Journal of Modern History* it was found to be "full of paradoxes which tend to leave the historian breathless. . . . as a synthesis of the malign forces which, working together, produced totalitarianism, it fails to carry conviction." The flagship journal in political science, *The American Political Science Review*, did not consider the book at all. Within that discipline, a contemporaneous review in *Political Science Quarterly* announced it to be marred by a major "defect" in causal reasoning, stating that "the pattern, the trend, the relation of cause and consequence, are not always clear." The fullest treatment in political science was published in *World Politics* only two decades after the book first had appeared. "An over-reliance on deductive reasoning and a disregard for data contribute to the tendency of *Origins of Totalitarianism* to lose touch with reality," the reviewer remonstrated, revealing "that Arendt is not a social scientist" and regretted that her work had not been "cast in terms compatible with the theory and method of modern comparative political analysis."[16]

Because her writing is so enclosed within a complicated, mostly German, idealist theoretical ancestry, scholars more inclined toward systematic Anglo-American philosophy or methodical social science have been prone to dismiss it. Isaiah Berlin, for example, assessed Arendt this way: "I do not greatly respect the lady's ideas. . . . She produces no arguments, no evidence of serious philosophical or historical thought. It is all a stream of metaphysical associations."[17] For the anthropologist Ernest Gellner, Arendt's "verbosity, logical untidiness, impressionism, and imprecision of her style make her contribution of dubious value."[18] The historian Walter Laqueur was equally dismissive, offering a scathing assessment of her "long and far fetched discourses on the Dreyfus Trial and French antisemitism, on Disraeli, Cecil Rhodes, Lawrence of Arabia, and

---

16. The reviews of *The Origins of Totalitarianism*, respectively are by Werner Baer, *The American Economic Review* 42 (June 1953): 437; C.H. Van Duzer, *The American Historical Review* 57 (July 1952): 934; Aileen Dunham, *The Journal of Modern History* 24 (June 1952): 184; Thomas I. Cook, *Political Science Quarterly* 66 (June 1951): 291; and Robert Burrowes, "Totalitarianism: The Revised Standard Version," *World Politics* 21 (January 1969): 280, 294.

17. Benhabib, *Arendt*, p. xxxvii.

18. Ernest Gellner, "Accounting for the Horror," *Times Literary Supplement*, August 6, 1982; reprinted in Ernest Gellner, *Culture, Identity, and Politics* (Cambridge, Cambridge University Press, 1987), p. 89.

British imperialism. . . . The reputation of the *Origins* as a path-breaking, let alone definitive work," he concluded, "seems unwarranted."[19] Arendt's own expressed disdain for the manner in which the social sciences had come to model themselves on the natural sciences in language and method[20] reciprocally has reinforced impressions of inexactness in her use and emplacement of evidence, concern about the opaque and elliptical elaboration of her causal arguments, and suspicion about such key choices as her focus on France and Britain in the late nineteenth and early twentieth centuries and her repression of differences between Nazi Germany and Bolshevik Russia in order to demonstrate their similarities as the paramount sites of totalitarianism.

Of course, there were, and are, other views. In February 1950, Heinrich Blücher, Arendt's husband, wrote to her in Germany to report that William Jovanovich, her publisher, had "handed your manuscript to Alfred [Kazin] after rereading it, with the comment that they are 'convinced of the greatness of the book'."[21] When *Origins* appeared its reception in broad intellectual circles was adulatory. Mary McCarthy "described Arendt's political acuity as 'amazing,' Kazin said her thinking had a 'moral grandeur,' and [Dwight] Macdonald dubbed her 'the most original and profound—therefore the most valuable—political theoretician of our time'."[22] Similarly, Abbott Payson Usher, the noted economic historian of technology, proclaimed *The Great Transformation* on the morrow of its publication to be a "remarkable book . . . a searching critical analysis" and a "critical revision of economics and of political theory . . . no less significant for the understanding of history than for the definition of current political and social aims."[23]

Despite the early, more common, dissent within the disciplines, it is these positive judgments that have endured. A half-century after the publication of *Transformation*, a list of 'the hundred most influential books since the war' reported by the *Times Literary Supplement* placed Polanyi's text next to George Orwell's *Animal Farm* and *1984* and R. G. Collingwood's *Idea of History* as leading books of the 1940s. It also located Arendt's study at the head of the list for the

---

19. Walter Laqueur, "The Arendt Cult: Hannah Arendt as Political Commentator," *Journal of Contemporary History*, 33 (October 1998): 486–487.

20. Hannah Arendt, *Between Past and Future* (New York: Viking Press, 1968), pp. 58–59.

21. Lotte Kohler, ed., *Within Four Walls: The Correspondence between Hannah Arendt and Heinrich Blücher, 1936–1968* (New York: Harcourt, Inc., 2000), p. 137. "It was Kazin who first arranged for the publication of *The Origins of Totalitarianism* when her original publisher backed out of the contract." Alan M. Wald, "Radical Evil," *Reviews in American History*, 9 (June 1981): 262.

22. Wald, "Radical Evil," p. 262; Dwight Macdonald, "A New Theory of Totalitarianism," *New Leader*, 34 (May 14, 1951): 17.

23. Abbot Payson Usher, Review of *The Great Transformation*, *Political Science Quarterly*, 59 (December 1944).

1950s that included Winston Churchill's *The Second World War*, Erik Erikson's *Young Man Luther*, and Boris Pasternak's *Doctor Zhivago*. With the exception of Karl Popper's *The Open Society and its Enemies* and Kenneth Arrow's *Social Choice and Individual Values*, no other volumes named in the social sciences have been as durably influential, certainly none that probed the origins of the West's dark times.[24] Both books remain touchstones of interpretation and understanding. Not a year passes without at least one major scholarly conference devoted to each. So we have something of a paradox to contend with. In trying to understand why the continuum of assessment by highly intelligent readers has been so broad, some of the most distinctive features of the political studies enlightenment can be brought into view, including the way its members sought to braid purpose, passion, and perception.[25] Seeking to "enlarge the field of vision" and advance "a new type of political knowledge" at the junction of history, social science, and political theory, these books are impossible to harness in conventional ways.[26]

Above all, what is compelling about their work is the manner in which they pursued historical periodization, the effort "to assign a meaning to historical phenomena by relating them either to sequential chains of other events or to webs of relationships, including institutions, social groups of one sort or another, or even mentalités that endure across a significant length of time."[27] This interpretive and analytical project, the historian Charles Maier has noted, tends to fall into one of two types of narrative: sequential and causal structural accounts or moral characterizations like those of twentieth-century atrocity.[28] In their quest for meaningful temporal understandings of modern western history, Polanyi and Arendt stand out for their risky, difficult, and compelling efforts to combine structural and moral periodizations, broadly in the manner of Alexis de Tocqueville's great studies of France and the United States and Barrington Moore's powerful account written some two decades after *Transformation* and *Origins* that sought to discern "the forces behind the emergence of Western par-

---

24. The list was compiled to assist East European scholars cope with the results of intellectual isolation by the Central and East Europe Publishing Project (including Ralf Dahrendorf, Lesek Kolakowski, and François Furet). "The Hundred Most Influential Books Since the War," *Times Literary Supplement*, June 10, 1995.

25. These are Kenneth Burke's terms. Kenneth Burke, *A Grammar of Motives* (New York: Prentice Hall, 1945). Ralph Ellison reports they structured his *Invisible Man*. Van Wyck Brooks, *Writers at Work: The Paris Review Interviews, Second Series* (New York: Viking Press, 1965), p. 328.

26. These goals for social inquiry are those announced by Karl Mannheim in *Ideology and Utopia* (London, Routledge & Kegan Paul, 1936), pp. 285, 170–171.

27. Charles Maier, "Consigning the Twentieth Century to History: Alternative Narratives for the Modern Era," *American Historical Review* 105 (June 2000): 809.

28. Maier, "Consigning," pp. 808–813.

liamentary versions of democracy, and dictatorships of the right and the left, that is, fascist and communist regimes."[29] Admixing "deep passion and cool analysis," their work was written out of a conviction and determination to confront their period's "mental and moral chaos." In this pursuit, they produced a "hybrid brand of history" that tied "an orientation toward beginnings, origins, foundations" and the analysis of events and their sequence to the fate of such fundamental values as freedom and the autonomous person based on the conviction that more ordinary historical scholarship could not comprehend the unprecedented occurrences their generation just had experienced.[30] It is this combination, I believe, that has proved the source both for the deep skepticism and the extravagant approbation announced by readers of *The Great Transformation* and *The Origins of Totalitarianism*.

I.

The analytical/moral histories in these books are well-known. Nineteenth-century civilization's institutional design, Polanyi argued, had been built on

---

29. Alexis de Tocqueville, *The Old Regime and the Revolution* (Chicago: University of Chicago Press, 1998 [1859]); Alexis de Tocqueville, *Democracy in America*. Vols. 1 and 2 (New York: Knopf, 1945 [1835, 1840]); and Barrington Moore, Jr., *Social Origins of Dictatorship and Democracy: Lord and Peasant in the Making of the Modern World* (Boston: Beacon Press, 1966), p. xi.. The spirit of this kind of history, refusing to sacrifice either analytical power or normative purpose, was addressed by Fritz Stern in an introduction to an anthology dedicated to a close examination of the historical method. While confirming that the historian's "obligation to the past, his complete, unassailable fidelity to it, must always claim his first loyalty, he must accept the fact that the choices he makes as a historian are not of consequence to him alone, but will affect the moral sense, perhaps the wisdom, of his generation. And since he knows that his own being, his intellectual capabilities and his critical faculties as well as his deeper sense of righteousness and love, are engaged in the writing of history, he knows that his work, too, is a moral act." Fritz Stern, "Introduction," in Fritz Stern, ed., *The Varieties of History* (Cleveland and New York: Meridian Books, 1956), p. 32.

30. Here, I am extending to Polanyi the characterization offered by Bernard Crick in "Hannah Arendt and the Burden of Our Times," *The Political Quarterly* 68 (January–March 1997) and by Leonard Krieger in "The Historical Hannah Arendt," *The Journal of Modern History* 48 (December 1976); the citations in Krieger come from pp. 675–678. Polanyi himself wrote that the "polarities" between "fact and value; empiricism and normativity . . . formed the permanent axis of my world of thought." Polanyi is cited by his daughter, Kari Polanyi-Levitt, "The Origins and Significance of *The Great Transformation* (Montreal: Black Rose Books, 1990), p. 17. Crick judged "*The Origins of Totalitarianism*, for all its faults, its bold but discomforting and alarming—not only to the empiricist— leaps from history to sociology to philosophy, and its mixture of factuality and speculation, is still Arendt's key work, possibly her master-work. It is a magisterial if untidy mixture of deep passion and cool analysis; many or most of her other works are like huge footnotes constructed to resolve differences left behind in the postwar urgency and immediacy of its exposition." (p. 80)

four pillars: the balance of power system, the international gold standard, the liberal state, and, most important, the self-regulating market, especially its labor market, and the ideas which sustained them. These regulatory institutions had produced contradictory effects. Though sources of global peace and European prosperity, they also provided the rootstock generating a new age of desolation. What had appeared for a long period as a durable formula to curb autocracy, advance prosperity, secure freedom, and procure peace only was an interlude between older and newer, more terrible, forms of despotism marked by special betrayals and heightened cruelty.[31]

Polanyi's story ordered the history of much of the nineteenth and twentieth centuries culminating in the world crisis of the 1930s and 1940s by distinguishing three broad overlapping moments: the establishment of a liberal institutional order in the early decades of the nineteenth century when state action made markets possible by securing the conditions needed for their functioning; a long period of relative success for such regimes spanning the middle of the nineteenth century, into the 1870's, when a global economic liberalism of free trade and the gold standard underpinned domestic markets and representative democracy; and an ensuing period of emergency, a terrible moment when the imperatives of markets and citizenship sharply clashed to make new forms of disaster possible. Price-markets and laissez-faire ideology were core components of nineteenth-century modernity. But they exacted too high a price for those who had to suffer the insecurities of labor markets. Accordingly, both those who lived from the land and worked for wages utilized the instrumentalities of citizenship made possible by political representation and the franchise to demand protection: from imports and from the vagaries of the labor market. These interventions produced a deep and terrible contradiction. Market rationality was impeded by this crusade for protection, but the effort to utilize politics to produce public policies to shield individuals, groups, and society as a whole from the consequences of market arrangements failed sufficiently to protect.[32] The consequence was a profound loss of faith in the efficacy of liberal regimes in the face of large-scale war, economic collapse, and seductive totalitarian alternatives. The result, liberal collapse and the rise of illiberal alternatives, thus was the consequence of failed attempts to control the disorder brought about by faltering efforts for security in a market economy.[33]

---

31. I agree with Goldfrank that it was this 'great transformation,' not the rise of the market economy in the nineteenth century, that was designated in Polanyi's title. W. L. Goldfrank, "Fascism and *The Great Transformation*," in Polanyi-Levitt, *Polanyi*, p. 87.

32. A similar analysis can be found in Adolf Sturmthal, *The Tragedy of European Labor, 1981–1939* (New York: Columbia University Press, 1943).

33. An excellent short summary of Polanyi's journalism between 1924 and 1938 can be found in Michele Cangiani, "Prelude to *The Great Transformation*: Karl Polanyi's Articles for *Des Oester-*

Arendt's origins narrative complemented Polanyi's. Whereas he had asked how a putatively successful liberal global and domestic political and economic order could have collapsed, Arendt probed the sources of its totalitarian arch-enemy. Rather than focus primarily on institutional features and legitimating ideas, she brought the subsurface elements of anti-Semitism, imperialism, and anti-liberal totalitarianism into view. Without making Jews mere victims or their situation a primary cause, she inserted their particularity inside a wider European experience to show how the relationship between Jews and the modern state did not, perhaps could not, survive the rise of strong nationalism, which was independent of the state, thus transforming "social discrimination," which had been the product of resistance to growing Jewish equality and economic success, "into a political argument" seeking to extrude Jews from the unit of the nation. "For more than a hundred years," she wrote:[34]

> antisemitism had slowly and gradually made its way into almost all social strata in almost all European countries until it emerged suddenly as the one issue upon which an almost unified opinion could be achieved. The law according to which this process developed was simple: each class of society which came into conflict with the state as such became antisemitic because the only social group which seemed to represent the state were the Jews.

By the latter third of the nineteenth century, political anti-Semitism had entered public life. In the face of anti-Semitic movements and political parties making mass appeals, mainstream bourgeois and working class parties alike increasingly became mute, "not only unprepared to integrate the Jewish issue into their theories, but actually afraid to touch the question at all."[35]

But it was imperialism, especially Europe's colonization of Africa, that had introduced racism into this brew. In part, of course, imperialism was an economic event, one that Arendt understood in surprisingly orthodox Marxist terms as a search for sites to invest capitalism's surplus. Equally important, she insisted, was the new life it gave to an otherwise archaic racism, once trumped, or so it had seemed, by Enlightenment liberality. "It is highly probable," Arendt averred, "that the thinking in terms of race would have disappeared in due time together with other irresponsible opinions of the nineteenth-century, if the 'scramble for Africa' and the new era of imperialism had not exposed western

---

reichische Volkswirt," in Kenneth McRobbie, ed., *Humanity, Society, and Commitment: On Karl Polanyi* (Montreal: Black Rose Books, 1994).

34. Arendt, *Origins*, p. 25.

35. Arendt, *Origins*, p. 41.

humanity to new and shocking experiences. . . . brutal deeds and active bestiality," including "the triumphant introduction of such means of pacification into ordinary, respectable foreign policies."[36] Further, she argued, imperialism not only reinvigorated but bureaucratized racism, bringing the race principle to the heart of the western body politic by joining the powerful discovery of race in South Africa to the modes of imperial bureaucracy elaborated in Algeria, Egypt, and India.[37] Pan-nationalist, then fascist, mobilizations in continental Europe collected and joined these elements of anti-Semitism and racism to create templates for totalitarian movements which convened classless mobs and masses "on the basis of racism" and a program of anti-legal, anti-constitutional hostility to existing states signified by the "extraordinarily rapid decline" of the post-1848 party system which largely had been based on class, rather than national and other primordial, divisions.[38] Soon, an atmosphere of disintegration became palpable. Its hallmark after the First World War was a growing crisis of statelessness accompanied by the loss of citizenship for those who were not deemed to fit into the national order. The abstractions of the Rights of Man collapsed, totalitarianism flourished, and its most characteristic institution, the concentration camp, opened its doors.

My purpose is not evaluate the particulars of these schematic histories, many of whose details have been superseded by subsequent scholarship.[39] Rather, I wish to comment on their periodization of western history and the character of their historical social science, underscoring compelling aspects of their writing that have been apprehended insufficiently but are central to their efforts to secure the Enlightenment by forging "a new beginning," as Arendt put it, "politically . . . identical with man's freedom."[40] For Polanyi, these qualities include the links he made connecting his analysis of liberal political and economic the-

---

36. Arendt, *Origins*: 183, 185.

37. Arendt, *Origins*, p. 207.

38. Arendt, *Origins*: 221, 265.

39. As examples: For recent work on the Dreyfus Affair, for example, contradicting Arendt in more than a few respects, see Pierre Birnbaum, ed., *La France de l'affaire Dreyfus* (Paris: Gallimard, 1994), and Pierre Birnbaum, *Le moment antisémite: Un tour de la France en 1898*. (Paris: Fayard, 1998). For scholarship differing substantially with Polanyi on Speenhamland, see Mark Blaug, *Economic History and the History of Economics* (New York: New York University Press, 1986); Gary F. Langer, *The Coming of Age of Political Economy, 1815–1825* (New York: Greenwood Press, 1987); and James E. Cronin, "The British State and the Structure of Political Opportunity," *Journal of British Studies* 27 (July 1988). But despite the attempts by an immense literature to render the concept of 'totalitarianism' obsolete, I agree fully with Jeffrey Isaac who, writing about how this concept "has disappeared from the lexicon of political theory," lamented its absence as "unfortunate both for political theory and for political understanding in general." Jeffrey C. Isaac, *Arendt, Camus, and Modern Rebellion* (New Haven: Yale University Press, 1992), p. 37.

40. Arendt, *Origins*: 478–479.

ory to institutions and public policy and his disregard for the usual boundaries separating international affairs from domestic studies. For Arendt, they include the global quality of her analysis of European affairs, quite unique at the time, and her combination of a probabilistic account of large-scale change with very focused 'normal science' empirical propositions about causation.

Read separately but especially together, these works written to make safe the Enlightenment by discerning the sources of its insecurity suggested a particularly appealing course for historical social science that subsequent practitioners have followed very incompletely. Both accounts of desolation's inception and lineage stand out for their sheer suggestive power, for their braiding of moral with analytical narration, and for their methodological self-consciousness in dealing with such vexing problems as those of teleology, and objectivity. Curiously, neither book has been considered and evaluated primarily as analytical and historical social science. In appraising how *The Great Transformation* and *The Origins of Totalitarianism* approached modern history and social science, we soon will discover that they have been understood and appreciated only partially, even by admirers, usually consigned, respectively, to boxes of political economy and political theory too small to contain them. Polanyi's writing mainly has inspired non-Marxist critics of economic liberalism and market society as a core contribution to the field of economic sociology celebrated for abjuring economic determinism and striking at market-centered nostrums.[41] Reacting against both Marxism and liberal economics, Polanyi indeed did seek to combat what he thought to be the proclivity to disconnect the zone of economics and to confer causal primacy to economic factors by overextending a materialist and instrumental rational actor view of human motivation. Rejecting timeless portrayals of market institutions and choice, Polanyi stressed instead how modern markets are not natural or free-standing, but historically contingent products of regulation by modern states. Even when markets appear autonomous and independent, he insisted, they never are.

This aspect of *Transformation* has been underscored, and both celebrated and condemned, the most. Of the volume's three parts—the first concerns 'the international system,' the second the 'rise and fall of market economy,' and the third the 'transformation in progress'—it is the middle one that tends to be read and remembered, thus effectively removing the volume from the context of the exigency that motivated and shaped it while severing the ties it makes attaching

---

41. For this orientation, see, Neil J. Smelser and Richard Swedberg, eds., *Handbook of Economic Sociology* (Princeton: Princeton University Press, 1994); Richard Swedberg, ed., *Explorations in Economic Sociology* (New York: Russell Sage Foundation, 1993); Mark Granovetter and Richard Swedberg, eds., *The Sociology of Economic Life* (Boulder: Westview Press, 1992); and Viviana Zelizer, *The Social Meaning of Money* (New York: Basic Books, 1994).

politics to economics and international to domestic institutions.[42] Further, Polanyi's attention to key issues in liberal and socialist thought tends to be ignored.[43] By contrast, it is the combination of these elements that marks the book's distinctive approach to social science.

Likewise, despite an explosion of commentary, Arendt has been considered in too truncated a manner, mainly contained within the field of political theory. Her scholarship, of course, has been enjoying a significant revival and has been the subject of an ever more extensive array of secondary treatments.[44] For some,

---

42. See, for examples, Fred Block and Margaret Somers, "Beyond the Economistic Fallacy: The Holistic Social Science of Karl Polanyi," in Theda Skocpol, ed., *Vision and Method in Historical Sociology* (Cambridge: Cambridge University Press, 1984); Bernard Barber, "All Economies are Embedded: The Career of a Concept, and Beyond," *Social Research* 62 (Summer 1995), and the special section on Karl Polanyi in *Telos* no. 73 (Fall 1987), whose two core articles concern "The Economy as an Institutional Process" (Alberto Martinelli) and "The Relation of State and Market" (Jean-Jacques Gislain). The secondary literature on Polanyi is relatively modest in scope; even when excellent, as in the work of Fred Block and Margaret Somers, it tends in the direction of advocacy and hagiography, avoiding issues and problems which have put *The Great Transformation* outside the ken of the main currents in history and social science. For examples, see Charles P. Kindleberger, "The Great Transformation by Karl Polanyi," *Daedalus*, no. 103 (Winter 1973); Margaret Somers, "Karl Polanyi's Intellectual Legacy," in Kari Polanyi-Levitt, ed., *The Life and Work of Karl Polanyi: A Celebration* (Montreal: Black Rose Books, 1990); William Waller and Ann Jennings, "A Feminist Institutionalist Reconsideration of Karl Polanyi," *Journal of Economic Issues* 25 (June 1991); Marguerite Mendell and Daniel Salee, eds., *The Legacy of Karl Polanyi: Market, State, and Society at the End of the Twentieth Century* (New York: St. Martin's Press 1991); Gregory Baum, *Karl Polanyi on Ethics and Economics* (Montreal: McGill-Queen's University Press, 1996); Kenneth McRobbie, ed., *Humanity, Society, and Commitment: On Karl Polanyi* (Montreal: Black Rose Books, 1994); J. R. Stanfield, *The Economic Thought of Karl Polanyi* (New York: St. Martin's Press, 1986); Tim Stroshane, "The Second Contradiction of Capitalism and Karl Polanyi's *The Great Transformation*," *Capitalism, Nature, and Society* 8 (September 1997); Kenneth McRobbie and Kari Polanyi-Levitt, eds., *Karl Polanyi in Vienna: The Contemporary Significance of the Great Transformation* (Montreal: Black Rose Press, 2000); and Allen Morris Sievers, *Has Market Capitalism Collapsed? A Critique of Karl Polanyi's New Economics* (New York: 1949). The best sympathetic short critique of *The Great Transformation* I know is Alberto Martinelli, "The Economy as an Institutional Process," *Telos*, no. 73 (Fall 1987).

43. For an exception, see Fred Block, "Marxism and Beyond: Karl Polanyi and the Writing of *The Great Transformation*," unpublished manuscript, 2002.

44. The literature on Arendt, of course, is considerable. For examples from the past two decades, see Bhikhu Parekh, *Hannah Arendt and the Search for a New Political Philosophy* (Atlantic Highlands, New Jersey: Humanities Press International, 1981); George Kateb, *Hannah Arendt: Politics, Conscience, Evil* (Totowa, New Jersey: Rowman and Allanheld, 1984); Dagmar Barnouw, *Visible Spaces: Hannah Arendt and the German-Jewish Experience* (Baltimore: Johns Hopkins University Press, 1990); Margaret Canovan, *Hannah Arendt: A Reinterpretation of Her Political Thought* (Cambridge: Cambridge University Press, 1992), a successor to her earlier book, *The Political Thought of Hannah Arendt* (London: Dent and Sons, 1974); Issac, *Arendt, Camus, and Modern*

she, too, has become an iconic figure, for others a candidate for dismissal, perhaps because "her experiences . . . read like a parable of this century: persecution, statelessness, exile, a brief internment in a detention camp, immigration, success and public recognition,"[45] perhaps because the absence of a system in her thought makes it possible to produce highly selective readings, each appropriating the Arendt that serves a particular purpose.[46]

This burgeoning literature treating Arendt almost exclusively as a social and political philosopher is partial in yet another respect. Theorists aside, social scientists have paid her writing little heed, rarely thinking of her as a compatriot. Despite the barriers Arendt herself placed in our way, this tendency to distance her from the social and political sciences is a serious mistake. In *Origins*, she combined three types of analysis: a macrohistorical account stressing the underdetermination of its main elements;[47] systematic propositions about such institutions as political parties; and, inside both, explanations of variations in the

---

Rebellion; Bonnie Honig, *Political Theory and the Displacement of Politics* (Ithaca: Cornell University Press, 1993); Lisa J. Disch, *Hannah Arendt and the Limits of Philosophy* (Ithaca: Cornell University Press, 1994); Maurizio Passerin d'Entrèves, *The Political Philosophy of Hannah Arendt* (London: Routledge, 1994); Hinchman and Hinchman, *Arendt*; Seyla Benhabib, *The Reluctant Modernism of Hannah Arendt* (Thousand Oaks, California: Sage Publications, 1996); Richard J. Bernstein, *Hannah Arendt and the Jewish Question* (Cambridge: MIT Press, 1996); Larry May and Jerome Kohn, eds., *Hannah Arendt: Twenty Years Later* (Cambridge: MIT Press, 1997); Hannah Fenichel Pitkin, *The Attack of the Blob: Hannah Arendt's Conception of the Social* (Chicago: University of Chicago Press, 1998); Dana R. Villa, *Politics, Philosophy, Terror: Essays on the Thought of Hannah Arendt* (Princeton: Princeton University Press, 1999); Reuben Garner, ed., *The Realm of Humanitas: Responses to the Writing of Hannah Arendt* (New York: Peter Lang, 1990); Dana Villa, ed., *The Cambridge Companion to Hannah Arendt* (Cambridge: Cambridge University Press, 2000); and Julia Kristeva, *Hannah Arendt* (New York: Columbia University Press, 2001). A curiously laudatory review of Arendt's *Between Past and Future* praising her for having changed the landscape of our thinking without advancing a single causal hypothesis (a view I am at pains to say below is wrong) was penned by Michael Oakeshott, *Political Science Quarterly* 77 (March 1962). The major biography remains that by Elisabeth Young-Bruehl, *Hannah Arendt: For Love of the World* (New Haven: Yale University Press, 1982). A recent representative appreciation of Arendt as political theorist is Ann M. Lane, "Hannah Arendt: Theorist of Distinction," *Political Theory* 25 (February 1997). Also see the special issue on Arendt, with essays by Bernstein, Kateb, Canovan , and others in *Revue Internationale de Philosophie* 53, no. 2 (1999).

45. Seyla Benhabib, "The Personal Is Not the Political," *Boston Review* (October/November 1999): 45.

46. I realize, of course, that my own particular treatment of Arendt risks this partiality, not least because I am limiting my attention to *Origins* and a small number of essays she wrote in the decade following the Second World War.

47. Her account of barbarity and slaughter, Seyla Benhabib has observed, "is not concerned to establish some inevitable continuity between the past and the present that would compel us to view what happens as what had to happen." Seyla Benhabib, *The Reluctant Modernism of Hannah Arendt* (Thousand Oaks, California: Sage Publications, 1996), p. xxxvii.

preferences, choices, and activities of historical actors. Moving amongst these levels, she sought to identify both the elements that made totalitarianism possible not in isolation as independent causal variables but in particular configurations; what she called the crystallization of elements. In so doing, she brought together the elucidation of necessary conditions with ample scope for the causal analysis of behavioral choices mediated by institutional arrangements. Just this combination, together with the charged anxiety, normative purpose, and effort to embed their historical and empirical scholarship inside political theory,[48] makes the work of Polanyi and Arendt worth considering as models both for contemporary historical social science and as guides to our own disquieting times. When read not simply as political economy or political theory but as contributions to a larger effort to deepen, protect, and renew the tradition of enlightenment, the range and purpose of their historical social science come into view.

II.

Like any such effort, this kind of enterprise is impossible without ordering the significance of historical time. Seeking to understand and defend the best features of the western political tradition without departing from the reason-based epistemologies and value commitments of the Enlightenment, Polanyi and Arendt underpinned their social science with a powerful conviction and claim: that the decades of total war, totalitarianism, and (for Arendt), holocaust causing the demise of what he called "nineteenth century civilization" and what she thought of as a new age marked by unprecedented facts and deeds marked a monumental breach, a rupture more deep and more fundamental than almost any other critical juncture in human history. Historical Europe had died and could not simply be revived. Because the break with the past had been so fundamental, shattering familiar categories and methods of analysis, the crisis in understanding was profound.[49] Writing about the three decades from 1884 to 1914 that separated the twentieth century from the nineteenth, Arendt observed,

---

48. German idealism, primarily, for Arendt; liberal and socialist political thought for Polanyi.. See, in this regard, Arendt's 1946 essay, "What is Existential Philosophy?," in Hannah Arendt, *Essays in Understanding, 1930–1954*, ed. Jerome Kohn (New York: Harcourt, 1994), pp. 163–187 (subsequently cited as Kohn, *Arendt*).

49. For discussions, see John McGowan, *Hannah Arendt: An Introduction* (Minneapolis: University of Minnesota Press, 1998), p. 14; d'Entrèves, p. 3; and Richard Wolin, *Labyrinths: Explanations in the Critical History of Ideas* (Amherst: University of Massachusetts Press, 1995), p. 163. Arendt returned to this theme in 1968, writing that "Totalitarian domination as an established fact, which in its unprecedentedness cannot be comprehended through the usual categories of political thought, and whose 'crimes' cannot be judged by traditional moral standards or pun-

"We can hardly avoid looking at this close and yet distant past with the too-wise eyes of those who know the end of the story in advance, who know it led to an almost complete break in the continuous flow of Western history as we had known it for more than two thousand years."[50] In a formulation at once more modest yet almost equally radical, Polanyi located this discontinuity against the foil of a prior break, the nineteenth-century "phenomenon unheard of in the annals of Western civilization, namely a hundred year's peace."[51]

Because their project entailed discerning the processes that had caused the old order to collapse and a new one to be born, the search for the historical sources of desolation had to be double-barreled. What, they asked, had brought about the breakdown and destruction of the West's first secular and 'enlightened' order based on broadly coherent international and domestic institutional arrangements and an expansion to the scope of liberal citizenship? Which elements had been available for collection by the enemies of Enlightenment to produce alternative designs for politics, economics, culture, and society?

Polanyi primarily explored the first of these questions by elucidating the breakdown of the 'long nineteenth century's' liberal order. Arendt, by contrast, mainly probed how new and terrible solutions drew their essentials from an anti-Enlightenment bricolage inherited from the past.[52] But there is more than this division of labor distinguishing the two volumes. The gap in substance and sensibility between *The Great Transformation* and *The Origins of Totalitarianism* is deeper than the divergence in their respective objects of explanation, the end of the old order and the birth of the new, or even the causal wagers they made as they conducted their inquiries. Ultimately, their objects of analysis were incommensurable. Polanyi wrote before the fate of Europe's Jews had become clear; Arendt, by contrast, began to work on *Origins* late in 1945 when their terrible circumstances had been discovered.[53] His periodization was defined by

ished within the legal framework of our civilization, has broken the continuity of Occidental history." Arendt, *Past and Future*, p. 26.

50. Arendt, *Origins*, p. 123.

51. Polanyi, *Transformation*, p. 5.

52. Of course, this distinction is a bit too sharp. Each volume contained both elements. Thus Crick, for example, takes note both of "her account of the growth of the ideology of Nazism and her account of the breakdown of traditional bourgeois values and expectations," observing that, "strictly speaking, the two accounts have no logical connection." Precisely because this is correct—the sources of breakdown may not be the same as the causes of a new form—it makes sense to underline the distinctive main task in each book. Bernard Crick, "On Rereading *The Origins of Totalitarianism*," *Social Research* 44 (Spring 1977): 110.

53. "What was decisive," Arendt told Günther Gaus on West German television in 1964, "was the day we learned about Auschwitz . . . That was in 1943. . . . It was as if an abyss had opened." Hannah Arendt, " 'What Remains? The Language Remains': A Conversation with Günther Gaus," in Kohn, *Arendt*, p. 13.

institutional change; hers by the eruption of evil from its subterraneous confines. Accordingly, Arendt's perception of a historical break ran deeper than Polanyi's. His cleft was her abyss.[54]

This discrepancy in emphasis and orientation provides each volume with a distinctive torque, effectively distinguishing Arendt's analysis of some of the same issues Polanyi had amply treated, most notably in the case of imperialism, from his. Arendt thus can be read as providing an unintentional rebuke to Polanyi, reproaching his, or any, political economy as insufficient on its own to comprehend the deformations of contemporary civilization.[55] Indeed, alone of all the members of the political studies enlightenment, it was Arendt who achieved a major work in historical social science arraying total war, totalitarianism, and holocaust in a single historical constellation.

My point of departure, however, is their common sense that an unprecedented fracture had developed dividing then from now. "The essential structure of all civilizations is at the breaking point," Arendt declared on her first page.[56] "Nineteenth century civilization has collapsed," Polanyi began.[57] Despite some linguistic ambiguity, both pursued what might be called a strategy of origins rather than an analysis of crisis.[58] What was required, both believed, was not the just the study of the period of emergency, implying a possible return to normalcy, but a deeper and more fundamental consideration of origins, a search by the means of historical social science for the sources and elements of a catastrophe so far reaching that, as they believed, the world had begun anew.

---

54. She was curiously silent about atomic weaponry in *The Origins of Totalitarianism*, especially in light of the development of a Soviet as well as an American bomb and the period's vibrant fear for the possibility of a nuclear exchange in the early Cold War. Writing in 1954, though, she made it clear that nuclear technology had reinforced her understanding of a basic breach between past and present. "With the appearance of nuclear weapons," she wrote, "both the Hebrew-Christian limitation on violence and the ancient appeal to courage have for all practical purposes become meaningless, and, with them, the whole political and moral vocabulary in which we are accustomed to discuss these matters. . . . The moment a war can even conceivably threaten the continued existence of man on earth, the alternative between liberty and death has lost its old plausibility." Hannah Arendt, "Europe and the Atomic Bomb," in Kohn, *Arendt, pp.* 421, 422; this essay first appeared in *The Commonweal*, September 24, 1954.

55. I say unintentional because there are no citations to Polanyi in *The Origins of Totalitarianism*. Certainly, though, Arendt knew his work. Arendt's retrospective awareness of doom, written in full knowledge of the holocaust, was the darker of the two. See, for a sense of this, her preface on post-holocaust Jewish historiography for the 1974 edition of her early work, *Rahel Varnhagen, The Life of a Jewish Woman* (New York: Harcourt, Brace, Jovanovich, 1974).

56. Arendt, *Origins*, vii.

57. Polanyi, *Transformation*, p. 3.

58. Polanyi, for example, used a more routine language of crisis in declaring that humankind was passing through "one of the deepest crises in man's history." Polanyi, *Transformation*, p. 4.

Had it? Which, and whose, world had begun anew? Are such claims for the existence of a qualitatively distinctive dark time, judged both against the longer and the shorter term persuasive or extravagant? Illiberal rule, organized killing and brutality, and fierce identities distinguishing 'us' from 'them' (including the targeting of Jews as 'other') long have been present, arguably prevalent, in human affairs; so much so, that over as wide an expanse of space as the world, and as great a span of time as the past millennium, they appear virtually as universals. If at all, how did the West's three decades of desolation stand out within this dismal record? Polanyi and Arendt were compelled to address such questions because their answers both motivate their projects and define what it is they wished to explain.

Further, many other historians and social theorists have divided human history into big temporal sections.[59] There exist more than a few such models and philosophies of history from which to choose. These attempts also distinguish 'critical junctures' marked by crises and uncertainty from periods of persistence and continuity.[60] Set alongside Marx's theory of epochal transformations based on changes to the mode of production, or Durkheim's breach between tradition and modernity, or Weber's account of the growth of rationalization, or more recent scholarship on break points in the development of the modern sovereign state,[61] what makes the assertions advanced by Arendt and Polanyi about temporality either distinctive or compelling? Can their claims about historical time not be subsumed into other, perhaps more familiar, approaches?

---

59. The task of periodization, Walter Dean Burnham observes, provides "an organized prioritization of a vast and otherwise unmanageable flow of raw data. . . . [by asserting] that certain facts are at the core of what is going on, while others are more or less subsidiary to them." Burnham, "Pattern Recognition and 'Doing' Political History: Art, Science, or Bootless Enterprise?," Lawrence C. Dodd and Calvin Jillson, *The Dynamics of American Politics: Approaches and Interpretations.* (Boulder: Westview Press, 1993), pp. 66–67. For an earlier discussion, see, Walter Dean Burnham, "Periodization Schemes and 'Party Systems': The System of 1896 as a Case in Point," *Social Science History* 10 (Fall 1976).

60. For discussions, see Ruth Berins Collier and David Collier, *Shaping the Political Arena: Critical Junctures, the Labor Movement, and Regime Dynamics in Latin America* (Princeton: Princeton University Press, 1991), especially chapters 1 and 8; and Sidney Verba, "Sequences and Development," in Leonard Binder, *et.al., Crises and Sequences in Political Development* (Princeton: Princeton University Press, 1971).

61. As examples, see Richard Bonney, *The European Dynastic States, 1494–1660* (Oxford: Oxford University Press, 1991); Thomas Ertman, *Birth of the Leviathan: Building States and Regimes in Medieval and Early Modern Europe* (Cambridge: Cambridge University Press, 1997); Hendrick Spruyt, *The Sovereign State and its Competitors* (Princeton: Princeton University Press, 1994); and Martin van Crevald, *The Rise and Decline of the State* (Cambridge: Cambridge University Press, 1999).

Certainly, there are ample grounds for empirical and historical skepticism. War, after all, has been an omnipresent feature of the human experience.[62] Pre-state peoples, we now know, fought as cruelly as moderns, and for similar 'rational' reasons.[63] Cultural contact long has gone hand in hand with deep violence against the 'other' in a compound of interest, power, and misunderstanding, often combining war with biological shock and aided by calculated and deliberately functional western ethnographies of the targets of conquest that presented these populations as beyond reason.[64] The Spanish conquest of Mexico cost the lives of some 11 million indigenous people; and its subjugation of the Andean Empire in Peru came at the expense of 8 million more.[65] Cruelty was not all one-sided. In a modest example, the Algonquian Indian rebellion against the Puritan settlers of southern New England in 1675 wiped out more than half the English towns, with battles marked by terrifying atrocities on both sides.[66] The 'Great War' of 1914–1918 was not the first, but the eighth, world war, if by that we mean a war fought on every inhabited continent; nor the first to be fought in set-pieces of senseless slaughter (the battle at Antietam in Sharpsburg, Maryland, for example, ending General Robert E. Lee's first invasion of the north, claimed more than 23,000 men killed, wounded, or missing in a single day, September 17, 1862). Twentieth-century wars, though vastly injurious, arguably do not top the league table of destruction. During the Thirty Years War, something like one-third the German-speaking population of Europe perished, even doubling the proportion of Russians killed between Hitler's invasion and the Red Army's victory.[67] Goya's etchings depicting the 'disasters of war' after the Spanish insurrection of 1808 and the Peninsular War with Napoleon

---

62. See the classic study by Quincy Wright, *A Study of War*. two volumes, Chicago: University of Chicago Press, 1942); Jeremy Black, *War and the World: Military Power and the Fate of Continents* (New Haven: Yale University Press, 1998); and Victor David Hanson, *Carnage and Culture: Landmark Battles in the Rise of Western Culture* (New York: Doubleday, 2001). I draw examples in the next two paragraphs from a treatment of human affairs on this scale: Felipe Fernández-Armesto, *Millennium: A History of Our Last Thousand Years* (London: Bantam Press, 1995), pp. 185, 195, 205, 253, 299.

63. Lawrence H. Keeley, *War Before Civilization* (New York: Oxford University Press, 1996).

64. Stuart B. Schwartz, ed., *Implicit Understandings: Observing, Reporting, and Reflecting on the Encounters Between Europeans and Other Peoples in the Early Modern Era* (Cambridge: Cambridge University Press, 1994). Also see Amartya Sen, "East and West: The Reach of Reason," *New York Review of Books*, July 20, 2000.

65. Mark Cocker, *Rivers of Blood, Rivers of Gold: Europe's Conquest of Indigenous Peoples* (New York: Grove Press, 1998), p. 5.

66. Jill Lepore, *The Name of War: King Philip's War and the Origins of American Identity* (New York: Alfred A. Knopf, 1998).

67. Andrew Cunningham and Ole Peter Grell, *The Four Horsemen of the Apocalypse: Religion, War, Famine, and Death in Reformation Europe* (Cambridge: Cambridge University Press, 2000).

marked by the famine of Madrid might well be adopted as emblems of human history.

There have been many lords of plundered peoples, as the fifteenth-century Rwozi Chief, Nyatsimka Mutota, was called after capturing the middle Zambezi valley. When the Goths seized Rome from a Byzantine garrison in 530, they executed some 30,000 male civilians.[68] To alleviate the stress on his own men when faced with how hard it was to overwhelm the Aztec, Cortés massacred more than 3,000 residents of Cholula; in the three-month siege of Tenochtitlan, a minimum of 100,000 and possibly 240,000 Mexicans died. Before the coming of Pizarro, the Incas had murdered 20,000 Caranqui Indians, tossing their bodies into Lake Yahuarcocha. Slave trading whites visiting the court of Dahomey approached the king's court by traversing paths of skulls to participate in ceremonies marked by human sacrifice. The largest part of early New World colonization was slave. Utterly deprived of rights and not ranked as truly human, hundreds of thousands died even before reaching the other side of the Atlantic. Racialized slavery was so deeply embedded in western economics, politics, and society that its trade in bodies, numbering some 11 million, achieved the status of the natural order of things. In liberal America, Tocqueville observed, "The legislation of the Southern states with regard to slaves presents at the present day such unparalleled atrocities as suffice to show that the laws of humanity have been totally perverted."[69] Just after 10,000 Chinese were killed in Batavia by the Dutch in 1740, a participant recorded, "When my boss, the master-carpenter, saw me [steal my Chinese neighbor's fat pig], he slapped me and told me to kill the Chinese first and then to plunder. I therefore took a rice-pounder and with it beat to death my neighbor with whom I had so often drunk and dined."[70] Each of these sites and moments of brutality, depicting only a fraction of the sum of human cruelty, could well have been transported to Arendt and Polanyi's, as well as our own, period without any loss of familiarity. So it is not cruelty as such that can define what had become new in the period spanning the twentieth century's two world wars.

Even the most European and Christian qualities of the West's dark times possessed both long and more proximate lineages. It was not Hitler, but the Fourth

---

68. David Nicholas, *The Growth of the Medieval City: From Late Antiquity to the Early Fourteenth Century* (London: Longman, 1997), p. 19.

69. Tocqueville, *Democracy in America*, vol. 1, p. 395. For a contemporary treatments of slavery as the central constitutive fact of antebellum American history, see John E. Cairnes, *The Slave Power: Its Character, Career, and Probable Designs* (London: Macmillan, 1863). A powerful recent account is Don E. Fehrenbacher, *The Slaveholding Republic: An Account of the United States Government's Relations to Slavery* (New York: Oxford University Press, 2001).

70. Fernández-Armesto, *Millenium*, p. 299.

Lateran Council guided by Pope Innocent III in 1215 that first required Jews to wear a visible, distinguishing badge on their clothing, specified as linen two fingers wide and four long, lest they be confused with Christians.[71] It was not nine-teenth- or twentieth-century codifications that first grounded anti-Semitism in wider, often estimable, projects, but Luther's 1543 text, *On the Jews and their Lies* that inscribed such hatred.[72] It was not National Socialist persecutors but both secular and ecclesiastical courts in early modern Europe that executed tens of thousands of women accused of witchcraft.[73] It was not the propagandists of the Reich who invented the Jew as "a foreigner, the repository and embodi-ment of all that was outside the established order of good," fulfilling "the mysti-cal social function of scapegoat, on which was bound the sins of the commu-nity." This, rather, in 1930 was Lionel Trilling's summary of how Jews were represented in English fiction from the *Canterbury Tales* to *Daniel Deronda*.[74] It was not the Nazi Behemoth but King Leopold II's sanction of staggering atrocities in the late-nineteenth- and early-twentieth-century Congo (a territory larger than Spain, Italy, Germany, France, and England combined) that over the course of a quarter-century halved its population, Adam Hochschild esti-

---

71. Gavin I.. Langmuir, "Continuities, Discontinuities and Contingencies of the Holocaust," *Studies in Contemporary Jewry* 13 (1997): 14. Though unevenly enforced, "reminders of this regu-lation were frequent in papal letters and conciliar decrees of every part of the Catholic world" during a period in which the Church pursued a policy of degradation "in the pursuit of a funda-mental Church policy . . . namely, that Jewish life must be such as to prove unmistakeably that God had spurned Judaism." Solomon Grayzel, *The Church and the Jews in the XIIIth Century: A Study of their Relations During the Years 1198–1254, Based on the Papal Letters and the Conciliar Degrees of the Period*. Vol. 1 (New York: Hermon Press, 1966), pp. 62, 41.

72. For a discussion, see Richard Marius, *Martin Luther: The Christian between God and Death* (Cambridge: Harvard University Press, 1999).

73. Erik H.C. Midelfort, *Witch Hunting in Southwestern Germany, 1562–1684: The Social and In-tellectual Foundations* (Stanford: Stanford University Press, 1972); Joseph Klaits, *Servants of Satan: The Age of Witch Hunts* (Bloomington: University of Indiana Press, 1985); Brian P. Levack, *The Witch-Hunt in Early Modern Europe* (London: Longman, 1987); Brian P. Levack, "The Great Witch-Hunt," in Thomas A. Brady, Jr., Heiko A. Oberman, and James T. Tracy, eds., *Hand-book of European History, 1400–1600: Late Middle Ages, Renaissance and Reformation* (Leiden: E. J. Brill: 607–640); Jonathan Farry, Marianne Hester, and Gareth Roberts, eds., *Witchcraft in Early Modern Europe: Studies in Culture and Belief* (Cambridge: Cambridge University Press, 1996); and Stuart Clark, *Thinking with Demons: The Idea of Witchcraft in Early Modern Europe* (Oxford: Clarendon Press, 1997).

74. Lionel Trilling, "The Changing Myth of the Jew," in Lionel Trilling, *Speaking of Literature and Society* (Oxford: Oxford University Press, 1982). This article was accepted by the *Menorah Journal*, set in type in 1931, yet not published. It first appeared almost a half century after it was composed in *Commentary*, August 1978.

mates, from some twenty to ten million;[75] and it was not the SS but the Special Organization of the effort to transform the Ottoman Empire into a Turkish state in 1915 that pioneered organized mass killing at the start of the thirty-year crisis on the scale of hundreds of thousands (there were at least 800,000; perhaps 1.3 million Armenian dead).[76]

This, of course, is only a very partial list, omitting the nineteenth-century genocidal conquest of Tasmania, the brutality of German conquest in Southwest Africa in the first decade of the twentieth century, the savageness of the war for Algerian independence, and the Rwandan genocide of 1994 (not to speak of the West's complicity by acts of omission and, especially in the case of the French, commission).[77] What then was so unaccustomed about twentieth-century catastrophes after 1914? Why were special origins stories required? Were not total war and totalitarianism, and even the holocaust, no more than extensions, perhaps radicalized enlargements, of the normal state of human affairs?

There is, of course, a Europe-centered aspect to Polanyi and Arendt's work. In part, of course, this feature reflects the assumptions of their time. Virtually all the instances of brutality I have listed either took place outside the confines of the West or occurred before the Enlightenment had helped reclaim Europe from barbarism. Clearly, both writers assayed the shock administered in the epoch of the two twentieth-century global wars in this spatial and historical context. What had occurred betrayed expectations about enlightened behavior *in the West.* Thus, Arendt's treatment of "the phantom world of the dark continent" does not call into question the dominant imagery of a civilizational hierarchy. While

---

75. Leopold treated the Congo as something a personal preserve (if at an abstract distance, as he never set foot in Africa) in pursuit of the riches of rubber and ivory. An indigenous Force Publique under Belgian command carried out many executions and mutilations while enforcing work discipline in near-slave conditions. John de Courcy MacDonnell, *King Leopold II, His Rule in Belgium and the Congo* (New York: Negro Universities Press, 1969); Adam Hochschild, *King Leopold's Ghost: A Story of Greed, Terror, and Heroism in Colonial Affairs* (Boston: Houghton Mifflin, 1998); for a discussion of population estimates, see p. 233. Remarkably, a huge, heroic statue of Leopold stands undisturbed in front of Zaire's Parliament in Kinshasa; apparently, he was a hero to President Mobutu.

76. Vahakn Dadrian, *Warrant for Genocide: Key Elements of Turko-Armenian Conflict* (New Brunswick: Transaction Books, 1999); Sarkisse Makaroff, ed., *Le deporte de Deir-Ez-Zor: la deportation des Armeniens ottomans en 1915* (Paris: Pensee universelle, 1998); and Richard Hovannisian, *Remembrance and Denial: The Case of the Armenian Genocide* (Detroit: Wayne State University Press, 1998). Also see, Alan S. Rosenbaum, ed., *Is the Holocaust Unique? Perspectives on Comparative Genocide* (Boulder: Westview Press, 1996).

77. Cocker, *Rivers*, Parts II and IV. Philip Gourevitch, *We Wish to Inform You That Tomorrow We Will Be Killed With Our Families* (New York: Farrar, Straus, and Giroux, 1998); Linda Melvern, *A People Betrayed: The Role of the West in Rwanda's Genocide* (London: Zed, 2000).

writing bitingly about the Boers, she observed without much reflection or irony that "The world of native savages was a perfect setting for men who had escaped the reality of civilization. Under a merciless sun, surrounded by an entirely hostile nature, they were confronted with human beings who, living without the future of a purpose and the past of an accomplishment, were as incomprehensible as the inhabitants of the madhouse. . . . What made them different from other human beings," she continued, "was not at all the color of their skin but the fact that they behaved like a part of nature." When white newcomers massacred many Africans, they thus were acting in consonance with the "extermination of hostile tribes [that] had been the rule in all African native wars."[78] For Polanyi, the modal individual in "the condition of some native tribes in Africa today" is "a nondescript being, without self-respect or standards, veritable human refuse."[79] I hasten to add that both Polanyi and Arendt were appalled by the brutality of the colonizers who "treated the natives as raw material and lived on them as one might live on the fruits of wild trees," and observed how individuals and groups who had been secure in their environments had "been transformed" by imperialism "into a human variety of half-domesticated animal."[80] Still, it is clear their sense of outrage was reserved primarily for the collapse of civilized standards within a putatively enlightened Europe itself. Their project probing the origins of dark times sought to understand what happened there, amongst 'civilized' western people, not between Europe and its colonized populations on their periphery.[81]

I say this less to condemn than situate their work. After all, their Eurocentrism is not celebratory. Rather, as Bernard Crick observed about Arendt, it was oriented "to set up a mirror by which European civilisation can recognise its faults and perhaps seize a last chance to renovate its house before some other great disaster . . . comes about."[82] The rupture in western history they probed was located spatially within Europe and temporally in their own time, the very moment, indeed, when colonialism began to crumble. But however parochial their perspectives, it also should be clear that the warrants for their claim about

---

78. Arendt, *Origins*: 190, 192. A stinging account is Anne Norton, "Heart of Darkness: Africa and African Americans in the Writings of Hannah Arendt," in Bonnie Honig, ed., *Feminist Interpretations of Hannah Arendt* (University Park: Pennsylvania State University Press, 1995).

79. Polanyi, *Transformation*, p. 157.

80. Arendt, *Origins*, p. 194; Polanyi, *Transformation*, p. 157. Polanyi likened this situation to "living death." (p. 292).

81. In this respect, they reproduced the pattern of 'liberal conventions and imperial exclusions,' the subtitle of chapter two in Uday Singh Mehta, *Liberalism and Empire* (Chicago: University of Chicago Press, 1999).

82. Crick, "Burden of Our Times," p.77.

a radical breach was based on a combination of bestial historical events and disappointed prospects. Unlike the main broad assessments of temporality in European history, theirs underscored that modernity had been sharply, suddenly, and nearly totally put into reverse. The sheer scale of violence, moral decay, and institutional malfunctioning had overwhelmed prior developments and understandings; "the moral structure of Western society," Arendt remarked, had been "laid waste."[83] If we are careful to keep this periodization in harness as geared to the analysis of European history's unexpected fate after the seeming triumph of Enlightenment, rather than either as a more narrowly targeted form of analysis or as a more global set of claims, the most perceptible bases for empirical skepticism about the radical shift to the level and character of uncertainty disappear, and the case Polanyi and Arendt made about the impact of total war, totalitarianism, and holocaust becomes compelling.

With regard to historicity, their core point, moreover, was not that other Europe-centered theories of temporality and change are wrong but that they had become radically insufficient. To be sure, there are *marxisant* and Weberian aspects to both texts, and both authors draw liberally on a variety of philosophical, historical, and social scientific traditions. Notwithstanding, for Polanyi and Arendt these tools and historical frameworks simply had become inadequate, for they possessed virtually no means that could be utilized even to name, let alone explain, the core elements of the new desolation. They had become convinced, in addition, that the rupture they were addressing could not be apprehended in the quite common language of crisis. At the time, most scholars and intellectuals considered current events as exaggerated versions of 'normal' irrationality and uncertainty, believing that correct diagnoses could conduce effective cures; that is, a relatively smooth return to enlightened rationality. Polanyi and Arendt thought such views to be hopelessly naïve. Unless fresh tools of analysis and rectification could be invented, they believed, humankind (that is, western humankind) would be condemned to a new age of barbarism and to the permanent defeat of enlightenment.

Each sought to defend this tradition by analyzing the negation of freedom and illiberal attacks on the moral person that had been so fierce as to threaten continuing degradation. "The issue on which they divide," Polanyi wrote about broadly liberal regimes and their adversaries, "is whether the idea of freedom can be upheld or not; is freedom an empty word, a temptation, designed to ruin man and his works, or can man reassert his freedom in the face of that knowledge and strive for its fulfillment in society without lapsing into moral illusionism? This

---

83. Hannah Arendt, "The Aftermath of Nazi Rule: Report from Germany," in Kohn, *Arendt*, p. 248; this essay first appeared in *Commentary* 10, no. 10 (1950).

anxious question," he concluded, "sums up the condition of man," adding that "the spirit and content of this study should indicate an answer."[84] For Arendt, the radical newness of the challenge produced a situation in which "we actually have nothing to fall back on in order to understand a phenomenon that nevertheless confronts us with its overpowering reality and breaks down all standards we know."[85] Both depicted this "radical evil, previously unknown to us,"[86] in terms of the decay of old institutions based on Enlightenment values and the creation of new ones hostile to this heritage and motivated by the terrifying "fundamental belief . . . that everything is possible."[87]

To pursue their protective tasks, Polanyi and Arendt sought to shift 'evil' from a location in theology concerned with death and judgment to the secular zone of modern social science where analytical reason could be put to work, but not without seeking to transform the character of such inquiry on the understanding that, as P.G. Tait and Balfour Stewart had put it, in 1875, in their attempt to reconcile science and religion, that "the greatest of all mysteries" is "the origin of evil."[88] For Polanyi, the simultaneous collapse of capitalism's promise of prosperity and liberal democracy's stability and claims to legitimacy invoked a deep challenge to orthodox economic categories, especially the axiomatic status of free markets. For Arendt, totalitarian violence, especially the holocaust, demanded an even broader reconsideration. "Every science," she indicated,[89]

> is necessarily based upon a few inarticulate, elementary, and axiomatic assumptions which are exposed and exploded only when confronted with altogether unexpected phenomena which can no longer be understood within the framework of its categories. The social sciences and the techniques which they have developed during the past hundred years are no exception to this rule. . . . [T]he institution of concentration and extermination camps, that is, the social conditions within them as well their functions in the larger terror apparatus to totalitarian regimes, may very likely become that unexpected phenomenon, that stumbling block on the road

84. Polanyi, *Transformation*, p. 258A.
85. Arendt, *Origins*, p. 459.
86. Arendt, *Origins*, p. 443.
87. Arendt, *Origins*, p. 437. Arendt and Polanyi drew slightly different lines between freedom and unfreedom. She distinguished between the absolute totalitarianism of Nazism and Stalinism, marked by an all-embracing nihilism, and all other regimes including authoritarian-fascist ones, while he focused on the distinction between liberal states and all others.
88. P. G. Tait and Balfour Stewart, *The Unseen Universe* (London: 1875, vii., p. 269).
89. Hannah Arendt, "Social Science Techniques and the Study of Concentration Camps," in Arendt, *Understanding*. The paper first appeared in *Jewish Social Studies* 12, no. 1 (1950), thus written at the same time as *Origins*.

toward the proper understanding of contemporary politics and society which must cause social scientists and historical scholars to reconsider their hitherto unquestioned fundamental preconceptions regarding the course of the world and human behavior.

These critical impulses solicited attention to what was new about twentieth-century western desolation and invoked Arendt and Polanyi's efforts to create broad accounts of these historical dynamics braced by precise causal claims, all the while holding tight to a charged normative purpose.

Arendt and Polanyi's comprehension and analysis of radical evil had more in common with medieval and early modern notions of Purgatory than of Hell.[90] In Roman Catholic thought, individuals consigned to Hell possess no possibility of escape. Like those who ascend to Heaven, their place, once fixed, is immutable. Purgatory, by contrast, is an in-between place, where the imperfect dead endure great pain. As a spectral location marked by fear, misery, and torment, Purgatory is distinguished from Hell by prospects of rescue and release (this journey is powerfully portrayed by Hieronymus Bosch's "Vision of the Otherworld" in an image akin to a birth canal in which angels lead the now-worthy to the light of Heaven). Correct diagnosis and action could extricate individuals from agony and suffering.[91]

Polanyi and Arendt sought to know the origins of dark times in order to make release from an earthly Purgatory possible. Both shared the sense that the West faced more than a crisis that could be resolved by returning to traditional or familiar ideas and institutions without profound revision grounded in a new realistic understanding that humankind had become doomed to live irreversibly in dark times. For once Purgatory has been inscribed on earth in new human institutions after the Enlightenment, it had come to exist as a permanent option. They thus aimed their efforts to comprehend the origins of the deep cleft between then and now as a contribution to putting an end to illusions, whether associated with liberal conceits about unfolding reason and liberty, Marxist conceits about class struggle producing progress, conservative conceits about the bulwarks of tradition, or imperial conceits mapping the West as a zone of civilization at the top of the globe's hierarchy of cultural difference, achievement, and privilege.[92]

90. Though, to be sure, Arendt wrote that "the reality of concentration camps resembles nothing so much as medieval pictures of Hell." But this is not contradictory, because from these camps, unlike Purgatory, there was no escape. Arendt, *Origins*, p. 447.

91. I draw here on Stephen Greenblatt, *Hamlet in Purgatory* (Princeton: Princeton University Press., 2001).

92. On the latter, see Fernando Coronil, "Beyond Occidentalism: Toward Nonimperial Geohistorical Categories," *Cultural Anthropology* 11, no. 1 (1996).

III.

Their efforts to make sense of the West's catastrophic decades were just two of many works by analysts of the period's deep crisis. Best-seller lists of the day were dotted with tens of now-forgotten books like Emery Reves' *The Anatomy of Peace*, a rather banal utopian plea to replace the nation state with a universal legal order,[93] and many highbrow but shallow tracts like Robert MacIver's[94] 1938 Edward Douglass White Lectures, written in a state of apprehension that rarely moved beyond historical redescription written in semi-abstract, often pontificating tones, found their way into print.[95] Leading up to the Second World War, there were a host of crisis accounts written in this vein belonging to a line of anxious writing that had begun to appear in the aftermath of the First

---

93. Emery Reves, *The Anatomy of Peace* (New York: Harper and Brothers, 1945).

94. A noted political sociologist, then at Columbia University's Barnard College, MacIver later wrote the Foreword introducing Karl Polanyi's *The Great Transformation* to a wide American audience.

95. MacIver's lectures focused on the battle between democracy and dictatorship under the rubric of 'leviathan and the people.' Parsing his subject in three—the state, dictatorship, and democracy—he sought, first, to account for the modern state's "vast proportions" and "great new functions and powers." Why, he asked, "has Leviathan expanded again in democracy and dictatorship alike?" The state's responsibilities for domestic activities, including mass education, labor conditions and employment, social insurance, public health, and business regulation had expanded, he argued, "because the whole civilization changed." Until the First World War, he argued, social and economic change had been corralled and controlled by the growth of democracy, but now "the sudden revulsion" of modern dictatorship, "congenial to emergency conditions," was making a strong running by providing solutions to "the universal crisis" in "catastrophic conditions under which democracy cannot flourish or even endure." Robert M. MacIver, *Leviathan and the People* (Oxford: Oxford University Press, 1940), pp. 6, 8, 9, 12, 18, 20. A similar British example is provided by the 1937 Hibbert lectures on 'liberality and civilization' by the noted classicist Gilbert Murray. Focusing on total war and the association of war with illiberalism, he simply counseled the avoidance of a new global war as the means to protect the heritage of political liberalism. Gilbert Murray, *Liberality and Civilization: Lectures Given at the Invitation of the Hibbert Trustees in the Universities of Bristol, Glasgow, and Birmingham in October and November 1937* (London: George Allen and Unwin, 1938). Written before Nazi anti-Semitism had reached the apex of its fury and before the carnage of the Second World War had taken its measure, these texts oscillated between understandings of the situation convened by the First World War as an acute crisis shaped by familiar elements of despotism and geopolitics requiring diagnosis and cure and as a novel situation made especially disquieting by such new features of modernity as technological advances, mass politics, and new forms of social control that had introduced unaccustomed elements into the equation, especially in fascist and communist political systems. In addition to this ambivalence, this body of writing shared other traits: rather short, proximate, time horizons, a penchant for explanations of pathological outcomes by reference to exceptional pathological causes, and attachment to the medical imagery of crisis which implied the prospects of a cure and a return to a prior healthy equilibrium.

World War and the ebbing of liberal expectations for peaceful and rational possibilities in reflective considerations like those of the American journalist Harold Stearns. His 1919 *Liberalism in America: Its Origin, Its Temporary Collapse, Its Future* assessed the feasibility of toleration, open-mindedness, liberal democracy, and anti-militarism in the face of wartime hysteria, the collapse of liberalism as an organized political force in the West, and a broader disintegration of European civilization. Charged by a vague fear hard to pin down, this volume recognized the fragility of freedom and sought to discover how to continue to carve out a space for reason despite the virulence of conflict between states, the mobilizing capacities of states at war, the fierce antagonism of capital and labor, and the plasticity, even jingoism, of mass opinion.[96]

The better the effort to analytically tame the period's bewilderment and disillusionment, the more likely it was to illuminate the immediate situation by deploying tools drawn from a larger kitbag. Often written by émigré intellectuals who combined first-hand experience with deep learning in more than one field,[97] these more accomplished works included *State of the Masses*, the refugee sociologist Emil Lederer's explication of the view that classlessness had come to underpin a new kind of volatile mass society; *Behemoth*, Franz Neumann's massive probe of National Socialism's odd but still capitalist political economy, the constellation of interests under Nazism, and, more originally, the manner in which the movement character of the regime had supplanted traditional forms of German stateness; and *The Political Collapse of Europe*, Hajo Holborn's powerful account of nineteenth- and twentieth-century geopolitics.[98] Yet what is

---

96. Harold Stearns, *Liberalism in America: Its Origin, Its Temporary Collapse, Its Future* (New York: Boni and Liveright, 1919).

97. For discussions, see H. Stuart Hughes, *The Sea Change: The Migration of Social Thought, 1930–1965* (New York: Harper and Row, 1975); and Anthony Heilbut, *Exiled in Paradise: German Refugee Artists and Intellectuals in America from the 1930's to the Present* (New York: Viking Press, 1983).

98. Emil Lederer, *State of the Masses: The Threat of the Classless Society* (New York: Norton, 1940); Franz Neumann, *Behemoth: The Structure and Practice of National Socialism* (New York: Oxford University Press, 1942); and Hajo Holborn, *The Political Collapse of Europe* (New York: Knopf, 1951). Such considerations, of course, hardly were limited to the United States.

Arendt reviewed Holborn for the *Journal of Modern History* in the same number where a review of *Origins* appeared, approving his claim that historical Europe had died and was beyond resurrection. She noted positively that "this book is inspired by a sincere political concern and a truly political passion. As such, its value depends on the precision of the political judgment which guides the historical analysis; and it is this judgment which gives the book its excellence." *Journal of Modern History*, 24 (June 1952).

The noted French liberal historian of England Élie Halévy submitted "The Era of Tyrannies, a deliberately provocative communication for discussion by the Société Française in November 1936, arguing that the First World War had reshaped the states of all the belligerent countries in

striking even about these excellent texts, and what distinguishes them from the books by Polanyi and Arendt, is their more focused and narrow compass, their linear causal diagnoses, their rather straightforward programs of rectification, and, most important, their assumption that the present crisis was an aspect, albeit an especially difficult one, of what might be called normal periodization.

We can see the strengths but especially the limits of the more conventional approach in the important writings of Karl Mannheim which come closer than most to the more radical rupture perspective of Arendt and Polanyi.[99] Lecturing in Holland in 1933 after his emigration from Germany to England following the collapse of the Weimar Republic and the loss of his academic chair, Mannheim addressed "The Crisis of Culture in the Age of Mass Democracies and Autarchies" in Spenglarian terms, observing the decay of civilization at a time of chaos and noting the harnessing of sadism for public purposes.[100] A year later, announcing themes he soon was to develop far more extensively, his Hobhouse Memorial Lecture at the University of London, which sought to comprehend the "rational and irrational elements in contemporary society," promoted non-totalitarian planning as the main instrument of rectification.[101] If properly named and analyzed, Mannheim claimed, the crisis, despite its intensity, could be resolved.

---

decisively illiberal directions as a result of their adoption of similar measures extending state control in the sphere of economics and in the intellectual sphere through a mix of repression and the "organization of enthusiasm." Élie Halévy, *The Era of Tyrannies* (New York: Doubleday, 1965), p. 266.

99. Offered a post in New York at the New School for Social Research in 1933, he had opted, to his later regret, for a lectureship at the London School of Economics. "You will understand," Mannheim wrote to University of Chicago sociologist Louis Wirth, in July 1933, "that one would rather go where one has the feeling or the illusion of being needed, and that one is not called simply out of pity for one's troubles." This was something of a misstatement of motives. After his German patron Emile Lederer had agreed to join the new University in Exile at the New School, he and the institution's president, Alvin Johnson, composed a list of target colleagues. Both traveled to London to interview these prospects. During this trip, Mannheim insisted the New School create a distinctive 'school' oriented to advance his own body of sociological thought. Though he was not turned down out of hand, Johnson's coolness to the proposition probably offended Mannheim. David Kettler and Volker Meja, *Karl Mannheim and the Crisis of Liberalism: The Secret of these New Times* (New Brunswick: Transaction Publishers, 1995), pp. 178, 190. As it turned out, the LSE, New School, and Columbia émigrés, if not always without tension, maintained something of a robust cross-Atlantic intellectual community. Mannheim also had had a long-standing relationship with Karl Polanyi, and his brother Michael, dating back to their years together in Budapest.

100. The paper based on these talks is Karl Mannheim, "The Crisis of Culture in the Age of Mass-Democracies and Autarchies," *Sociological Review* 26 (April 1934).

101. Karl Mannheim, *Rational and Irrational Elements in Contemporary Society. L.T. Hobhouse Memorial Trust Lectures No.4* (London: Humphrey Milford for Oxford University Press, 1934).

At its core, he argued, lay a disproportion between the development of humankind's advanced "technical powers over nature" and "the development of [its] moral faculties and [its] knowledge of the guidance and government of society." Accordingly, his "first proposition" argued that "contemporary society must break down unless this disproportionality is eliminated; that is to say, unless we can made the rational control of our individual selves, of the society in which we move, and of the things we handle keep pace with the rationality attained in the spheres of technique and industry." To this uneven distribution of human capacities he added the problem of unequal distribution of "the social division of rational and moral qualities." In past times, he argued, this division of knowledge and moral forces could smoothly prevail because it was based on despotism. Now, "the fundamental democratization of the masses" and a social situation in which "the very same industrial society which, through its industrialization, causes more and more individuals and spheres of human life to become functionally rationalized, compresses the large masses into cities, and creates the greatest stimulus to irrationality." This makes unevenness ominous by making it likely that a "democracy of reason" will be replaced by a "democracy of moods" as "accumulated irrationalities" come to be "directed into the public sphere." Force thus replaces reason; instrumental rationality, reaching its highest levels in modern bureaucracies, also supplants the substantive rationality of considered judgment. The extension of functional reason had been "perfected," he argued, "so far as to make the planned control of the social mechanism feasible," but, he believed, under conditions of the democratization of society, planners, dictators, and demagogues enjoying mass support are able to deploy these means for irrational, even sadistic ends. Changes to personality, social structure, human abilities, and political arrangements thus had combined to produce a dangerous situation. Therein, he argued, lies the main substance of the crisis.[102]

But it was not beyond rectification. The critical question Mannheim asked was whether human beings could harness reason's techniques in the face of these trends to rescue enlightened liberal values. "I, as a sociologist," he wrote in 1936 to Oscar Jászi, his Budapest mentor in the 1910s, who had led the reform-oriented Society for Social Science and had founded the Radical Citizens Party

---

102. Mannheim, *Rational and Irrational*, pp. 5, 6, 7, 8, 14, 19, 22, 24, 25, 30, 34. Mannheim contrasted this dangerous moment with the pre-First World War "liberal era [which] offered a much more favourable soil for the rearing of substantial rationality. Since this period of industrialization knew only relatively small economic units and individual property ownership, there was a much wider industrial *élite* which, through the control of its property, had acquired the habit of assuming individual responsibility and of calculating events for short periods ahead. This period, therefore, was also more enlightened in the sense that it produced more individuals who thought for themselves and it interposed a wide middle-layer of intelligent people between the passive masses and the cultured few" (pp. 18–19).

(in which Karl Polanyi had served as a General Secretary), "would like to learn by close observation the secret (even if it is infernal) of these new times, because I believe this is the only way we can remain masters over the social structure, instead of it mastering us. To carry liberal values forward with the aid of the techniques of modern mass society," he continued, "is probably a paradoxical undertaking; but it is the only feasible way, if one does not want to react with defiance alone."[103] Forcefully advancing planning as the basis of a solution, he wagered in the affirmative, especially in *Man and Society in an Age of Reconstruction*,[104] even after the Second World War had begun and the urgency of the crisis had accelerated. In mid-war, when Polanyi was presenting his own account of 'the political and economic origins of our time,' deliberately transcending the language and analysis of crisis, Mannheim collected his wartime papers under the heading of 'diagnosis.'[105]

Present trends, for Mannheim, were cumulations of past developments that affected both the dictatorships and democracies of the period alike. He thus placed these regimes, as it were, on the same analytical plane. The uneven advance of reason and the growth of mass society had widened the space for illiberalism while providing the means to reconstruct liberalism. For Mannheim, there was no fundamental break separating the past and the crisis he diagnosed. Nor, for that matter, between the present and a better future to be convened by the solutions he proffered to move humanity to a more healthy phase in its history. However exigent his times, they still could be located under the broad penumbra of the ordinary. The language of crisis Mannheim borrowed from medicine implied prospects for a successful resolution based on prompt rational intervention. Though designating the unusual, such language nonetheless in-

---

103. Letter of Oscar Jászi, November 8, 1936; cited in Kettler and Meja, *Mannheim*: 18, 165.

104. Karl Mannheim, *Man and Society in an Age of Reconstruction* (London: Routledge and Kegan Paul, 1940).

105. Karl Mannheim, *Diagnosis of Our Time: Wartime Essays of a Sociologist* (London: Kegan, Paul, Trench, Treubner, 1943). Like Arendt and Polanyi, and indeed the other members of the group I characterize as members of the American political studies enlightenment, Mannheim was committed to the powers of social science as sources of understanding, rectification, and defense. Just as he was moving to England, in 1933, he requested a large grant, $50,000, from the Rockefeller Foundation (which then was underwriting the rescue of oppressed German scholars to the New School) for a collaborative, cross-disciplinary, empirical study, to be conducted by a senior staff composed, among others, of his former students and assistants Franz Neumann, Sigmund Neumann, Hans Gerth, Albert Salomon, and Norbert Elias, on the theme of "The Sociological Causes of the Cultural Crisis in the Era of Mass-Democracies and Autarchies." After some interest, the proposal was rejected. See Kettler and Meja, *Mannheim*, pp. 178–181.

vokes prognostication and supports intervention based on assumptions that are commonplace and customary.[106]

Polanyi and Arendt understood the rupture of these decades in qualitatively different terms. Like Mannheim, they feared the erosion of possibility for free and moral persons and they bemoaned the period's streak of irrationality. But the break between past and present was too multifaceted, too encompassing, and too charged by the scope and depth of its radical divergence from the West's doctrines and institutions of enlightened reason, they believed, to be apprehended by traditional crisis narratives. The break with the past had been too radical. Even the standard, and, on the face of things, unobjectionable dating of the onset of the crisis in the Great War of 1914–1918, was, they came to think, too flat, since by connoting a crisp beginning it implied the possibility of an equally crisp end to the period's upheavals.[107] By contrast, *Transformation* and *Origins* each identified the break between past and present as entailing a breach so fundamental that even the best contemporary work written in terms of crisis was underestimating the novelty of the situation. For Polanyi, the character of the shift lay in the totality of institutional destruction; for Arendt in the erasure of moral and juridical personhood.

"World War I and the postwar revolutions," Polanyi submitted, "still formed part of the nineteenth century." The deep break with the past came in the 1930s, he argued, marked by a far-reaching institutional collapse, symbolized by the decisions Britain and the United States took in 1931 and 1933 to go off the gold

---

106. Mannheim died in January 1947. He was Jewish, part of the assimilated Jewish communities in his native Budapest and Frankfurt and lived among Jews in London. "He took distance from Eastern Jews," Kettler and Meja observe, "and left no record of recognition of the Holocaust." This, they add, "does not distinguish him from most members of his Budapest or Weimar era circles," including Karl Polanyi, a Christian social-liberal, who likewise never made the fate of Europe's Jews constitutive of his scholarly analyses of the origins of his time. Polanyi was born to Jewish parents in 1886 who had been part of a self-conscious movement to assimilate in Hungarian society. Though his father, Mihaly Pollacek, kept his name and religion, at least nominally, he "changed the names of his children to Polanyi and their religion to Protestant (Calvinist)." Kari Polanyi-Levitt and Marguerite Mendell, "Karl Polanyi: A Biographical Sketch," *Telos*, no. 73 (Fall 1987): 121.

107. I find this unconvincing, or at least excessive, as a claim, understating the impact of its range of destruction: "shattered empires, crushed regimes, millions of deaths, ruined economies, landscapes blasted beyond recognition, and political and social convulsions." Paul Kennedy, "In the Shadow of the Great War," *New York Review of Books*, 46 (August 12, 1999), p. 39. Rather more persuasive is the approach of François Furet, who treats the First World War and especially the Russian Revolution as continuous with older traditions and practices, but who stresses that both fascism and bolshevism never would have become grand ruling systems if not for the war which thus, for him, is best seen as a the last of the old and the start of the new. Furet, *Illusion*.

standard, so profound that it left the all the globe's key international and domestic political and economic institutions in disarray. "The political *and* economic system of the planet disintegrated conjointly."[108] This institutional dissolution was no mere crisis—crises had been a recurrent feature of the global order, especially since the early 1870's—since its constellation of elements, he believed, could not be put back together again. Past this threshold the development of human freedom had lost its liberal substructure. Now, it was vulnerable both to fascism, which refused to play or be constrained by the old rules, and to bolshevism, which, after 1929, had been transformed from a radical effort to complete the ideals of 1789 to an entirely new collectivized system. After this second Russian revolution, both fascism and bolshevism represented the negation of a liberal order that had shattered mainly from internal pressures, tensions, and shortcomings, but not in the same way. After the key institutional pillars of the market economy, the liberal state, the balance of power system, and the international gold standard had broken down, bolshevism mainly served as a potential holistic alternative to liberal capitalist democracy; hence as a source of fear. Fascism, by contrast, actually was present in the West, actively storming the "the bulwarks of *democracy and constitutional liberties*" whose defenses were "found wanting in . . . spectacular fashion."[109]

What had ushered in the great transformation of the 1930s was the tightly knit relationship between the institutions that had defined the mechanisms of nineteenth-century international and domestic politics. By the start of that fateful decade, the problems of unemployment and class tension, global imperialist rivalries, and pressures on exchange rates combined to delegitimize the institutions of liberal political regimes which now were found wanting in all these spheres, considered separately but especially together. Under these conditions, fascism in different forms (which, like communism, "was rooted in a market society that refused to function") became appealing in countries that had both lost and won the First World War. Across a wide swath of the West, what Polanyi called the 'fascist situation' combined "irrationalistic philosophies, racialist esthetics, anticapitalist demagogy, heterodox currency views, criticism of the party system, widespread disparagement of the 'regime,' or whatever was the name given to the existing democratic set-up."[110] By the 1920s, anti-Enlightenment versions of counterrevolution and nationalism had made an appearance, but both the degeneration of the liberal order and a growing disillusionment with the Enlightenment as inadequate and credulous vastly accelerated after the Great Depression.

---

108. Polanyi, *Transformation*, pp. 20, 244.
109. Polanyi, *Transformation*, pp. 247, 237.
110. Polanyi, *Transformation*, pp. 239, 238.

Likewise with communism. Taking a somewhat heretical position, Polanyi viewed the Russian Revolution of 1917–1924 as concluding rather than beginning an era, thinking it to be "the *last* of the political upheavals in Europe that followed the pattern of the English Commonwealth and the French Revolution." This Revolution, he observed, "achieved the destruction of absolutism, feudal land tenure, and racial oppression—a true heir to the ideals of 1789." But the 1930s marked a deep rupture here as well with the ruthless imposition of a completely socialist economy, the erosion of any space between public and private, and the massive increase in terror and political oppression, trends which were accelerated by the breakdown of the world economy, making autarchy seem the only feasible option.[111]

"The very possibility of freedom" now was "in question," he concluded, because the institutional pillars of the first modern western institutional system had collapsed, having "disintegrated as the result of . . . the measures which society adopted in order not to be, in its turn, annihilated by the action of the self-regulating market." Now, "the reality of society" is starkly defined by "the dividing line between liberalism, on the one hand, fascism and socialism, on the other." The issues on which they divide, he averred, are "not primarily economic," but the "moral and religious" standing of compulsion and freedom.[112] Any hope for the triumph of freedom required understanding the sources of the prior institutional collapse and inventing social analysis to direct a reinscription of liberal institutions within the embrace of an Enlightenment without illusions. Polanyi hardly was sanguine.

Neither, it must be said, was Arendt who was even more explicit than Polanyi in identifying exactly what she thought was so threateningly new in the human condition. In her discussion of "Totalitarianism in Power," she addressed the question of continuity directly, observing that "Many things that nowadays have become the specialty of totalitarian government are only too well known from the study of history," which she proceeded to enumerate:[113]

There have always been wars of aggression; the massacre of hostile populations after a victory went unchecked until the Romans mitigated it by

---

111. Polanyi, *Transformation*, p. 247.

112. Polanyi, *Transformation*, p. 257.

113. Arendt, *Origins*, p. 440. As an aspect of the effort by 450,000 British troops to subdue Boer force five times smaller, the British commander, Lord Kitchener, coerced women and children into concentration camps. Some 28,000 died of disease and hunger. They are memorialized in a monument in Bloemfontein, one of the two most important Afrikaner nationalist shrines. Recent work has also discovered sites of black concentration camps where some 20,000 perished. See Thomas Pakenham, *The Boer War* (London: Seven Dials, 1999).

introducing the *parcere subjectis*; through centuries the extermination of native peoples went hand in hand with the colonization of the Americas, Australia, and Africa; slavery is one of the oldest institutions of mankind and all empire of antiquity were based on the labor of state-owned slaves who erected their public buildings. Not even concentration camps are an invention of totalitarian movements. They emerge for the first time during the Boer War, at the beginning of the century, and continued to be used in South Africa as well as India for 'undesirable elements'; here, too, we first find the term 'protective custody' which was later adopted by the Third Reich.[114] These camps correspond in many respects to the concentration camps at the beginning of totalitarian rule; they were used for 'suspects' whose offenses could not be proved and who could not be sentenced by ordinary process of law.

What was different about totalitarianism and about the human condition after the cruelties administered during the Second World War, she argued, were not the originality of the period's instruments of domination, which had been enlarged, hardened, and borrowed from extant instruments, or even the "nihilistic principle that 'everything is permitted,'" for this, too, had "inherited and already take for granted."[115] What was new, rather, were two, interrelated, elements of transformation and invention. When totalitarian regimes take over traditional instruments of control and "wherever these new forms of domination assume their authentically totalitarian structure they transcend . . . utilitarian motives and self-interest of the rulers, and try their hand in a realm that up to now has been completely unknown to us: the realm where everything is possible." Once this zone is entered, its scope, reach, and action "cannot be limited by either utilitarian motives or self-interest, regardless of the latter's content."[116] From this perspective, the quest to understand the origins of totalitarianism, total war, and holocaust is not a probe for evidence that humans suddenly have become dishonorable or prone to cruelty; rather, it is a search for how evil doing

---

114. Here, Arendt's history was almost right. Concentration camps aiming at the reconcentration of civilians in camps to cut them off from supporting guerrilla insurgency were first introduced in Cuba in 1895 by the Spanish, uprooting so many that by some estimates 200,000 reconcentrated rural Cubans died between 1895 and 1898. This strategy was employed by the British in the Boer War and not long after by the Americans in the Philippines and in South-West Africa by the Germans. For a discussion, see Anne Applebaum, "A History of Horror," *New York Review of Books*, October 18, 2001, which reviews Joël Kotek and Pierre Rigoulot, *Le Siècle des camps* (Paris: J.C. Lattés, 2001).
115. Arendt, *Origins*, p. 440.
116. Arendt, *Origins*, p. 440.

became detached from the advancement of traditional motives of normative or material gain; that is, when its impetus became autonomous.[117]

The culmination of the disconnection between interests and actions was the ultimate site of "manufactured unreality," the concentration and extermination camps, "the most consequential institution of totalitarian rule." It was at this site of radical evil, Arendt argued, that the ultimate difference with past times could be discerned:[118]

> There are no parallels to the life in the concentration camps. Its horror can never be fully embraced by the imagination for the very reason that it stands outside of life and death. It can never be fully reported for the very reason that the survivor returns to the world of the living, which makes it impossible for him to believe fully in his own past experiences. It is as though he had a story to tell of another planet, for the status of the inmates in the world of the living, where nobody is supposed to know if they are alive or dead, is such that it is as though they had never been born. Therefore all parallels create confusion and distract attention from what is essential. Forced labor in prisons and penal colonies, banishment, slavery, all seem for a moment to offer helpful comparisons, but on closer examination lead nowhere.

It was their "uselessness . . . their cynically admitted non-utility"[119] that was so distinctive about the camps, she asserted. This quality divorced them from functional and pragmatic calculations (the massive effort required to administer the death factories we know detracted significantly from the German war effort, even as the camps had been integrated into the war economy of the Third Reich[120]). Their hallmark was the manner in which human beings caught up in them were made fully superfluous, first by putting the both the dominating and dominated individuals enmeshed in them outside of normal law and rights,

---

117. That is, as Canovan puts the point, when "certain political phenomena had become detached from utilitarian motives and had gathered their own momentum," drifting "away from solid, down-to-earth motivation." These, she added, "were not states protecting specific interests, but movements interested in remaking reality for ideological reasons on a global scale." Canovan, *Arendt*, pp. 52, 58. This approach, of course, is radically different from the 'crisis' and interest orientation of Neumann's *Behemoth*.

118. Arendt, *Origins*, p. 444.

119. Arendt, *Origins*, p. 456.

120. See Franciszek Piper, "Auschwitz Concentration Camp: How it was Used in the Nazi System of Terror and Genocide and in the Economy of the Third Reich," in Michael Berenbaum and Abraham J. Peck, eds., *The Holocaust and History: The Known, the Unknown, the Disputed, and the Reexamined* (Bloomington: Indiana University Press, 1998).

thus killing the juridical person; then by a thoroughgoing, willful attack on the moral person. These two processes also ushered in a third, the complete loss of human spontaneity, what she believed to be the hallmark of what it means to be human, often preceding physical death which then served as a kind of ratification of nonhuman status in a design organized to conduct a descent to nonpersonhood. Of course, Arendt knew full well that this utopian process never could be fully realized. Still, what was wholly new was "the society of the dying established in the camps, . . . the only form of society in which it is possible to dominate man entirely. Those who aspire to total domination must liquidate all spontaneity, such as the mere existence of individuality will always engender, and track it down in its most private forms, regardless of how unpolitical and harmless these may seen."[121] By targeting the Jews, this organized program by a legitimate, modern state created a more universal danger.[122]

With all conventional, constraining standards having collapsed in this effort to kill every single member of a specific ethnic and religious group, unlimited power ran free.[123] Arendt dated the moment of the full eruption of absolute, rad-

---

121. Arendt, *Origins*, p. 456. For a fine discussion of Arendt on Nazi death camps, see. Bernstein, *Arendt*, pp. 88–100. His chapter opens with a citation of Arendt's first reaction to hearing reports about Auschwitz: "That was in 1943. At first we didn't believe it—although my husband and I always said that we expected anything from that bunch. But we didn't believe this because militarily it was unnecessary and uncalled for. . . . And then a half-year later be believed it after all, because we had proof. That was the real shock. Before that we said: Well, one has enemies. That is entirely natural. Why shouldn't a people have enemies? But this was something different. It was really as if an abyss had opened. . . . *This ought not to have happened*. And I don't mean just the number of victims. I mean the method, the fabrication of corpses and so on—I don't need to go into that. This should not have happened. Something happened there to which we cannot reconcile ourselves. None of us ever can." " 'What Remains? The Language Remains': A Conversation with Günter Gaus," in Arendt, *Understanding*, pp. 13–14; also cited in Bernstein, *Arendt*, p. 88.

122. With these insights, Arendt clearly resisted two quite different ways to read the Jewish character of the Holocaust either as an important feature of a more universal development by situating it within the context of Nazi killings of other groups, thus disinheriting its particularity, or make it wholly incomparable, thus depriving it of its universality.

123. It is in this regard that Richard Bernstein argues there is a tight link, not a contradiction, between Arendt's formulation of 'radical evil' in *Origins* and her controversial account of the 'banality of evil' in her reportage from the Eichmann trial. "Radical evil," he writes, "differs from the main traditional Western understanding of evil because it has nothing to do with 'evil motives'— indeed it has nothing to do with *human* motives. And this is precisely what Arendt says about Eichmann when she speaks of the 'banality of evil'!" Richard J. Bernstein, "Did Hannah Arendt Change Her Mind? From Radical Evil to the Banality of Evil," in Kohn, *Arendt*, p. 136. This paper appears as a retitled chapter 7, "From Radical Evil to the Banality of Evil: From Superfluousness to Thoughtlessness," in Bernstein, *Arendt*. In this version, the exclamation point in the passage I have cited drops out.

ical evil quite precisely, "when the SS took over the administration of the camps." Then,[124]

> the old spontaneous bestiality gave way to an absolutely cold and system-
> atic destruction of human bodies, calculated to destroy human dignity;
> death was avoided or postponed indefinitely. The camps were no longer
> amusement parks for beasts in human form, that is, for men who really
> belonged in mental institutions and prisons; the reverse became true:
> they were turned into 'drill grounds,' on which perfectly normal men
> were trained to be full-fledged members of the SS.

Both inside the camps and in killing fields outside their perimeters, average and normal individuals were in institutional conditions that made them willing to behave day after day, not just in spasms of fury, as if they existed outside of normal times, places, and constraints.[125]

But if the camps both were the central and most condensed institution of totalitarianism, the core of the system's invention, human superfluousness, was not contained by its bounds: "We may say that radical evil has emerged in connection with a system in which all men have become equally superfluous." This was the development, Arendt believed, that forced a confrontation with origins.[126] Once such systematic depravity had made an appearance, "we actually

---

124. Arendt, *Origins*, p. 454. Three years before the publication of *Origins*, Arendt had taken up this theme: "Behind the blind bestiality of the S.A., there often lay a deep hatred and resentment against all those who were socially, intellectually, or physically better off than themselves, and who now, as if in fulfillment of their wildest dreams, were in their power. This resentment, which never died out entirely in the camps, strikes us as a last remnant of humanly understandable feeling." Hannah Arendt, "The Concentration Camps," *Partisan Review* 15 (July 1948): 758; cited in Bernstein, *Arendt*, p. 132.

125. Christopher Browning, *Ordinary Men: Reserve Police Battalion 101 and the Final Solution in Poland* (New York: Harper Collins, 1992); Larry May, "Socialization and Institutional Evil," in Kohn, *Arendt*, pp. 83–105.

126. Presciently, alas, Arendt projected that the nonutilitarian features of totalitarian camps, whether Nazi or in the Gulag, would transfer when placed in a more traditional interest-grounded utilitarian calculus into a growing heedlessness toward human life and a more instrumental use of totalitarian instruments, including genocide. "The danger of the corpse factories and holes of oblivion," she wrote, "is that today, with populations and homelessness everywhere on the increase, masses of people are continuously rendered superfluous if we continue to think of our world in utilitarian terms. . . . Totalitarian solutions," she cautioned, "may well survive the fall of totalitarian regimes in the form of strong temptations which will come up whenever it seems impossible to alleviate political, social, or economic misery in a manner worthy of man." Arendt, *Origins*, p. 459. Fittingly, the last substantive chapter of a major overview of the twentieth century is a survey of "Genocide." Ponting, *Twentieth Century*, pp. 502–527.

have nothing to fall back on in order to understand a phenomenon that nevertheless confronts us with its overpowering reality and breaks down all standards
we know."[127] Writing in 1891 on "the idea and forms of the state," the political
scientist John Burgess had ratified the view that was still largely in place when
Arendt penned her text, to the effect that Aristotle's "classification of states, as to
form, into monarchies, aristocracies, and democracies is both correct and ex-
haustive."[128] Totalitarianism in all its aspects broke this mold;[129] hence invention was required that broke both with traditional narrative forms of history, with
standard treatments of large-scale change in political sociology, and with the
limited features of studies of political behavior in political science.

---

127. Arendt, *Origins*, p. 459. Writing to Karl Jaspers after he had reacted to reading the pre-
publication copy of *Origins* she had sent to her former teacher, Arendt observed, "Evil has proved
to be more radical than expected. In objective terms, modern crimes are not provided for in the
Ten Commandments. Or: The Western Tradition is suffering from the preconception that
the most evil things human beings can do arise from the vice of selfishness. Yet we know that the
greatest evils or radical evil has nothing to do anymore with such humanly understandable, sinful
motives. *What radical evil really is I don't know but it seems to me it somehow has to do with the following phenomenon: making human beings as human beings superfluous (not using them as
means to an end, which leaves their essence as humans untouched and impinges only on their
human dignity; rather, making them superfluous as human beings).* [Italics in original] Hannah
Arendt and Karl Jaspers, *Correspondence, 1926–1969* (New York: Harcourt, 1992), p. 166; cited in
Bernstein, *Arendt*, p. 141. Bernstein observes that while Arendt paid homage to Kant for his invention of 'radical evil,' she also distanced her usage from his. Although he "at least must have
suspected the existence of this evil . . . he immediately rationalized it in the concept of a 'perverted ill will' that could be explained by comprehensible motives." Arendt, *Origins*, p. 459;
Bernstein, *Arendt*, p. 143. Kohn observes that a leading aspect of the concept of superfluousness
for Arendt was "the loss of *common sense*. When individuals are, for whatever reasons, rejected
form the plurality of men, no longer sharing common interests but thrown back among themselves, then the common world begins to break down. That is just another way of naming the loss
of common sense." Jerome Kohn, "Evil and Plurality: Hannah Arendt's Way to *The Life of the
Mind*," in Kohn, *Arendt*, p. 159.

128. John Burgess, *Political Science and Comparative Constitutional Law*, 2 vols. (Boston: Ginn
and Company, 1891); reprinted in a shortened version as "The Idea and Forms of the State" in
James Farr and Raymond Seidelman, eds., *Discipline and History: Political Science in the United
States* (Ann Arbor: University of Michigan Press, 1993), p. 57.

129. "The obviously outstanding contribution Hannah Arendt made to political philosophy,"
Hans Morgenthau observed, "is the understanding of totalitarianism as a new form of government. That is to say, the Aristotelian distinctions among different types of government from which
our classifications of types of government derive do not suffice to understand the phenomenon of
totalitarianism as it appears in Nazism and Bolshevism. For modern totalitarianism has added to
the traditional characteristics of tyranny two novel qualities: an ideology which, when thought
through to its logical conclusions, makes the outrages of totalitarianism inevitable; and second,
the bureaucratization of terror in particular and political power in general, which gives political
power an efficacy it did not have before." Hans Morgenthau, "Hannah Arendt on Totalitarianism
and Democracy," *Social Research*, 44 (Spring 1977).

In circumstances of a historical fracture, when deeds had replaced delibera-
tion and ethics had dissolved in the face of action, political studies as ordinary
science, Arendt thought, were doomed to fail, "denying the outrageous, deduc-
ing the unprecedented from precedents, or explaining phenomena by such
analogies and generalities that the impact of reality and the shock of experience
are no longer felt."[130] The clash between disorienting desolation and simple political knowledge had become so great that a new approach had to be crafted. "It
means, rather, examining and bearing consciously the burden which our century has placed on us—neither denying its existence nor submitting meekly to
its weight. Comprehension, in short, means the unpremeditated, attentive, facing up to, and resisting of, reality—whatever it may be." *The Origins of Totalitarianism*, the Preface thus averred, "was written out of the conviction that it
should be possible to discover the hidden mechanics by which all traditional elements of our political and spiritual world were dissolved into a conglomeration
where everything seems to have lost specific value, and has become unrecognizable for human comprehension, unusable for human purpose."[131] And yet, it
was just this tradition that even total war, totalitarianism, and holocaust could
not—and must not—render obsolete.

IV.

Writing after magnified suffering and stunning revelations of depravity, Polanyi
and Arendt accordingly were compelled to wrestle with the vexing problem of
how to write about 'origins.' Any effort to comprehend the origins of dark times
had to face difficult intrinsic challenges of the kind Marc Bloch, the great historian of feudalism executed by the Nazis for his role in the French Resistance, had
underscored. 'Origins' itself, he noted, is a congested term, uncertainly combining claims about causes with avowals about beginnings. For this reason, Bloch
had warned about "this idol of the historian tribe . . . the obsession with origins,
. . . the explanation of the very recent in terms of the remotest past," an approach,
he believed, that blemished such major works as Ernest Renan's *The Origins of
Christianity* and Hippolyte Taine's *The Origins of Contemporary France*.[132] If 'origins' simply denotes beginnings, he observed, elusive issues of definition and justification are posed. If 'origins' means causes, "there will be no difficulties other
than those which are always inherent in the nature of causal inquiry." The main

---

130. Arendt, *Origins*, p. viii.
131. Arendt, *Origins*, p. viii.
132. Ernest Renan, *Origins of Christianity* (New York: Carleton, 1870); Hippolyte Taine, *The Origins of Contemporary France* (New York: P. Smith, 1932 [1876]).

problem, he believed, lies in the "frequent cross-contamination of the two meanings, the more formidable in that it is seldom very clearly recognized. In popular usage, an origin is a beginning which explains. Worse still, a beginning which is a complete explanation. There lies the ambiguity, and there the danger!"[133]

We have seen how just this conflation lies at the heart of Horkheimer and Adorno's *Dialectic of Enlightenment*. From its very start, they argued, the Enlightenment had established conditions, once dominant, that conduced "disaster triumphant" because of its disenchantment of nature by knowledge. With myth turned "into enlightenment, and nature into mere objectivity," humankind came to "pay for the increase of their power with alienation from that over which they exercise their power." The result, they claimed, was the production of a new and terrible correspondence between the way "Enlightenment behaves toward things" and how "a dictator [behaves] toward men."[134] Twentieth-century barbarism thus was entailed in the origins, and dominion, of Enlightenment.

As it turned out, this approach vitiated one of the Frankfurt School's own most cherished goals, the aim "of synthesizing a broad spectrum of disciplines" by integrating "speculation and empirical research."[135] In the 1940s, this link was severed. The Institute of Social Research continued to be interested in both, contributing after the war to important empirical studies of prejudice, demagoguery, and authoritarianism[136] while continuing to be develop social theory, most notably Horkheimer's *Eclipse of Reason*,[137] but these enterprises

---

133. Marc Bloch, *The Historian's Craft* (Manchester: Manchester University Press, 1992), pp. 24–25. Bloch wrote the bulk of this volume in 1941–1942, soon after the publication of his magisterial two volumes, *Feudal Society*. He finished the book after joining the Resistance (the Germans captured and shot him days before the Allies landed at Normandy). It was published in France in 1949. For a discussion of Foucault's later "assault upon the hidden teleological assumptions contained in the notion of 'origins,'" see Gareth Stedman Jones, "Anglo-Marxism, Neo-Marxism, and the Discursive Approach to History," in Alf Lüdtke, ed., *Was bleibt von marxistischen Perspektiven in der Geschichtsforschung?* (Göttingen: Wallstein Verlag, 1997), p. 185.

134. Max Horkheimer and Theodor W. Adorno, *Dialectic of Enlightenment* (New York: Continuum, 1994 [original edition 1944]), pp. 3, 9.

135. Martin Jay, *The Dialectical Imagination: A History of the Frankfurt School and the Institute of Social Research, 1923–1950* (Boston: Little, Brown, 1973), p. 253.

136. Including, Leo Loewenthal and Norbert Guterman, *Prophets of Deceit: A Study of the Techniques of the American Agitator* (New York: Harper, 1949); Theodor W. Adorno, Else Frenkel-Brunswik, Daniel J. Levinson, and R. Nevitt Stanford, *The Authoritarian Personality* (New York: Harper, 1950).

137. Max Horkheimer, *Eclipse of Reason* (New York: Oxford University Press, 1947) Later, Arendt also severed this linkage of the theoretical and empirical in her own work. I am indebted to Craig Calhoun for making this point.

grew increasingly distinct because the theoretical construction of origins in *Dialectic* left no room for this linkage.

If Horkheimer and Adorno recognized the origins of their time in the Enlightenment's structure of ideas and ambitions, Polanyi's and Arendt's approach to periodization was radically different. They reconstructed nineteenth- and early-twentieth-century developments to identify far more near-term and contingent configurations of causal elements that had made total war, and, especially, totalitarianism and holocaust possible. Rejecting a division between theory and empirical scholarship, they declined a strategy of genetic determination combining long-ago beginnings with ineluctable causality of the kind that characterized not only the writings of Horkheimer and Adorno but also other learned texts by Karl Popper and Jacob Talmon tracing the sources of current tribulations to Plato, Rousseau, and Marx.[138] Crucially, though, these refusals did not extend to a repudiation of origins marked by periodicity and causality, the combination Bloch had counseled historians to cast aside. Rather, both Polanyi and Arendt marshaled analyses combining broadly permissive accounts of large-scale processes and probabilities with tight causal versions of contemporary history, the two aspects in "the word 'origins' " Bloch had thought "disturbing because . . . ambiguous."[139] By contrast, they thought just such a conjunction was necessary and just such a composite of elements had to be kept in tension to show how Europe had crossed the nearly impassable rupture dividing the removed past from the near past. Only then could the pathway of origins be traveled as the best available course with which to navigate what a German historian, Reinhart Kosseleck, has called the "aporetic situation" of scholars confronted by situations so radical (he was writing about the holocaust) they face "the necessity of making comparisons as well as the need to leave these comparisons behind."[140]

In the face of such difficulties, Polanyi and Arendt neither lapsed into stunned silence nor treated totalitarianism and the holocaust simply as exaggerations of modernity's normal features. They rejected the notion that 'modernity,' understood whole, could be held responsible for recent events, as in Zygmunt Bauman's too-bulky formulation that "without modern civilization and its most

---

138. Karl Popper, *The Open Society and its Enemies*. 2 vols. (London: Routledge & Sons, 1945); and Jacob Talmon, *The Origins of Totalitarian Democracy* (London: Secker & Warburg, 1952).
139. Bloch, *History*, p. 25.
140. In such circumstances, Kosselleck observed, scholars must maneuver through a thicket of moral demands whose drumbeat "does not gain in strength through repetition." Since religious interpretations take us outside the realm of the systematic and analytical, and normal political analysis is "too limited to explain what happened." A letter to Saul Friedländer, June 29, 1989, cited in Friedländer, *Memory, History, and the Extermination of the Jews of Europe* (Bloomington: University of Indiana Press, 1993), p. 57.

central essential achievement, there would be no Holocaust,"[141] a statement so true as to be tautological, but so slack as to lack causal bite. Nor were they content with analyses pointing distinctively at German exceptionalism, German guilt, German indifference, or German anti-Semitism, as if the search for causes could possibly be enclosed wholly within this particular national story.[142] Writing immediately at the close of the Second World War, Arendt warned of the need to distinguish between guilt and responsibility, between Nazis and Germans. "The true problem, however" she wrote,[143]

> is not to prove what is self-evident, namely that Germans have not been potential Nazis ever since Tacitus' times, nor what is impossible, that all Germans harbor Nazi views. It is rather to consider how to conduct ourselves and how to bear the trial of confronting a people among whom the boundaries dividing criminals from normal persons, the guilty from the innocent, have been so completely effaced that nobody will be able to tell in Germany whether in any case he is dealing with a secret hero or with a former mass murderer. . . . The number of those who are responsible *and* guilty will be relatively small. There are many who share responsibility without any visible proof of guilt. There are many more who have become guilty without being in the least responsible.

141. Zygmunt Bauman, *Modernity and the Holocaust* (Ithaca: Cornell University Press, 1989), p. 87.
142. Of course, this does not rule out attempts to grasp specifics of the German situation such as the eclipse of the Weimar Republic and the rise and consolidation of the Third Reich; nor does it dislodge the need to grapple with the character and causal impact of German elite and mass anti-Semitism. The literature on both topics is enormous, of course. For an overview of "The Historiography of National Socialism," see the essay by that title by Jane Caplan, in Michael Bentley, "Companion to Historiography," (London: Routledge, 1997). For a still useful collection of collection of papers on the transition to Nazism, see Hajo Holborn, ed., *Republic to Reich: The Making of the Nazi Revolution* (New York: Pantheon Books, 1972). Arguably, the most penetrating and original recent historian of Nazism was Tim Mason. See, in particular, his treatment of "The Primacy of Politics: Politics and Economics in National Socialist Germany" and "Intention and Explanation: A Current Controversy about the Interpretation of National Socialism," in the collection of his essays edited by Jane Caplan, *Nazism, Fascism, and the Working Class* (Cambridge: Cambridge University Press, 1995). German anti-Semitism and its Nazi variant are thoughtfully considered in Jonathan Frankel, ed., *The Fate of the European Jews, 1939–1945: Continuity or Contingency? Studies in Contemporary Jewry* (Oxford: Oxford University Press, vol. 13, 1997); and Albert S. Lindemann, *Esau's Tears: Modern Antisemitism and the Rise of the Jews* (Cambridge: Cambridge University Press, 1997). What certainly is clear, is that the kind of argument about mass and elite 'exterminationist' anti-Semitism mounted by Daniel Goldhagen will not stand careful scrutiny. Daniel J. Goldhagen, *Hitler's Willing Executioners* (New York: Knopf, 1996).
143. Hannah Arendt, "Organized Guilt and Universal Responsibility," in Kohn, ed., *Arendt*, p. 125; this essay first appeared in *Jewish Frontier*, no. 12 (1945).

Instead, both without abjuring objectivity or erasing the plurality of vantage points on this and other key issues, she and Polanyi sought to disclose the configurations of nineteenth- and twentieth-century elements that had shattered the *Britannica's* treasured triad of knowledge, rational social organization, and a reduction in social violence that, in *extremis*, had not proved able to stop the worst from happening. Using language Arendt soon was to echo, Polanyi cautioned that the "face of demoniac violence is merely superimposed on a swift, silent current of change which swallows up the past often without so much of a ripple on the surface! A reasoned analysis of the catastrophe must account both for the tempestuous action and the quiet dissolution."[144] Though Polanyi and Arendt selected different starting points from which to set forth on journeys in search of origins, and while each knew their choice semi-arbitrarily conferred special status on a particular antecedent starting point, they rightly were persuaded that without what Edward Said calls the necessary fiction of a beginning—what he designated as transitive, project-directed beginnings[145]—they, and we, would be at a loss to mount any kind of systematic explanations for situations so novel and extreme as to lie beyond the ken of ordinary reason.

Since traditional history and social science manifestly were inadequate in these circumstances, they chose to run the risks of origins identified by Bloch. Yet to succeed, they also knew they had to avoid the simple conformance of origins with impersonal, often invisible, material or ideational structures common to such great nineteenth-century works as Darwin's *Origin of Species*, Marx's *Capital*, and Nietzsche's *Genealogy of Morals*. "What is interesting here," Said notes, "is a transformation that takes place in the concept of beginnings" which "now requires, not beginning as event, but beginning either as *type* or *force*—for example, the unconscious, Dionysus, class and capital, or natural selection." In such approaches, "beginnings perform the task of differentiating material *at the start*: they are *principles* of differentiation which make possible the same characteristic histories, structures, and knowledges they intend."[146]

Still, it must be acknowledged, the dangers inherent in origins stories were not easy to avoid. Like Arendt, Polanyi did not supplant events and decisions with abstract ideas or remote processes. But he did come perilously close to fixing outcomes in beginnings. In the train of Darwin's *Origins*, which had become something of a model for prewar history and social science, the twin temptations of teleology and analyses of change motored by functional adaptations without human motivation or intention had become quite common. Importing concepts

---

144. Polanyi, *Transformation*, p. 4.

145. Edward Said, *Beginnings: Intention and Method* (Baltimore: Johns Hopkins University Press, 1975), p. 50.

146. Said, *Beginnings*, p. 51.

and metaphors drawn from evolutionary biology, Polanyi's account of the origins of dark times was pulled at times in this direction, thus running the risk of insufficiently identifying and specifying the actual causal mechanisms that were at work.[147] Though aware of these hazards, he often combined description and analysis in such a manner as to imply that no other outcome but catastrophe was possible. At best, the causal status of the elements he implicated in the making of dark times is ambiguous in his text, as in his very first paragraph which reads: "Nineteenth century civilization has collapsed. This book is concerned with the political and economic origins of this event, as well as with the great transformation which it ushered in." If 'origins' can 'usher,' with what degree of necessity? Moreover, he often wrote about large-scale social and political processes as if they were self-motored, as in his much-cited claim about laissez-faire and the reaction to it: "Our thesis," he summarized,[148]

is that the idea of a self-adjusting market implied a stark utopia. Such an institution could not exist for any length of time without annihilating the human and natural substance of society; it would have physically destroyed man and transformed his surroundings into a wilderness. *Inevitably, society* took measures to protect itself, but whatever measures it took impaired the self-regulation of the market, disorganized industrial life, and thus endangered society in yet another way. It was this dilemma which *forced* the development of the market system into a definite groove and finally disrupted the social organization based on it.

This paragraph's causal statements invite, though they do not mandate, a teleological reading without specifying the agents and mechanisms shaping the collision between markets and politics.[149] Such passages recur in his text. Thus, for example, in writing about the origins of mercantilism in the fifteenth and sixteenth centuries, Polanyi argued "the centralized state was a new creation called forth by the Commercial Revolution" and that "in external politics, the setting up of sovereign power was "the need of the day."[150]

By contrast, these post-Darwinian temptations are almost entirely absent from Arendt's writing. Replying, in 1953, to a critique by Eric Voegelin, who had thought her work to be teleological, she backed away from the term, though not

---

147. Jon Elster, *Explaining Technical Change: A Case Study in the Philosophy of Science* (Cambridge: Cambridge University Press, 1983).
148. Polanyi, *Transformation*: 3–4 (emphasis added).
149. Similarly, Franz Neumann wrote that "Every social system must somehow satisfy the primary needs of the people," Neumann, *Behemoth*, p. 37.
150. Polanyi, *Transformation*, p. 65.

the project, regretting the misperception implied by the naming of *Origins*: "The book," she wrote, "does not really deal with the 'origins of totalitarianism' — as its title unfortunately claims — but gives a historical account of the elements which crystallized into totalitarianism."[151] And yet, her own too-terse exposition of method in the very brief Preface to *Origins* can leave the impression that she, too, had fallen into the trap of failing to clarify sufficiently the nature of the causal relationship linking what she called the "elements and origins" of totalitarianism. "This sentence," Lisa Disch remarks, "is the problem. Arendt writes as if 'elements' and 'origins' meant the same thing," thus leaving "her work open to misinterpretation" as an ineluctable and agentless story in which the explanation of totalitarianism is embedded in its genesis, which, in fact, Disch rightly observes, is "the very epistemic framework she claims to write against."[152]

Despite these instances of slippage, each book effectively addressed the problem of origins posed by Bloch. This accomplishment was the product of their approaches to large-scale historical social science. They avoided getting trapped into teleological reasoning by a probabilistic orientation to causation. Their work was not finely geared to explain particular outcomes on particular days in particular places. Rather, they composed their analytical histories to understand the changing organization of possibilities in early- to mid-twentieth-century Europe, leaving "open the question whether people are doing what people would invariably do in these uniquely complicated circumstances, or are doing one of the comparatively few things which people (usually free) choose to do in such circumstances."[153] The products of this work were not narrowly crafted causal propositions about regularities in motivation and action but guarded generalizations about how alterations to institutions and ideas had transformed probabilities.

Even though *Origins* did so more successfully than *Transformation*, both fashioned approaches to temporality and causality that advanced their purpose of coming to grips with the shock of desolation by developing nonteleological causal accounts of its sources. Although neither author expended much prose on methodological issues, Arendt explicitly addressed this set of issues in her

---

151. Hannah Arendt, "A Reply to Eric Voegelin," in Arendt, *Understanding*, p. 403. This text first appeared in *The Review of Politics*, January 1953. The term 'crystallization' is not innocent, of course, as it is borrowed from Kant's *Third Critique*, where he had introduced it to refer to contingency. For a discussion, see Lisa J. Disch, "More Truth than Fact: Storytelling as Critical Understanding in the Writings of Hannah Arendt," *Political Theory* 21 (November 1993): 683.

152. Disch, "More Truth," pp. 677–678.

153. Hugh Stretton, *The Political Sciences: General Principles of Selection in Social Science and History* (London: Routledge & Kegan Paul, 1969), p. 215.

response to Voegelin.[154] She made clear that the object of her analysis was not a lineage of ideas that made western civilization hospitable to totalitarianism, but "the *event* of totalitarian domination itself," a form of domination "unlike all forms of despotism and tyranny we know of" representing "a much more radical liquidation of freedom as a political and human reality than anything we have ever witnessed before." It is this distinctiveness that challenges historical analysis because "the deeds of its considered policies have exploded our traditional categories of political thought . . . and the standards of our moral judgment (totalitarian crimes are very inadequately described as 'murder' and totalitarian criminals can hardly be punished as 'murderers')."

To understand this quite special object of analysis, she argued, it is necessary to eschew the teleological temptation inherent in tracing "intellectual affinities and influences." It also is important to be wary of claims about the unchangeability of human nature and to avoid the kind of functionalism inherent in such claims, as the one Voegelin made, that totalitarianism is a substitute for absent religion and lost creeds. Rather, Arendt insisted, on facticity and historicity. "Historically," she cautioned, "we know of man's nature only insofar as it has existence, and no realm of eternal essences will ever console us if man loses his essential capabilities." In comprehending such existence in specific situations, it is imperative that distinctions be attended. Writing against the backdrop of her period's growing fascination with structural-functionalism, the quest for behavioral propositions that are portable across time and space, and the Frankfurt School's effort to read the ugliest features of the present backwards into the founding of the Enlightenment itself, Arendt favored a more precise, more analytical historical venture, noting that,[155]

> my chief quarrel with the present state of the historical and political sciences is their growing incapacity for making distinctions. Terms like nationalism, imperialism, totalitarianism, etc., are used indiscriminately for all kinds of political phenomena (usually just as 'highbrow' words for aggression), and none of them is any longer understood with its particular historical background. The result is a generalization in which the words themselves lose all meaning. Imperialism does not mean a thing if it is used indiscriminately for Assyrian and Roman and British and Bolshevik history; nationalism is discussed in times and countries which never experienced the nation-state; totalitarianism is discovered in all kinds of tyrannies or forms of collective communities, etc. This kind of confusion—where everything distinct disappears and everything that is new and

---

154. The citations in the next two paragraphs are found in Arendt, "Reply," pp. 401–408.
155. Arendt, "Reply," p. 407.

shocking is (not explained but) explained away either through drawing some analogies or reducing it to a previously known chain of causes and influences—seems to me to be the hallmark of the modern historical and political sciences.

This was the context for Arendt's discussion of what she called the "problem of method." Her book, she noted had been reproached for a certain lack of unity, but that criticism missed its central methodological conception: "to discover the chief elements of totalitarianism and to analyze them in historical terms, tracing these elements back in history as far as I deemed proper and necessary." These are not the subjects of inquiry but means to a focused understanding. "I did not write a history of anti-Semitism or of imperialism," she continued, "but analyzed the element of Jew-hatred and the element of expansion insofar as these elements were still clearly visible and played a decisive role in the totalitarian phenomenon itself." In her account, anti-Semitism and imperialism did not 'cause' fascism, nazism, and bolshevism, but rather combined in distinctive configurations to compose "the elementary structure of totalitarianism," running through it "like red threads through the whole."

As it happens, the basic strategy employed by Polanyi was nearly identical, though in a mirror image. If Arendt sought to show how diverse elements within the West's past, often hidden from view, had combined under distinctive historical conditions to produce an unprecedented form of tyranny, Polanyi wished to understand how institutional configuration of the balance of power, gold standard, domestic market, and liberal state had come apart to put an end to the hundred years' peace to make war and totalitarianism possible. As for Arendt, his object of explanation concerned the conditions for change on an immense scale: "No less than a complete destruction of the national institutions of the nineteenth century accompanied the crisis in a great part of the world, and everywhere these institutions were changed and re-formed almost out of recognition. The liberal state," he enumerated, "was in many countries replaced by totalitarian dictatorships, and the central institution of the century—production based on free markets—was superseded by new forms of economy."[156] The result was a remarkable bifurcation between countries assaulting and defending freedom, his core value. Though there were vast differences between the outcomes in Russia, Germany, Italy, Britain, France, and the United States, all had been affected by "their relation to the underlying social process" he sought to identify and account for.[157]

---

156. Polanyi, *Transformation*, p. 28.
157. Polanyi, *Transformation*, p. 29.

Twentieth-century events, he insisted, were "too big to have been caused" by single causes like the collapse of the gold standard. Like Arendt, therefore, his work also was an enterprise of shifts in the configuration of elements to the effect of altering thresholds for the probabilities of outcomes. In the historical social science of both Arendt and Polanyi, in short, the quest for origins neither was a search for strong linear causal statements where evidence could satisfy theories composed of tightly linked hypotheses nor was it simply an effort to name factors present in the 'old' world and the 'new.' Rather, both sought to show[158] that the probability of a given set of outcomes had been altered by a reconfiguration of macro-historical elements well above any prior probability.[159]

V.

"Whether the ancient Western dream of a free and rational society will always remain a chimera," Barrington Moore mused at the end of *Social Origins of Dictatorship and Democracy*, no one can know for sure. But if the men of the future are ever to break the chains of the present, they will have to understand the forces that forged them."[160] This kind of search, Arendt and Polanyi had understood, demanded the (re)invention of a historical social science marked by new links between understanding the past, empirical research, and political theory. They pioneered work in this vein a quarter-century before Moore, as well as Immanuel Wallerstein and Perry Anderson, among others, placed this kind of analysis of large processes and major moments of historical inflection at the center of contemporary academic sociology and political science.[161] Unlike their successors, who were concerned primarily to grasp the origins of political modernity in the creation of sovereign states and global markets in late medieval and early modern Europe (both to address and revise Marx's notion of a transi-

---

158. In a broadly Bayesian approach.

159. The evidence is not so strong as to qualify as veridical, but is far stronger than artful storytelling, thus akin to what Peter Achinstein, a philosopher of science, calls potential evidence. Peter Achinstein, *The Book of Evidence* (New York: Oxford University Press), pp. 6–31.

160. Moore, *Social Origins*, p. 508.

161. Moore, *Social Origins*; Immanuel Wallerstein, *The Modern World System: Capitalist Agriculture and the Origins of the European World-Economy in the Sixteenth Century* (New York: Academic Press, 1974); Perry Anderson, *Passages from Antiquity to Feudalism* (London: New Left Books, 1974). For discussions, see Paul Pierson and Theda Skocpol, "Historical Institutionalism in Contemporary Political Science," in Ira Katznelson and Helen Milner, eds., *Political Science: The State of the Discipline, Centennial Edition* (New York: W.W. Norton for the American Political Science Association, 2002); and James Mahoney and Dietrich Rueschemeyer, eds., *Comparative Historical Analysis in the Social Sciences* (New York: Cambridge University Press, 2002).

tion from feudalism to capitalism), they tackled the more difficult pressing task of grasping the sources of a contemporary breach with the past they considered to be more prodigious than any prior juncture of transformation. Now, Arendt observed, "the essential structure of all civilizations is at the breaking point." Decent possibilities, after this rupture, had become dependent "on political forces that cannot be trusted to follow the rules of common sense and self-interest—forces that look like sheer insanity, if judged by the standards of other centuries." The globe, she continued, now found itself divided "between those who believe in human omnipotence (who think that everything is possible if one knows how to organize masses for it) and those for whom powerlessness has become the major experience of their lives."[162] Linking analytical determination and normative purpose, Polanyi and Arendt believed that in such circumstances the analysis of origins and burdens of obligation to posterity had to go hand in hand. For only with persuasive histories of the inception of desolation could human beings renew their responsibility for the world and reclaim a realm for worthy human action inside, and in defiance of, the difficult structural conditions with which they had been presented.

The basis for their reinvention of a normatively charged historical social science was the work of Tocqueville and his desire to produce "a new science of politics . . . for a new world."[163] Self-describing as a "liberal of a new kind," his pioneer efforts combining structural and moral narratives while searching both for origins and future prospects were written to understand French and American failures, achievements, and possibilities.[164] Pursing the goal he announced to John Stuart Mill—"I have meant to depict the general features of democratic societies, for which there is not yet a complete model"[165]—Tocqueville was concerned in *The Old Regime and the Revolution* and in his earlier text on *Democracy in America* to work out the relationship between equality and freedom. Obsessed with the oscillation between anarchy and despotism in France and concerned to understand why "France alone could give birth to a revolution so sudden, so radical, so impetuous in its course, and yet so full of backtracking, or contradictory facts and contrary examples,"[166] *Regime* developed a layered account of freedom's failures by portraying the semi-ruination of medieval institutions by monarchical absolutism, by showing the doleful impact of the centralization of the sovereign state across early modern Europe, and by addressing the

162. Arendt, *Origins*, p. vii.

163. Tocqueville, *Democracy*, p. 7.

164. Arendt refused to call herself a liberal, but Aileen Dunham persuasively located Arendt in a group of "liberals all too well acquainted with Hitler's Germany." Dunham review, p. 184.

165. Olivier Zunz and Alan S. Kahan, eds., *The Tocqueville Reader: A life in Letters and Politics.* (Oxford: Blackwell, 2002).

166. Tocqueville, *Old Regime*, p. 247.

particularly intense application of these processes in pre-Revolutionary and rev-olutionary France. The 'causes' of the French Revolution thus extended in his analysis to processes far beyond France, yet their particular combination within France accounted for the country as the site of revolution in 1789. The relevant causal factors both were located broadly in the West but combined in highly particular ways in eighteenth-century France.

It was this kind of duality that characterized the historical social science of Polanyi as well as Arendt as they linked large-scale, cross-national processes not contained within the borders of particular countries to developments inside each. "It may be comprehensible, but it is not the less dangerous," she cau-tioned, "that the horrors of the Hitler regime have led people to ignore the . . . interrelated factors which made Hitler possible."[167] As the structure of her work and the locus of her empirical analysis indicate, this was no standard call to avoid the pitfalls of single causes. Her designation of European desolation as a combination of the long-term working out of anti-Semitism and imperialism that had been partially obscured by nineteenth- and early-twentieth-century lib-eral regimes and her focus on the twentieth-century collapse of universal citi-zenship and the inclusive state in the face of ultra-nationalist movement as-saults were paralleled in Polanyi's account by the steady but concealed internal decay of older institutional forms at the turn of the century that soon were de-stroyed utterly by revolutionary fascist and communist regimes. In treading this course, both scholars broadly duplicated the analytical path that had been fol-lowed by Tocqueville that combined historically distant and temporally near el-ements to understand the sources of political disappointment in France within a larger European historical context.

Methodologically, the work of Polanyi and Arendt also tracks the manner in which Tocqueville considered the United States in *Democracy* as a complex configuration of elements and as an elaboration of the archetype of social and political equality. That text identified ante-bellum America as highly distinctive, even exceptional, yet it also regarded the young republic in relation to larger trends and processes which affected the modern, western world more generally; especially those of social and political equalization. Tocqueville studied the United States as a harbinger of things to come at a moment of enormous change. Moreover, his text carefully distinguishes levels of causation: those fac-tors specific and limited to the American milieu and those shared broadly by the larger thrust in the West toward social equality and the movement of masses into politics. Throughout, individual and group dispositions and patterns of collec-

---

167. Arendt, Holborn review, p. 187.

tive action are understood to have been shaped by large-scale structural and ideological arrangements and trends. For Tocqueville, human nature is not fixed either as benevolent or as interest-seeking; rather, human behavior is conditioned on the structural and institutional shaping of values and mores which, in turn, remake contextual conditions for action. Motivated by broadly liberal values and fears in a revolutionary world, Tocqueville combined classification and typological thinking with the dense historical, sociological, and political depiction of a single, complicated case. He understood that out of context, the factors deployed in his analysis would lose their relational quality; yet he insisted that a thick study of the United States could contain deeply comparative lessons.[168]

Like Tocqueville, Polanyi and Arendt constructed their analytical histories by focusing less on the causal importance of this or that specific factor contrasted with others than on how variables are joined together in specific instances. Their

---

168. As Aron has noted, Tocqueville "wanted to make history intelligible, but he did not want to do away with it," thus rejecting transhistorical syntheses which claimed either to tame or predict history's vagaries. Raymond Aron, *Main Currents in Sociological Thought* 1 (London: Penguin Books, 1968), p. 232. There is a close affinity between Tocqueville's mix of modesty and assertion and Max Weber's guidelines for historical sociology in the essay he published on objectivity in the social sciences on the occasion of the appearance of the new *Archiv fur Sozialwissenschaft und Sozialpolitik* which he edited. Social science, he argued, should aim to construct situations so that individuals can ascertain the possible, either in the past or the present; that is, what they or other actors can, as opposed to what they must, do. This orientation considers ethical imperatives not as independent motivators or explanations but only as operative inside determinate situations analytically ordered by social and political analysts who reveal "constellations of norms, institutions, etc" by focusing on the conceptually organized interconnections of elements in conjunction with narratives of events. Understanding that our values condition our interest in particular problems and in specific analytical narratives, Weber argued the case for what he called the analysis of 'configurations.' Such a social science, he wrote,

> seeks to transcend the purely *formal* treatment of the legal or conventional norms regulating social life. The type of social science in which we are interested is an *empirical science* of concrete *reality* (*Wirklichkeitswissenschaft*). Our aim is the understanding of the characteristic uniqueness of the reality in which we move. We wish to understand on the other hand the relationships and the cultural significance of individual evens in their contemporary manifestation and on the other the causes of their being historically *so* and not *otherwise*. . . . It too concerns itself with the question of the *individual* consequence which the working of these 'laws' in an unique *configuration* produces, since it is these individual configurations which are *significant* for us. Every individual constellation which it 'explains' or predicts is causally explicable only as the consequence of another equally individual constellation which has preceded it. As far back as we may go into the grey mist of the far-off past, the reality to which the laws apply always remain equally *individual*, equally *unreducible* from laws. (italics in original)

Max Weber, *The Methodology of the Social Sciences* (New York: Free Press, 1979), pp. 64, 72.

work is "fugue-like, . . . repeating its opening themes in multiple variations across a series of topical as well as temporal domains."[169] For Polanyi, each institutional pillar of the liberal nineteenth century was distinct, yet once brought into a relationship a set of deep tensions, as for example between the requirements of the price system and citizen-based impulses for protection, which fashioned fresh possibilities for anti-liberal, even evil, outcomes. For Arendt, anti-Semitism, imperialism, and totalitarianism were partially concurrent. Each had to be understood in its own terms, to be sure, but the big payoff in understanding came as a result of considering how they interacted to mutually constitute a new set of possibilities unknown until they combined. Both scholars thus wagered on the intersection of key ideas and, above all, the conjunction of institutions whose interaction transformed the likelihood of different forms of human action.

This Tocquevillian orientation prefers realist and concrete rather than nominalist and abstract treatments of such categories as markets or imperialism, never divorcing their treatment from concrete instantiations. Thus Polanyi considered the development of free labor markets by assessing the impact of English Poor Law reform, and Arendt understood the new late-nineteenth-century relationship between nationalism and the state in terms of the bureaucratization of racism convened by the imperial scramble for Africa. Throughout, there is a recurring oscillation in both texts between the manner in which large processes were transformed by big developments and an almost pointillist processing of instances, with both analytical levels guided by self-conscious criteria of selection.

Thus in a passage that might have been composed by Tocqueville, Polanyi explains that[170]

> Ours is not a historical work; what we are searching for is not a convincing sequence of outstanding events, but an explanation of their trend in terms of human institutions. We shall feel free to dwell on scenes of the past with the sole object of throwing light on matters of the present; we shall make detailed analyses of critical periods and almost totally disregard the connecting stretches of time; we shall encroach upon the field of several disciplines in the pursuit of this single aim.

---

169. Kirstie M. McClure, "The Odor of Judgment: Exemplarity, Propriety, and Politics in the Company of Hannah Arendt," in Craig Calhoun and John McGowan eds., *Hannah Arendt and the Meaning of Politics* (Minnesota: University of Minnesota Press, 1997), p. 67.
170. Polanyi, *Transformation*, p. 4.

Arendt's reliance on Tocqueville as a model and guide was more explicit.[171] She was particularly drawn to his work because he grappled with an utterly new historical challenge. She cited[172] a passage from the concluding chapter to *Democracy in America*, where Toqueville had observed that[173]

> Although the revolution that is taking place in the social condition, the laws, the opinions, and the feelings of men is still very far from being terminated, yet its results already admit of no comparison with anything that the world has ever before witnessed. I go back from age to age up to the remotest antiquity, but I find no parallel to what is occurring before my eyes; as the past has ceased to throw its light upon the future, the mind of man wanders in obscurity.

Earlier in the text, Tocqueville had remarked that the degree of difference between the American and the ancient republics was such that he was "tempted to burn my books in order to apply none but novel ideas to so novel a condition of society."[174]

Margaret Canovan has discovered that Arendt's unpublished 1955 University of California, Berkeley, lecture notes "contain a heavily emphasized quotation from J.P. Mayer's book on Tocqueville recording how he had himself read Plato, Machiavelli, Burke, etc. while trying to understand his own time: 'He felt a need to measure the wealth of his American observations against the whole Western heritage of political doctrine'."[175] So, too, did Arendt. She found it

---

171. A useful discussion, overstraining a bit to demonstrate similarities, is Margie Lloyd, "In Tocqueville's Shadow: Hannah Arendt's Liberal Republicanism," *The Review of Politics* 57 (Winter 1995). A comparative treatment that strives to demonstrate differences while also identifying parallels (their shared view that traditional modes of thinking about politics are inadequate; that the historical tendencies of their time—respectively democratic revolutions and the rise of society—are sources of deep concern; that historical determinism is to be eschewed; and that the zone of the public is to be cherished and nurtured) is Suzanne D. Jacobitti, "Individualism and Political Community: Arendt and Tocqueville on the Current Debate in Liberalism," *Polity* 23 (Summer 1991).
172. Arendt, *Past and Future*, pp. 7, 283; Arendt, *Dark Times*, p. 193.
173. Alexis de Tocqueville, *Democracy*, Vol. 2, p. 349.
174. Tocqueville, *Democracy*, Vol. 1, p. 327.
175. Canovan, *Arendt*, p. 67. Late in life, Arendt commented on how it had been Tocqueville who had pioneered the notion of a radical break convening dark times: "This business that the tradition is broken and the Ariadne thread is lost. Well, that is not quite as new as I made it out to be. It was, after all, Tocqueville who said that 'the past to throw its light onto the future, and the mind of man wanders in darkness.' This is the situation since the middle of the last century, and, seen from the viewpoint of Tocqueville, entirely true." In Melvyn Hill, ed., *Hannah Arendt: The Recovery of the Public World* (New York: St. Martin's Press, 1979), p. 337. A discussion of Tocqueville's influence on Arendt also can be found in Bernard Crick's "Rereading."

wanting in the face of 'radical evil.' "It is inherent in our entire philosophical tradition," she contended, "that we cannot conceive of a 'radical evil,' and this is true both for Christian theology, which conceded to the Devil himself a celestial origin, as well as for Kant, the only philosopher who, in the word he coined for it, at least must have suspected the existence of this even though he immediately rationalized it in the concept of a 'perverted ill will' that could be explained by comprehensible motives." In consequence, her mid-century epistemological conundrum was profound. "The originality of totalitarianism is horrible," she wrote soon after the publication of *Origins*, "not because some new 'idea' came into the world, but because its very actions constitute a break with all our traditions; they have clearly exploded our categories of political thought and our standards for moral judgment."[176] Arendt's response was not to invent a new philosophical stance, at least not here; it was, rather, to craft a Tocquevillian historical and institutional political science oriented to the purpose at hand as a means to avoid the pitfalls inherent in the conflation of beginnings with causation. Indeed, Arendt returned to this theme, remonstrating against tight linear causality in historical scholarship. Such an approach, she wrote,[177]

> can be concealed in the application of general categories to the whole course of happenings, such as challenge and response, or in the search for general trends which supposedly are the 'deeper' strata from which events spring and whose accessory symptoms they are. Such generalizations and categorizations extinguish the 'natural' light history itself offers and, by the same token, destroy the actual story, with its unique distinction and its eternal meaning, that each historical period has to tell us. Within the framework of reconceived categories, the crudest of which is causality,[178] events in the sense of something irrevocably new can never happen.

These doubts about determination did not push Arendt, or Polanyi, in the direction of traditional historical narratives which either eschew causality for description or discover 'causes' in temporally short sequences and confined geographies.[179] Instead, they opted to construct a historical social science marked by a layer of discontinuity like that separating a lake's upper, relatively warm, layer

---

176. Hannah Arendt, "Understanding and Politics (The Difficulties of Understanding)," in Kohn, *Arendt, pp.* 309–310. The paper was first published in *Partisan Review* 20, no. 4 (1954).
177. Arendt, "Understanding," p. 319.
178. Here she rails in a footnote against the conflation of causation and necessity. Arendt, "Understanding," p. 326.
179. For the former, I have in mind the synoptic view offered by Piers Brendon, *The Dark Valley: A Panorama of the 1930s* (New York: Knopf, 2000). Regarding the latter, Canovan observes Arendt's "leaving aside the particular histories of Germany and Russia, in which others have tried

of water from its lower, cooler, layer.[180] Above it lay 'normal' politics; obscured below, as Polanyi put it, were the period's powerful, if hidden, deep tides of change.[181]

In refusing both traditional narrative history and tight determining accounts of elements and processes, both scholars, but especially Arendt, echoed Walter Benjamin's "Theses on the Philosophy of History."[182] Benjamin had cautioned historians to refuse "to be drained by the whore called 'Once upon a time' in historicism's bordello" or to tell "the sequence of events like beads of a rosary." Instead, he counseled, they should grasp "the constellation which [their] own era has formed with a definite earlier one."[183] This combination of deconstructive and reconstructive history was the type of portrait identifying and combining elements that Polanyi and Arendt produced. Inside their philosophically guided frames, they elaborated many specific propositions about institutions, mechanisms, and behavior of the sort most familiar to mainstream social scientists. Often masked by their own language (which reflected a distaste for the innocence, limited boundaries, and hyper-positivist scientific style of mainstream sociology and political science), they thus developed a quite powerful and compelling alliance of large-scale analytical history with testable empirical claims, including the ones Arendt and Polanyi deployed about European party systems that focused on the contrast between multiparty and two-party electoral systems to address the seeming displacement of cause and effect.

In *Origins* and in *Transformation* there is a vexing distance between the main *explananda*—the collapse of an old, more decent, order, and the creation of a new one, consonant with the triumph of radical evil—and the physical and institutional locations the authors identify as the deep sources of catastrophe. At the center of their analytical accounts of what Polanyi called "critical phases of history, when a civilization has broken down or is passing through a transformation"[184] lay total war, totalitarianism, and (for Arendt) the holocaust. Yet

---

to find explanations for Nazism and Stalinism." Margaret Canovan, "Arendt's Theory of Totalitarianism: A Reassessment," in Villa, *Companion*, p. 30.

180. This discontinuity (the thermocline), separates the warmer epilimnion from the cooler hypolimnion.

181. Polanyi, *Transformation*, p. 4.

182. Which Arendt later edited for the English edition of Walter Benjamin, *Illuminations: Essays and Reflections* (New York: Harcourt, 1968). See her stunning chapter, "Walter Benjamin, 1892–1940" in *Dark Times*.

183. Thus, he continued, the historian "establishes a conception of the present as the 'time of the now' which is shot through with chips of Messianic time." Benjamin, *Illuminations*, pp. 262–263. For Arendt's rich account, see her "Walter Benjamin, 1892–1940," in Arendt, *Dark Times*, pp. 153–206.

184. Polanyi, *Transformation*, p. 155.

Polanyi's disquisition on how the broadly liberal "political *and* the economic system of the planet disintegrated conjointly"[185] to produce deep, possibly permanent, unfreedom treated England as his empirical pivot while ranging across its landscape of poor laws, extensive markets in land, money, and especially labor, nineteenth-century political and economic liberal thought, the gold standard, and early pressures on behalf of a protective welfare state. Likewise, Arendt identified the progenitors of Italian, German, and Soviet totalitarianism in late-nineteenth-century French anti-Semitism and British imperialism.

What is striking is how she placed 'normal science' hypotheses inside the frame of her far from typical synoptic analysis. Thus Arendt utilized variations in party-systems, a staple institutional issue for her period's political science, to explain why Great Britain, in spite of having been the globe's foremost imperial power and a leading innovator of racist thought and bureaucratic practices of native control, never produced anti-system fascist or communist movements of consequence outside the normal party system. European constitutional regimes, Arendt argued, had been toppled under the pressure exerted by anti-state movements originating in the domain of overseas imperialism. These authoritarian, pan-national, and fascist movements had organized masses of people outside the party system under the banner of slogans claiming to be 'above the parties' while appealing to members of the nation in all the existing parties, supplanting the claim of the existing state to speak for the public or national purpose. These movements, she averred, which had brought the continent's party systems down, had successfully aimed to replace liberal notions of the representation based on the diversity of society inside the state with the incorporation of society into the state itself, thus erasing, to the extent that it was possible, the very boundary separating state and society.

In the midst of a powerful discussion of how imperialism had come home to Europe from Africa, Arendt sought to make sense of British exceptionalism by noting that "one can hardly avoid concluding that the difference between the Anglo-Saxon and the Continental party system must be an important factor."[186] Writing as a political scientist, she advanced a hypothesis about the logic of particular institutional arrangements: "When it came to pass that movements began successfully to compete with the nation-state's party system, it was also seen they could undermine only countries with a multiparty system."[187] But she was not content merely to explain the incongruity at hand, but sought to further specify the mechanisms and assumptions that undergirded the range of outcomes produced by institutional variation.

---

185. Polanyi, *Transformation*, p. 244.
186. Arendt, *Origins*, p. 252.
187. Arendt, *Origins*, p. 250.

In two-party systems, she argued, the party in power always makes up the government and actually rules, thus eroding, symbolically and practically, the distinction between government and state. Moreover, since rule is time-limited, the opposition party is quite sure it will soon get its chance. A multiparty system, by contrast, "supposes that each party defines itself consciously as part of the whole, which in turn is represented by a state above parties." In consequence, "a one-party rule can only signify the dictatorial domination of one part over all others. Government formed by alliances between party leaders are always only party governments, clearly distinguished from the state which rests above and beyond them."[188] In two-party systems, parties try to draw links between the particular interests they represent and national interests; in multiparty-systems, where the state hovers outside the party system, however, the parties are more readily tempted by ideology linking their interests to claims that these coincide "with the more general interests of humanity." In settings where such systems fail to deliver decent results, even if for reasons outside their control, there is a greater likelihood of a popular shift in identification, legitimacy, and enthusiasm from parties to movements making comparable claims but which also promise a fusion, capable of solving problems the party system failed to address, between the party and the state via the institution of the mass movement.

Totalitarianism, from this perspective, conflates liberalism's key distinction between state and society by identifying the state with the nation rather than elevating it above nationality and by substituting the mass movement based on national identity for a system of representation based on interests. Arendt knew, of course, that this conflation took different forms under Italian fascism, German Nazism, and Soviet Communism, but she underscored that what joined these diverse experiences together at a slightly higher level of abstraction was their rejection of the differentiation of state and civil society which lies at the heart of all liberal political formulations.

Similarly, if less fully, Polanyi looked to the party system, and especially the nature and timing of the expansion of the franchise, to account for differences between the relative invulnerability to anti-system initiatives in England as compared to other European countries where, he believed, the contradictions connecting liberal politics to liberal economics had burst liberal regimes asunder. "On the Continent," he observed,[189]

trade unions were a creation of the party of the working class; in England the political party was the creation of the trade unions. While on the Continent unionism became more or less socialist, in England even political

---

188. Arendt, *Origins*, p. 253.
189. Polanyi, *Transformation*, p. 176.

socialism remained more or less trade unionist. Universal suffrage, there-fore, which in England tended to increase national unity, had sometimes the opposite effect on the Continent. There, rather than in England, did Pitt's and Peel's, Tocqueville's and Macaulay's misgivings come true that popular government would involve a danger to the economic system.

Thus for both scholars, the hinge connecting their accounts of long-term processes to specific historical outcomes in particular times and places lay in the character of the details characterizing political institutions, understood both as formal organizations and as codes of rules, and the sequence of their devel-opment, practices, and policies. Most important was the manner in which, be-neath the surface of events, the modern state's capacities to shape events and se-cure loyalties had eroded.

VII.

At the heart of *The Great Transformation* and *The Origins of Totalitarianism* lay the ruins of the great majority of European states based on a liberal creed. With their radical decline as the standards of Enlightenment broke down, the makeup of elites and masses changed, the character of institutions altered, the content of political preferences modified, and the meaning of words mutated. The "traditional elements of our political and spiritual world were dissolved into a conglomeration where everything seems to have lost specific value, and has become unrecognizable for human comprehension, unusable for human pur-pose."[190] Yet just across the Atlantic, the United States—stable, liberal, enlight-ened—offered, or seemed to offer, the most inviting of alternatives. For Arendt, the American Revolution, not the French, best enlarged the potentiality of free-dom. For Polanyi, it had been the New Deal, and only the New Deal, that ex-tended the hope that liberty and security might be reconciled effectively.[191] For the political studies enlightenment at large, the United States stood tall as the great historical counterfactual, thus soliciting close scrutiny of its political tradi-tion, fresh accounts of its liberal regime, and focused inquiry about the singular personality of its liberal state.

---

190. Arendt, *Origins*, p. viii.
191. Hannah Arendt, *On Revolution* (New York: Viking, 1963); Polanyi, *Transformation*, pp. 23, 29, 202, 227, 229, 244.

Three

A SEMINAR ON THE STATE

In 1986, the historian William Leuchtenburg, a former member of a faculty workshop at Columbia University, founded in 1945 and calling itself the Seminar on the State, delivered a presidential address to the Organization of American Historians on "The Pertinence of Political History: Reflections on the Significance of the State in America." Leuchtenburg promoted 'the state' as the best available analytical and historical object historians might use to revive political history, then in the doldrums, having lost its commanding position in the discipline.[1] A half-decade later, he penned a brief memoir in which he recalled his move to Columbia in 1952. "I had hardly arrived," he recollected, " . . . when I was invited to join a faculty seminar. Its members included my colleague in history, Richard Hofstadter, but it was chaired by a political scientist, David Truman, . . . and was called significantly, The State. . . . We felt ourselves to be part of one community."[2]

"And was called significantly, The State." Read against standard histories of political science, history, and sociology, there is something odd about this exercise of memory, especially how it underscored the Seminar's name. After all, the

1. William E. Leuchtenburg, "The Pertinence of Political History: Reflections on the Significance of the State in America," *The Journal of American History* 73 (December 1986).
2. William E. Leuchtenburg, "The Uses and Abuses of History," *History and Politics Newsletter* 2 (Fall 1991): 6–7.

members of the Seminar on the State and the larger group of leading postwar students of American politics in the disciplines of which they were a part usually are remembered for having refused to place the state at the center of their work. Indeed, the word 'state' rarely appears in their texts, much as it had not made an appearance a quarter-millennium earlier in John Locke's *Two Treatises of Government*. The papers and topics Columbia's Seminar discussed lend superficial credence to the view that the use of the term 'state' in its title might merely have been an anachronistic conceit. Seymour Martin Lipset considered social mobility; George Stigler, anti-trust policy; Daniel Bell, communism in American unions; Nathan Glazer, Jewish political behavior; Richard Hofstadter, the neglect of ethnicity in American historical writing; and William T. R. Fox, "The Impact of the Study of the Behavioral Sciences on Political Science and the Study of Inter-National Relations." Leuchtenburg himself presented an essay called "Problems of Writing New Political History in Light of New Theoretical and Methodological Developments in the Behavioral Sciences." With the possible exception of C. Wright Mills, a radical sociologist who self-consciously grounded his work in nineteenth- and early-twentieth-century social theory dealing with modern states, the seminar's members rarely announced themselves to be students of this subject, whether understood in traditional constitutional terms, or in Marxist terms as a capitalist state, or in Weberian terms as a highly autonomous administrative state. But it is just this jarring juxtaposition of name and subjects by the Columbia group that should prepare us to be surprised.

I.

Nation states claim exclusive sovereignty over a given territory and its population. They possess a distinctive ensemble of institutions, and justify their monopoly of coercion by deploying narratives to explain why their claims to rule are legitimate. How they exercise their sovereignty, which institutions they deploy, and how they justify their rule are the distinguishing, and contested, hallmarks of stateness.[3] What makes a liberal state distinctive is how its legal codes, institutions, and normative stories are oriented to protect citizens against arbitrary rule, enforce juridical equality among included members of the polity, and ensure that the boundaries of the state are permeable to the preferences, values, beliefs, and interests of participants in political life. A historical, analytical, and moral lament for the demise of such states lies at the center of *The Great Trans-*

---

3. A suggestive elaboration of these points is J. P. Nettl, "The State as a Conceptual Variable," *World Politics* 20 (July 1968).

formation and *The Origins of Totalitarianism*.[4] Both books share in the ironic view that excessive skepticism about the modern state by nineteenth-century liberals who feared its predatory tendencies helped undermine the prerequisites for an effective liberal political order. At issue in the postwar reconstruction, therefore, was whether it could be possible to discover a proper balance between overweening and insufficient political authority.

Polanyi identified the liberal state in England as the progenitor of the first effective framework for market economies, arguing that it had been the inability of this and other such states to bring about effective public policies to ensure the economic security of their populations while permitting markets to operate efficiently that had helped doom such regimes, opening the door to totalitarian alternatives. Arendt characterized the collapse of most European constitutional democracies, especially after their imperialist adventures, as having been marked by "the transformation of the state from an instrument of the law into an instrument of the nation," thus making it possible to render stateless those who did not fit within a strong national design. Minorities now could be extruded, denied citizenship, and placed "outside the pale of law."[5] Unrecognized and unprotected, members of these groups, especially the Continent's Jews, had lost far more than their legal standing or their identities as, say, Hungarian or German or Austrian citizens, but, most important, their protected access to the Rights of Man; for without membership in a state, such standards, she argued, become both abstract and meaningless, and radical evil marked by human superfluity and homelessness, can triumph:[6]

> The conception of human rights, based upon the assumed existence of a human being as such, broke down at the very moment when those who professed to believe in it were for the first time confronted with people who had indeed lost all other qualities and specific relationships—except that they were still human. The world found nothing sacred in the abstract nakedness of being human. . . . If a human being loses his political status, he should, according to the implications of the inborn and inalienable rights of man, come under exactly the situation for which the declarations of such general rights provided. Actually, the opposite is the case. It seems that a man who is nothing but a man has lost the very qualities which

---

4. This was not an unfamiliar theme in this period, especially in light of the supra-national commitments of the Third Reich, the USSR, and still-extant European colonialism. For a contemporaneous discussion, see W. Friedmann, *The Crisis of the National State* (London: Macmillan & Company, 1943).

5. Hannah Arendt, *The Origins of Totalitarianism* (London: George Allen and Unwin, 1951), pp. 275, 277.

6. Arendt, *Origins*, pp. 299–300, 302.

make it possible for other people to treat him as a fellow-man. . . . The paradox involved in the loss of human rights is that such loss coincides with the instant a person becomes a human being in general.

An effective liberal state thus is the necessary, if hardly the sufficient, condition for a decent social, economic, and political life. In the absence of such a state, the table of institutions mediating, and protecting, relations linking states and their citizens cannot be set. Without such a state, an authentic plurality of interests and cultures promoted by political representation is supplanted by anti-liberal movements organizing masses on the basis of total, often unthinking, loyalty to national identities, causes, and regimes. In these circumstances, totalitarian elites make mobs out of the mass population who join with them to claim "to have abolished the separation between private and public life and to have restored a mysterious irrational wholeness in man."[7] The new illiberal polity is a state only in appearance, for at its core is not the set of routines, codes, or institutions that comprise a genuine state, but a party-movement and its myths. At the heart of such pseudo-states lie camps, terror, and secret police.

In the doleful context of such transformations, the United States stood out for the durability of its liberal regime. "With all its shortcomings," Arendt remarked, "America . . . knows less of the modern psychology of masses than perhaps any country in the world." Only in the United States, Polanyi observed, had the state constructed a "moat around labor and land, wider than any Europe had known."[8] Probing the character, durability, and elasticity of the American case to better understand how to cope with the widespread collapse of the pillars of liberal civilization on terms that might still secure human freedom thus became a pressing task for the political studies enlightenment. Such inquiries, however, demanded detailed knowledge of the United States and analytical tools neither Polanyi nor Arendt possessed. In a useful division of labor, the task of making sense of the globe's largest and most successful liberal state was undertaken by historians and social scientists who specialized in American politics and its liberal state, set in comparative perspective and charged by apprehension about its capacities and its fate.

II.

Two principal convictions braced this effort to understand the distinctive qualities of the American regime: the uncontested status of the basic contours of the

7. Arendt, *Origins*, p. 336.
8. Arendt, *Origins*, p. 316; Polanyi, *Transformation*, p. 202.

country's liberal order, and its exposed position. "Americans of all national origins, classes, regions, creeds, and colors, have something in common," Gunnar Myrdal asserted at the outset of his great study of the Negro problem and American Democracy, "a social *ethos*, a political creed. . . . a humanistic liberalism developing out of the epoch of Enlightenment" that, at once, is under challenge and stress by far more than an imperfection since, as he put it, the country's racial patterns of domination are "an integral part of, or a special phase of, the whole complex of problems in the larger American civilization."[9] The same year that Harold Lasswell published a study of liberal democracy and public opinion, arguing, in effect that democracy is justice, understood as "respect for human dignity pursued by majority rule," he published a deep dystopian warning that not just the totalitarian regimes but those with liberal polities like the United States risked becoming a 'garrison state' in which "the specialists on violence are the most powerful group in society," displacing "specialists on bargaining," thus rendering nugatory the actions of legislatures, the main site of liberal representation.[10]

Most famously, this recurring combination of assurance about the country's liberal hegemony and disquiet about the tradition's qualities and safety was articulated in Louis Hartz's historical account of *The Liberal Tradition in America*. He argued that the most important underlying force in American history, the standing and power of its political liberalism, had been constituted by the nonappearance of feudalism on American soil. By contrast to the embattled standing of liberalism in Europe, he claimed, in the United States this tradition is fixed and, in its innocence and safety, also dogmatic, even absolutist, in character. As a country without the fissures of class that struggles about feudalism had generated in Europe, the United States now had little room for fundamental conflict, competing ideologies, or moments of genuine self-reflection. There has been a good deal of visible conflict in American politics, but this noise can mislead us about its range and intensity. In the main, adversaries are distinguished by only relatively modest differences as they disagree about a comparatively narrow range of options. Lacking an adversary, he argued, the contractual, individualist, constitutional liberalism identified most closely with John Locke enjoyed free sway in the United States and possessed the power to snuff out non- and anti-liberal impulses of various kinds. Hartz admired this security but did not celebrate these uncontested limits on discourse and choice since the consequence of the hegemony

---

9. Gunnar Myrdal, *An American Dilemma: The Negro Problem and American Democracy* (New York: Harper and Row, 1944), vol. 1, pp. 3, 8, lxxvii.

10. Harold Lasswell, "The Garrison State," *American Journal of Sociology* 46 (January 1941): 455. The characterization of his views on democracy is drawn from David Easton, "Harold Lasswell: Policy Scientist for a Democratic Society," *The Journal of Politics* 12 (August 1950): 455.

of political liberalism, he believed, was a dangerous level of provincialism in a hazardous world. "Can a people 'born equal' ever understand peoples elsewhere that have to become so? Can it ever understand itself?"[11]

In the second half of the 1940s and the first half of the 1950s, two groups of multidisciplinary scholars—members of Columbia University's Seminar on the State and founders of modern policy studies teaching at Yale—led efforts by the political studies enlightenment to grapple with the qualities and insecurities of American liberalism by focusing on the environment, composition, processes, and policies of the country's state. As the 'wing' of the political studies enlightenment specializing in the United States, they differed in many respects from the Europe-oriented students of the origins of dark times. Unlike Polanyi and Arendt, who never entered their adopted country's academic mainstream despite appointments at Columbia, the New School, and the University of Chicago, Richard Hofstadter, David Truman, Harold Lasswell, Robert Dahl, and Charles Lindblom, the figures on whom I primarily concentrate, defined the very center of studies of American history and American politics at mid-century. Though contemporaries of Polanyi and Arendt (some were acquaintances), their tacit knowledge, empirical sensibilities, systematic research methods, limpid language, and American networks distinguished them as a group apart. Uncomfortable with philosophical abstraction, they preferred observation and induction. Also interested in reaching wider publics, they primarily addressed the research and teaching communities in their own fields. Thus, by contrast to their Europe-born colleagues, their work could seem parochial. Writing in an American idiom, addressing American audiences, deploying American literatures, and seeking to influence American understandings, their scholarship was enclosed to a far greater degree within the milieu of the United States. Their references, moreover, to the subjects Polanyi and Arendt frontally addressed, including the holocaust, total war, and totalitarianism, were more indirect, widely spaced, often elliptical.

Notwithstanding, the U.S.-focused members of the political studies enlightenment shared key sensibilities and ambitions, even some analytical proposi-

---

11. Louis Hartz, *The Liberal Tradition in America: An Interpretation of American Political Thought since the Revolution* (New York: Harcourt, 1955), p. 309. Earlier versions of the argument appeared in Louis Hartz, "American Political Thought and the American Revolution," *American Political Science Review* 46 (June 1952), and Louis Hartz, "The White Tradition in Europe and America," *American Political Science Review* 46 (December 1952). His deep concern about the lack of cosmopolitanism in the American liberal tradition and the dangers it posed as the country engaged with a heterogeneous globe was a theme to which he returned in Louis Hartz, "The Coming of Age in America," *American Political Science Review* 51 (June 1957).

tions with Polanyi, Arendt, and other émigré scholars who had sought to understand the origins of dark times. Writing during the second half of the 1950s, the journalist and sociologist Daniel Bell, a member of the Columbia Seminar, reflected on the political mood of the postwar period, especially the welcome fall by American scholars and activists "from a singular innocence about politics." Faced with depredation in the West on an unprecedented scale, they now were compelled to reconcile this desolation with the more mundane, civil politics of the United States where divergent issues and interests were reconciled and provisionally adjudicated inside a " 'liberal culture,' receptive to ideas, critical in its outlook and encouraging of . . . dissent."[12] To address these challenges and probe these questions, the Columbia and Yale groups sought to identify how the liberal state actually worked in order to better fortify its standing, deepen its capacity for self-examination, and improve its engagement with democracy. They were motivated to create political knowledge after the catastrophic and illiberal decades of devastation in order to discern means to guard and secure the best features of the West's patrimony. Their empirical scholarship assessed the globe's most assuredly liberal regime as soberly as Arendt and Polanyi had probed European politics, and they were equally concerned for liberalism's fate in a world of predators. Like the more explicitly philosophical and comparative members of the political studies enlightenment, the American group aimed to create scientifically credible but usable political knowledge.[13]

This chapter appraises their work. I first examine the Seminar on the State, underscoring the creative field tension stipulated by the its named purpose and the largely behavioral means of its member's enterprise. Focusing mainly on the contributions offered by Hofstadter, troubled by his discipline's innocence and by the skewed and insufficient content of American liberalism, and Truman, haunted by Weimar's fate and looming challenges based on deep inequality, I show how each, the leading historian and political scientist, respectively, of the postwar generation, wanted to accomplish no less than a vast reorientation of his field to create new forms of analysis appropriate to the challenges at hand.

---

12. Daniel Bell, *The End of Ideology* (New York: Free Press, 1960), pp. 307, 308, 314. Bell wrote these words in an appraisal of the political mood of the 1940s that pivoted on the writing of Dwight Macdonald and the journal, *Politics*, he edited from 1944 to 1949. In 1968, when these forty-two issues were reprinted, Hannah Arendt wrote the Introduction where she, too, self-identified as a radical searching for the root of things, thus echoing the remark of the young Marx. Hannah Arendt, "Introduction," *Politics, volume 1, 1944* (New York: Greenwood Press, 1968), p. iii.
13. This challenge has remained especially central to the work of Charles Lindblom. See, for example, his 1979 book, written with David K. Cohen, *Usable Knowledge: Social Science and Social Problem-Solving* (New Haven: Yale University Press, 1979); and his *Inquiry and Change: The Troubled Attempt to Understand and Shape Society* (New Haven: Yale University Press, 1990).

Common to both was a fierce commitment not only to a liberal political order but also to the value of civility and the rules within which conflicts could be permitted to appear without jeopardizing the dominant but vulnerable liberal regime. I then turn to Lasswell, Dahl, and Lindblom to assess the origins, and purposes, of modern policy studies. Lasswell and Dahl are 'hinge' figures. Like Truman, they determined the boundaries and content of postwar political science. Lasswell's scholarship on elites, political psychology, rhetoric, power, and decisions, and Dahl's on political parties, Congress and foreign policy, and democratic theory offered landmark contributions that serve as the backdrop to the manner in which they sought to create a normatively oriented yet scientifically capable set of tools with which to discern and orient public policymaking at a time of unprecedented emergency. At stake was how to link the values of Enlightenment to effective action without an undue sacrifice of liberty. Lasswell and Dahl were concerned, one might even say rightly obsessed, with the darkest possibilities imposed, as they wrote, by the Cold War and nuclear weapons. Both, too, developed analytical and programmatic statements (Dahl, with Charles Lindblom, an economist who had written on the role of unions as a threat to market-oriented capitalism and who later became celebrated for a reciprocal treatment of the distorting powers of business[14]) that could redefine what it meant to plan in a liberal political and economic order.

For all the differences in subjects, style, and manner that distinguish the highly individual writings of these scholars, they plaited a thick braid of ideas to which Polanyi and Arendt also could subscribe. In reviewing these achievements, I identify two misconceptions and a glaring omission. The first misunderstanding falls in the domain of intellectual history. This period is commonly thought to be a barren one for studies of the state. In standard chronologies, this moment corresponds to the disappearance of the state as a self-conscious concept and as an object of analysis in political studies. "Among contemporary social scientists," the young political scientist Frederick Mundell Watkins wrote in 1934, "it is a virtually unquestioned assumption that the state forms the basic concept of political science." His little book, *The State as a Concept of Political Science* counseled his colleagues to abandon the state to favor, instead, behavioral studies of action and power. Writing in 1968 as the author of the entry on "The State" in the *International Encyclopedia of the Social Sciences*, Watkins declared victory. The idea that political science begins and ends with the state, he announced, "no longer corresponds . . . to the theory and practice of contemporary political scientists." In this chronology, the moment of the political

---

14. Charles Lindblom, *Unions and Capitalism* (New Haven: Yale University Press, 1949); Charles Lindblom, *Politics and Markets: The World's Political-Economic Systems* (New York: Basic Books, 1977).

studies enlightenment corresponds to the disappearance of the state as a self-conscious concept and as an object of analysis in political studies. This view is wrong.

Unfortunately, the idea that the state was displaced as an object of analysis by behaviorism and thus exiled into political theory has become a truism. So, too, is the cognate understanding that the state has been recovered as an object of analysis only since the early to middle 1970s by scholars dissatisfied with the complacency and intellectual blinders of mainstream political science, sociology, and history and with the inability of these disciplines to anticipate or explain political turmoil.[15]

This perspective gained institutional force and legitimacy when the Social Science Research Council created a new research committee devoted to the theme 'States and Social Structures' in 1982.[16] The key word was 'state.' Utilizing the behavioral revolution in the social sciences as our target, the Committee urged an effort to revive studies focusing on the modern state's goals and capacities. Concurrently, though quite separately, another research orientation centered mainly in France, though with affinities to some strands of postbehavioral thinking in the United States, likewise sought to rescue studies of the state from the apparent innocence and superficiality of simple behaviorism as Jacques Donzelot and especially Michel Foucault, among others, began to publish studies of stateness which treated the state as the site of social power deployed to control civil society by constraining and governing mass populations. In the past two decades, each of these tendencies has secured considerable followings in the American academy. Nourished by the energy of large cohorts of graduate students and young scholars, each has broadened its scope and deepened its intellectual range.[17] The state, in short, has been brought back in, but based on a mistaken premise since the key figures in the political studies enlightenment

---

15. These, certainly, were the convictions I carried in my head when I earned a doctorate in history in the late 1960s and took up a post as an assistant professor of political science at Columbia in 1969. I identified with, indeed was excited by, what I then believed to be that moment's self-conscious efforts to restore the state to the core of political analysis. For a jaundiced view of this effort, arguing, in effect, that with the exception of a brief moment in early-twentieth-century pluralism, American political scientists never abandoned the notion of a sovereign state, possessing a great deal of autonomy, in transaction with the economy, civil society, and other states, see Gabriel A. Almond, "The Return to the State," *American Political Science Review* 82 (September 1988).

16. Peter Evans, Albert Hirschman, Peter Katzenstein, Stephen Krasner, Dietrich Rueschemeyer, Theda Skocpol, Charles Tilly, and I were its founding members.

17. There have been many offspring. A subgroup in political science, for example, calling itself American Political Development, forcefully has advanced historical and institutionalist efforts to understand the country's central state. Another instance is the venture advanced largely in Foucauldian terms to understand the particularities of the postcolonial state.

after the Second World War did place the state at the center of their scholarship, and they did so despite wide differences in style and subject as aspects of a single, coherent, powerful analytical agenda.

My revisionist intellectual history underscoring the tight linkage between studies of behavior, policy, and the state by members of the political studies enlightenment is not offered, however, simply as a corrective to defective histories of ideas. Scholarship about the state by the political studies enlightenment generation, I have come to see, is superior in important respects to the more recent neostatist effort which, rather credulously, has assumed that the stronger the state the greater the prospects for human welfare, and to efforts by Foucault and his followers to rethink the modern state in ways that unduly endanger its Enlightenment foundations.

In 1986, the Middle East specialist Leonard Binder, then at the University of Chicago, scolded the Social Science Research Council group seeking to 'bring the state back in' for having failed to connect analyses of the state to normative issues, especially to liberalism's values and goals. From a premise that "the original if not the chief problem of politics is the necessity of the state," Binder wrote that[18]

the task of comparative government is . . . to find ways and means of determining the degree of stateness that exists and to find out what difference it makes. Normally, if one is concerned with the values of security, material well-being, social order, risk-sharing, sociability, and culture, then one concludes that more stateness is better than less stateness. On the other hand, when one is more concerned with equality, freedom, justice, and self-esteem, one concludes that less stateness is better than more stateness.

Thus, he observed,

there are two, usually implicit, simple definitions of political development . . . The first defines it as an increase in stateness and the second as a decrease in stateness. It might be possible to define political development in yet a third way, that is, as the increase in the objective prevalence of all the values mentioned: equality, freedom, justice, security, material well-being, risk sharing, etcetera. To take this latter definition simply restates the dilemma as an internal contradiction, transforming an issue of value preference into a logical problem.

---

18. Leonard Binder, "The Natural History of Development Theory," *Comparative Studies in Society and History* 28 (January 1986): 4–5.

Making the problem of the state into "an internal contradiction" and "a logical problem," I believe, is precisely what political studies enlightenment work
on the state tried to accomplish. If this reading is persuasive, it would be per-
ilous to ignore their patrimony or to overlook their sensibility that history and social science "practiced by mature minds," as Richard Hofstadter put the point,
"forces us not only to be aware of complexity but of defeat and failure."[19]
The second misunderstanding believes the distance between speculative,
semi-philosophical, brooding texts like Hannah Arendt's *Origins of Totalitarianism* and systematic, doggedly empirical, social science treatises like David Truman's book, *The Governmental Process*,[20] both published in 1951, to be so great
that they inhabit separate universes. Not only does such a division impoverish
our intellectual resources, but it also misapprehends what both sought to
achieve in common despite their considerable differences in subject, style, and
method. After all, their efforts, and those by other members of the political studies enlightenment, to come to terms with desolation and the modern state were
similarly motivated and substantively complementary. We should learn to read
them, and works like theirs, together.
The members of the political studies enlightenment who addressed the state
overcame the stylized and limited 'American' and 'European' idioms characteristic of scholarship at the time they were writing. Often, the contrast between these
two modes was so great that even when scholars shared subjects and concerns
they could not communicate effectively, at least not without a great deal of trans-
lation. European scholars working on the sociology of knowledge, for example,
Robert Merton observed in 1949, evinced an interest in structures of knowledge,
ideas, and doctrines, focusing on their affinity to positions in the social structure,
while Americans studying public opinion and communications focused on aggre-
gates of information and mass belief, paying special attention to establishing the
facts and probing them reliably. "The European variant with its large purposes,"
he observed, "almost disdains to establish the very facts it purports to explain."
Conversely, "the American variant, with its small vision, focuses so much on the
establishment of fact that it considers only occasionally the theoretical pertinence
of the facts, once established. . . . The American talks about . . . more trivial matters in an empirically rigorous fashion."[21] By contrast, work by members of the political studies enlightenment, ranging from Arendt, arguably its most 'European'

---

19. Richard Hofstadter, *The Progressive Historians: Turner, Beard, Parrington* (New York: Knopf,
1968), p. 466.
20. David B. Truman, *The Governmental Process: Political Interests and Public Opinion* (New
York: Knopf, 1951).
21. Robert K. Merton, *Social Theory and Social Structure* (Glencoe: Free Press, 1949), pp.
443–444.

member, to Truman, arguably the most 'American,' declined these options. From Arendt to Truman, the political studies enlightenment situated rigorous, tightly reasoned social science inside theoretically organized macroscopic stories about large-scale patterns of structures and ideas.

If Arendt was concerned to understand Europe's descent into barbarism, Truman was anxious to prevent such a collapse in the United States. The concluding chapter of *The Governmental Process*, his landmark study of interest groups in American democracy, cautions about what he called "morbific politics," the archaic term first used in the seventeenth century to connote that which either is diseased or causes disease. "The existence of a going polity," he advised, "testifies to [its] present effectiveness . . . but it does not justify the projection of a present equilibrium into the indefinite future." Clearly bearing in mind the collapse of Weimar and Hitler's accession, Truman cautioned his American readers that "No political system is proof against decay and dissolution."[22] Liberal political systems, too, can break down when stark inequality in society comes to be married to insufficient or ineffective means of mass participation in regular politics. Weak links to the state can combine to erode faith in the character and legitimacy of the state and make the population vulnerable to mobilization by demagogues who question the basic and essential neutrality of the state.

Truman geared *The Governmental Process*, a study of interest groups in American politics, to understand how group politics and representative democracy could be made legitimate and stable, capable of holding its own against totalitarian options. Drawing on social anthropology, social psychology, and the work of early-twentieth-century American and English pluralist thinkers, most notably Arthur Bentley, he sought to make the group—which he understood as a unit of individuals in interaction with each other—rather than the individual alone or society as a whole the main unit of political analysis. Organized in four sections—"groups in the political process," "group organization and problems of leadership," "the tactics of influence," and a conclusion on "group politics and representative democracy"—Truman's book was written, much like the work of the late-nineteenth and early-twentieth-century English New Liberals such as T.H. Green and L.T. Hobhouse, to thicken liberalism by making its social analysis more realistic by becoming less simply individualistic. Arguing that the absence of "a consistent conception of the political role of interest groups, their functions, and the ways in which their powers are exercised" had been the result of the hegemony of nineteenth-century individualism, Truman sought to build a more realistic and capable political science in tune with his organizational age. Anticipating future work focusing on impediments to collective action, he identified various mechanisms to overcome these barriers, noting that

22. Truman, *Governmental Process*, pp. 516, 524.

"Among other influences greatly facilitating group formation are such major national efforts as a war mobilization or a collective attack upon problems of industrial depression. In recruiting the national resources for such emergency, the Government stimulates interaction throughout the nation."[23] Most important, he projected these moves in order to watch over the security of America's liberal regime by grounding a defense against a Weimar-style breakdown in a realistic account of what actually happens inside American politics, the globe's most important liberal, anti-totalitarian regime.

Indeed, it was Weimar's mix of the characteristics Juan Linz has identified as common to the end of democracy in numerous settings that not only haunted Truman and his colleagues but also underpinned virtually all the topics their Seminar on the State considered. These included, "unsolvable problems, a disloyal opposition ready to exploit them to challenge the regime, the decay of democratic authenticity among the regime-supporting parties and the loss of efficacy, effectiveness (particularly in the face of violence), and ultimately of legitimacy [that led] to a generalized atmosphere of tension, a widespread feeling that something has to be done . . . reflected in widespread politicization."[24]

Weimar, as well as its collapse and replacement by Nazi rule, Hannah Arendt, of course, had experienced first-hand. Like such fellow refugee scholars as Franz Neumann and Otto Kirscheimer, who attended Columbia's Seminar on the State, Arendt understood that Weimar had posed the question of whether and how a liberal democratic state can coexist with a fractured society and with social movements seeking to transcend them. Totalitarianism, she grasped, could not simply be dismissed as reprehensible, for both fascism and bolshevism offered up attractive, even exhilarating, alternatives to political liberalism under conditions of duress. Further, bolshevism's class state and nazism's racial state produced many new winners, and justified their advance with hypnotic rhetoric and ideology and by deploying policies of militarized economic mobilization which, in the context of capitalism's more general collapse, seemed to work.

Read this way, Arendt and Truman shared a common normative concern for the breakdown of liberal democratic regimes. They shared even more, an institutional analytic with which they sought to elaborate propositions about the linkages connecting citizens and the state that best could resist totalitarian racist and violent prospect.

When Arendt is read by empirically oriented political scientists, they tend to be so mesmerized by the speculative sweep of her argumentation and by her

---

23. Truman, *Governmental Process*, p. 55.
24. Juan J. Linz, *The Breakdown of Democratic Regimes: Crisis, Breakdown, and Reequilibration* (Baltimore: Johns Hopkins University Press, 1978), p. 75.

Heideggerian style that they usually miss her analytical motivation and intellectual underpinnings. They also fail to see, as I have noted, that she elaborated a good many specific 'social science' propositions about institutions, mechanisms, and behavior which she embedded as motoring causal mechanisms inside her attractively underdetermined configuration of the macro-situation. Often masked by her own language, which reflected her distaste for the conventional boundaries and style of hyper-positivist social science, Arendt in fact performed like a very good political scientist of comparative politics, elaborating claims and hypotheses which function, we have seen, as links connecting the elements she identified as the building-blocks of modern times to actual history in specific times and places.

When we read Arendt this way, we can see why and how David Truman's *Governmental Process* is the proverbial coin's tail to Arendt's head. She was keen to understand how modern constitutional liberal regimes and party systems had collapsed to produce totalitarianism. Meshing an underdetermined historical-structural account with specific propositions about behavior and institutions, she sought to secure a usable past to make a nontotalitarian future possible. Truman, by contrast, directed his attention inside the liberal state threatened from without to focus far less on its macroscopic constellation than on specific behavior and institutions within its ken. Arendt worried about whether and how the modern liberal state could survive in the face of totalitarianism in an era marked by catastrophe. So, too, did Truman.

The omission I seek to rectify follows from these misconceptions. The postwar generation understood, and showed how, the modern state provides the cord by which the Enlightenment and desolation are tethered, yet virtually no one today interested in the origins, history, character, institutions, activities, policies, personnel, lawfulness, legitimacy, and fate of modern sovereign states draws from the well of resources furnished by these members of the political studies enlightenment. This self-denial constitutes a missed opportunity to modify, shade, or offset the proclivity in the various neo-Weberian, neo-Marxist, and Foucauldian strands of work on the state in play today to underwrite the Enlightenment too innocently or traduce it unmercifully. We, too, could benefit from a new seminar focusing on the questions that concerned the seminar that gathered a half-century ago about the character and security of liberal states and their abilities to advance pluralism while coping with its perils; picking up where it left off: with the attempt to create a realistic, nonmetaphysical, institutional, and behavioral understanding of the practices and vulnerabilities of such states, all the while refusing to distinguish too tightly between scientific and normative analysis.

III.

The Seminar on the State was founded at Columbia University in 1945 as the successor to a short-lived Seminar on Bureaucracy.[25] In its first year, the discussion of bureaucracy continued, focusing on similarities and differences in bureaucratic forms and behavior in the United States, Nazi Germany, and the USSR. What is striking in reading the minutes is the robust role played by the dialogue between Merton and Franz Neumann, and how small was the gap in their sensibilities, questions, and concerns. Neumann, who had recently published *Behemoth*, the best extant study at the time on the Third Reich,[26] set the agenda at an early session by distinguishing three sets of issues: bureaucracy as institution; bureaucracy as a site of behavior; and bureaucracy and the problem of power. These foci—institutions, behavior, and power—remained the centerpiece issues for the next decade, setting American-style behavioral inquiry in the context of large-scale analysis of regimes and institutions central to the kind of inquiry written by Europeans like Neumann.[27] Merton similarly called for theories of the middle range; less abstract than grand theory, focused

---

25. For access to the minutes of these meetings and especially those of the Seminar on the State, on which I draw below, I thank the late Aaron Warner. The Seminar on Bureaucracy, though technically the precursor, tended to discuss texts and historical developments at some remove from current events. Gathering from early October 1944 to January 1945, among the topics it considered were Ptolemaic bureaucracy and standardization in ancient China. In doing so, however, members set these questions in the context of recent scholarship by Max Weber, John Dewey, and Harold Laski. Robert Merton and Arthur Macmahon, who attended regularly and soon became leaders of the successor Seminar on the State, habitually turned many of these discussions in the direction of contemporary issues.

26. Franz Neumann, *Behemoth: The Structure and Practice of National Socialism* (New York: Oxford University Press, 1942). An important collection of his writings is Franz Neumann, *The Democratic and the Authoritarian State*. Edited with a Preface by Herbert Marcuse (Glencoe: Free Press, 1957).

27. For a discussion by Neumann of the impact of the influx of European scholars into the social sciences in the United States, see Franz L. Neumann, "The Social Sciences," in Franz L. Neumann, et al., *The Cultural Migration: The European Scholar in America* (Philadelphia: University of Pennsylvania Press, 1953). Two other notable essays in this volume are Paul Tillich's "The Conquest of Theological Provincialism," and Erwin Panofsky's "The History of Art." On this subject, also see Hans Speier, "The Social Conditions of the Intellectual Exile," in Speier, *Social Order and the Risks of War: Papers in Political Sociology* (New York: George Stewart Publishers, 1953); H. Stuart Hughes, *The Sea Change: The Migration of Social Thought, 1930–1965* (New York: Harper and Row, 1975); and Anthony Heilbut, *Exiled in Paradise: German Refugee Artists and Intellectuals in America from the 1930's to the Present* (New York: Viking Press, 1983).

on particular subjects, committed to the consolidation of hypotheses and empirical claims, and capable of grounding comparative and normative evaluations.[28]

The first chair of the new Seminar, the political scientist Arthur Macmahon, a New Dealer, a specialist in public administration and American federalism, and a student of German affairs, explained to the Committee on Instruction in December 1946, that the meetings serve "as a clearing house of ideas. . . . Those in attendance," he wrote, "have included Brebner (History), Gellhorn (Law), Goldfrank (Mrs. Wittfogel, anthropologist), Macmahon (Public Law and Government), Merton (sociology), Mills (Sociology) Neumann (School of International Affairs), Schiller (Law), Solomon (substituting for Lynd in Sociology), Wittfogel (Director, Chinese History Project)." In addition to this early group, the Seminar's fluctuating membership in its first decade included political scientists Richard Neustadt, Herbert Deane, Julian Franklin, William T.R. Fox, David Truman, and Gabriel Almond (the latter visiting from Princeton); sociologists Daniel Bell and Seymour Martin Lipset; historians Walter Metzger, Peter Gay, and Richard Hofstadter. Substantively, their discussions covered a very wide range, as topics included civil-military relations, the impact of public policy on social mobility, the role of labor movements in capitalist countries, discussion of the structure of political parties, congressional voting behavior, social movements, theoretical models for the study of Communism, assessments of the American presidency, polling on McCarthyism, the role of elites in shaping public opinion, the psychological underpinnings of various forms of political ideology, the history of academic freedom, scholarship on the authoritarian personality, class analysis and the American Constitution, and leadership and image-making. There also were a good many discussions of new ideas and methodologies in social science, including considerations of the work of visitors like Harold Lasswell and local members, including Lipset, Hofstadter, and Almond.

The minutes record easy movement from discussions of social theory, as, say, in the work of Roberto Michels or Gaetano Mosca, to statistical methods appropriate to probe recent events, to big regime questions concerning liberalism and totalitarianism. The various papers and books written by members of the group tended either to consider the historical and empirical requisites of a successful liberal regime across the swath of American history or define a particular domain of American political life like interest group politics, public opinion, or the policy process and probe these to better understand how key elements of the

---

28. Robert K. Merton, *Social Theory and Social Structure* (Glencoe: The Free Press, 1949).

linkage between civil society and the state, the centerpiece of normative liberal theory at least since Locke, actually work in the United States. Further, each assessed these sites and processes for their contributions to the health and security of American liberal democracy.

Social science and history as fixed by Neumann, Merton, and their Seminar colleagues were marked by engaged social knowledge, and motivated by foreboding about threats to the liberal democratic polity. Throughout, the deliberations and debates in the group were charged by anxiety, concerned for the stability and capacity of liberal democracy in the United States.[29] Distressed by the implications of the defeated fascist model, by the vitality of communism abroad (and to a far lesser extent at home), by the growth of a strident authoritarian right-wing populism, and by the uncertain qualities of mass political participation, members of the Seminar sought to bolster and refresh political liberalism by harnessing their values to a theory-driven and realist notion of science, one, they believed, that required more than one disciplinary revolution.

They also searched for sustenance for such realism outside their disciplines' credulous and meliorist lineage. At Columbia, many were influenced by the noted critic and Professor of English, Lionel Trilling.[30] His critique of socialist realism in the humanities appealed for an "active literature," geared to deepen and thicken American liberalism to recall it "to its first essential imagination of variousness and possibility, which implies the awareness of complexity and difficulty." To this end, Trilling also had sought a new realism, including a realism of human personality and motivation, turning for these purposes to Proust and to Freud, among others, an orientation that stands out in this period amongst

---

29. These concerns, of course, were not limited to the Columbia setting. Other leading scholars, like the political sociologist William Kornhauser who feared the consequences of what he thought to be the growing atomization of America's population into an undifferentiated mass vulnerable to mobilization by undemocratic and demagogic elites, and like Samuel Stouffer and other students of public opinion who discovered very weak popular support for civil liberties, also took up just these themes. William Kornhauser, *The Politics of Mass Society* (Glencoe: The Free Press, 1959); Samuel Stouffer, *Communism, Conformity, and Civil Liberties.* (New York: Doubleday, 1955). David Truman favorably reviewed Kornhauser's book, saluting his building "upon a set of analytical discriminations that permit coming to grips with the problem of mass society without lapsing into misguided complacency or embracing a more beguiling romantic pessimism." Kornhauser, he noted, had combined the aristocratic critique of Ortega y Gasset, Karl Mannheim, and Walter Lippmann with what he described as the more democratic version of Hannah Arendt. David B. Truman, review of Kornhauser, *Political Science Quarterly* 75 (December 1960): 591, 592.

30. About the "major debt" to Trilling owed by Hofstadter and Mills, see Richard Gillam, "Richard Hofstadter, C. Wright Mills, and 'the Critical Ideal'," *American Scholar* 47 (Winter 1977–8): 84.

124 THREE

the Seminar on the State participants especially in work by Hofstadter on the right wing in America and on the dangerous aspects of populist reform.[31]

History, Hofstadter believed, must recommit to the challenge of deepening while defending the Enlightenment by extending its reach into the social sciences, projecting that "the next generation may see the development of a somewhat new historical genre, which will be a mixture of history and the social sciences," a development that would make scholars better prepared to "cope with certain insistent macroscopic questions . . . with wars and social upheavals, with the great turning points in human experience, still tantalizingly unexplained or half-explained, still controversial."[32] Only in this way, he believed, could American liberalism be reformulated and toughened. In parallel moves, Daniel Bell, looking to questions of status anxiety, David Truman, looking to understand group behavior, and Gabriel Almond, looking to comprehend the attractions of communism, turned to social psychology, anthropology, and sociological theory for intellectual provisions.[33]

---

31. For a thoughtful reading of this impulse, see Benjamin DeMott, "Rediscovering Complexity," *The Atlantic Monthly*, (September 1988). He observed that "Robert Merton, Richard Hofstadter, and Lionel Trilling (a sociologist, a historian, and a *littérateur*) were well known to one another; occupied the same base, Columbia University; attained commanding reputations in their respective professions at early ages; and shared an unexpressed yet momentous goal: emancipating American liberalism from naiveté." (p. 68). Arthur Schlesinger, Jr. *The Vital Center: The Politics of Freedom* (Boston: Houghton Mifflin, 1949), pp. 1, 8, 243, 256; Lionel Trilling, *The Liberal Imagination: Essays on Literature and Society* (New York: Harcourt, Brace, 1950), pp. 284, vii; Richard Hofstadter, "The Pseudo-Conservative Revolt," in Daniel Bell, ed., *The New American Right* (New York: Criterion Books, 1955); Richard Hofstadter, *The Age of Reform* (New York: Knopf, 1955).

32. Richard Hofstadter, "History and the Social Sciences," in Fritz Stern, ed., *The Varieties of History* (Cleveland and New York: Meridian Books, 1956), p. 370.

33. Bell, *End of Ideology*; Gabriel A. Almond, *The Appeals of Communism* (Princeton: Princeton University Press, 1954). Hofstadter averred that the scholarly ideal he wished to pursue was "that sympathetic and yet somewhat alien and detached appreciation of basic emotional commitments that anthropologists bring to simpler peoples." Hofstadter, "History," p. 363. This stance allowed Hofstadter both to be 'detached' yet engaged as a political intellectual grappling with key issues of his times. The impact of psychological work by Freud, Adler, and Adorno on Hofstadter "was exerted on Hofstadter largely through the mediation of men in other fields," especially Karl Mannheim and Harold Lasswell. Daniel Walker Howe and Peter Elliot Finn, "Richard Hofstadter: The Ironies of an American Historian," *Pacific Historical Review* 43 (February 1974): 8. David Truman commented on behavioral work "at the borderland of psychology, sociology, and anthropology" in his 1955 Brookings Lecture, "The Impact on Political Science of the Revolution in the Behavioral Sciences," in Stephen K. Bailey, et al., *Research Frontiers in Politics and Government: Brookings Lectures, 1955* (Washington, D.C.: The Brookings Institution, 1955), p. 211.

By the mid-1950s, the program underwritten by members of Columbia's Seminar on the State had made very considerable advances in connecting the conceptualization of political problems to empirical theory and systematic research methods. Thus when David Truman delivered his presidential address to the American Political Science Association in 1965 he had good reason to celebrate this history of scholarly regeneration and underscore the achievements accomplished in the postwar period.[34] After all, he and his colleagues had carried through the project of creating a *political* science and a *political* history concerned with the dangers of mass politics and the terms of political participation based on the conviction the country needed analytical history, sociology, and political science if it were to secure its liberal regime against external and internal adversaries.

In his retrospective, Truman asserted the claim that something new and distinctive had happened in the discipline during the previous two decades. His lecture assessed the attributes of postwar political science by deploying Thomas Kuhn's then fresh concept of the paradigm[35] to contrast "the restless searching that has marked the field since 1945" to the earlier discipline. Truman made a persuasive case for an epistemological break inside what ordinarily is considered the single period of the behavioral revolution. From the 1880s through the 1930s, he claimed, both the initial abstract formalism of political science *and* the subsequent turn to behavioralism had shared the optimistic, reformist faith characteristic of the Progressive era's innocent version of Enlightenment. Subsequent catastrophes mocked this vision. Even when up to date methodologically, political science had come to seem old-fashioned, even beside the point. In consequence, Truman argued, members of his own generation ("whether as professionals or as citizens") had come to doubt the "uncritical optimism" of this inheritance which bordered on the ridiculous in the face of the challenge posed by totalitarianism's "open and effective repudiation of the expectations and practices that underlay the implicit agreements of the profession." Further, Truman observed, the transplantation of academic scholars to Washington during the New Deal and Second World War and from Europe to American shores had dislodged their parochialism.

Truman was devastating about the generation of his teachers (taking care to exempt his own 'Chicago School' instructors as heralds of the postwar revolution). They had lacked a concern "with political systems as such, including the

34. David B. Truman, "Disillusion and Regeneration: The Quest for a Discipline," *American Political Science* Review 59 (December 1965).

35. Thomas S. Kuhn, *The Structure of Scientific Revolutions* (Chicago: University of Chicago Press, 1962).

American system, which amounted in most cases to taking their properties and requirements for granted"; they had possessed "an unexamined and mostly implicit conception of political change and development that was blandly optimistic and unreflectively reformist"; they had neglected theory and, with it, had deployed "a conception of 'science' that rarely went beyond raw empiricism;" and they had failed to place the American case inside "an effective comparative method."[36] By contrast, he claimed post-1945 political science no longer took the properties of the American political system for granted; and it effectively deployed theory, guided by comparison and a realistic political psychology, to better understand the promise and perils of political change.

This new discipline, Truman made clear, was defined by the conjunction of two elements that previously had been kept apart. The first of these was "a recommitment to science in the broad sense." By this he meant a positivist orientation that could move the work of the discipline "cumulatively toward explanation, toward establishing relations of dependence between events and conditions" by aspiring "to explanations of classes of events . . . subject to the controls of empirical evidence and with sufficient systematic power at least to place its findings beyond complete invalidation by the day's events."[37] But, he insisted, empirical studies must not be disinterested. Political science is a science of moral purpose and choice. Calling for a revival of the study of political thought as more than a polite gesture, Truman sought to incorporate its ethical and normative impulses as integral aspects of the discipline. Political scientists must not stop with description, however accurate, he urged, but learn to marshal their emergent empirical and predictive capacities to clarify and assess the "probable consequences of proposals and events for the system and for the values implicit in it."[38]

This combination was deployed by the archetypal landmark works of the period to self-consciously advance this program; not least Truman's own *Governmental Process*. Cool in tone, realist in orientation, and behavioral in epistemology, the book sought to build bulwarks against what he described portentously as "the possibilities of revolution and decay"[39] by describing how interest representation actually works and by identifying the institutional and ideological conditions required to keep American democracy stable and secure. Like other major works written from the later 1940s and the 1950s, including such later books as Robert Dahl's *A Preface to Democratic Theory* and V.O. Key's

36. Truman, "Disillusion and Regeneration," p. 866.
37. Truman, "Disillusion and Regeneration," p. 872.
38. Truman, "Disillusion and Regeneration," p. 873.
39. Truman, *Governmental Process*, p. 516.

Public Opinion and American Democracy,[40] Truman and his colleagues sought to show how various naive elements of prewar political science had restricted the discipline's ability to protect liberal democracy against the challenges of other regime types.

In parallel fashion, Richard Hofstadter, the star historian of the Columbia Seminar, insisted by way of an account of "The Founding Fathers" that the country badly needed another "Age of Realism," one also marked by an appreciation for how the dark side of human possibility might be restrained less by virtue than by effective analysis and capable institutional design.[41] A critic of the liberal tradition without infirming its validity[42] and made anxious by "the rudderless and demoralized state of American liberalism," he concluded *The American Political Tradition*, a series of sardonic, reappraising, anti-heroic portrait essays, the majority about presidents, published in 1948, by warning that it "would be fatal to rest content with [a] belief in personal benevolence, personal arrangements, the sufficiency of good intentions, and month-to-month improvisation."[43]

Like Truman, Hofstadter sought to transcend the innocence that marked pre–Second World War historical inquiry.[44] Much as Truman thought pre-1945

---

40. Truman, *Governmental Process*; Robert A. Dahl, *A Preface to Democratic Theory.* (Chicago: University of Chicago Press, 1956); Robert A. Dahl, *Who Governs? Democracy and Power in an American City* (New Haven: Yale University Press, 1961); and V. O. Key, *Public Opinion and American Democracy* (New York: Knopf, 1961).

41. Richard Hofstadter, *The American Political Tradition and the Men Who Made It* (New York: Knopf, 1948), chapter 1.

42. In this dual stance, Hofstadter anticipated the critical history of liberalism Hartz later produced. Hofstadter wrote a favorable review of Hartz's *American Liberal Tradition* for the *New York Times Book Review*, "Without Feudalism," February 27, 1955, p. 34.

43. Hofstadter, *Tradition*, pp. vii, 352. From one vantage, the book, as Elkins and McKitrick note, "had at the outset no grand design." After he had written a small number of essays, an editor at Knopf solicited more, enough to make a book, and then encouraged him to add an introduction. So "the book simply grew." But underneath it lay a strong intellectual *marxisant* substructure suspicious of bourgeois capitalism's impositions on the range and character of political choices as well as an affinity for the approach and values Karl Mannheim had announced in *Ideology and Utopia*, a theme to which I return more generally in this book's concluding chapter. Stanley Elkins and Eric McKitrick, "Richard Hofstadter: A Progress," in Elkins and McKitrick, *The Hofstadter Aegis: A Memorial* (New York: Knopf, 1974), p. 308; Karl Mannheim, *Ideology and Utopia* (New York: Harcourt Brace, 1936 [1929]).

44. "To describe the young Hofstadter as a passionate revolutionary would be wrong; to underestimate the intensity of his Marxist conviction or the degree of his disillusion would be no less mistaken." Daniel Joseph Singal, "Beyond Consensus: Richard Hofstadter and American Historiography," *American Historical Review* 89 (October 1984). An undergraduate radical at Buffalo in the 1930s who later joined the graduate student unit of the Communist party at Columbia University,

political science to have been too ingenuous despite the discipline's methodological advances, Hofstadter brought into question the patrimony of the Progressive historians Frederick Jackson Turner, Charles Beard, and Vernon Parrington whose focus on conflict he thought simple and parochial.[45] Writing from the left, Hofstadter nonetheless thought it important to correct their reverence for individual striving, small farming, and entrepreneurial competitive business which he judged vastly inadequate for the complex, urbanized, and tragic world he inhabited. "Those of us who grew up during the Great Depression and the Second World War," he recollected, "could no longer share the simple faith of the Progressive writers in the sufficiency of American liberalism. We found ourselves living in a more complex and terrifying world."[46] A meaningful liberalism, he insisted, must be shadowed by apprehension and capable of an understanding of interests, tradition, and psychology and confront the country's liberal consensus without complacency.

Recoiling from the kind of absolutism displayed by totalitarian thinkers and regimes and from that exhibited at home by evangelicalism and reformers who

---

Hofstadter became disillusioned and left the Party before the Hitler-Stalin pact of 1939. Later, he would identify himself as a "radical liberal," a realistic critic of liberalism but from the inside. Lawrence Cremin has observed that "Hofstadter's central purpose in writing history . . . was to reformulate American liberalism so that it might stand more honestly and effectively." Susan Stout Baker, *Radical Beginnings: Richard Hofstadter and the 1930s* (New York: Greenwood Press, 1985), pp. 89–90, 141–143; *Newsweek,* July 6, 1970, p. 19; Lawrence A. Cremin, *Richard Hofstadter (1916–1970): A Biographical Memoir* (Washington, D.C.: National Academy of Education, 1972), p. 8. Cremin rightly stressed Hofstadter's fierce commitment to free inquiry and liberal education, a subject about which he wrote quite a lot. See Richard Hofstadter and C. DeWitt Hardy, *The Development and Scope of Higher Education in the United States* (New York: Columbia University Press, 1952); Richard Hoftstadter, *Academic Freedom in the Age of the College* (New York: Columbia University Press, 1955); Richard Hofstadter and Walter P. Metzger, *The Development of Academic Freedom in the United States* (New York: Columbia University Press, 1955); and Richard Hofstadter, *Anti-Intellectualism in the United States* (New York: Knopf, 1963).
45. This break was later described by Hofstadter as "parricidal." Hofstadter, *Progressive Historians,* p. 299. For an earlier consideration, see Richard Hofstadter, "Beard and the Constitution: The History of an Idea," *American Quarterly* 2 (Autumn 1950). A useful discussion can be found in Charles Crowe, "The Emergence of Progressive History," *Journal of the History of Ideas* 28 (January–March 1966), which summarizes the main themes of the work of these historians as including a pragmatic orientation seeking to navigate between a simple empiricism and grand abstraction, the reduction of ideas to secondary status, presentism, epistemological relativism, a focus on economic and geographic variables, and a presentist emphasis on the social and moral utility of history. Crowe observed, anticipating Hofstadter, that "the violent and tragic events of this generation" have made the Progressive version of history seem "increasingly superficial and inadequate." (p. 123)
46. Hofstadter, *Progressive Historians,* p. xv.

were moral crusaders, Hofstadter insisted that enlightened liberalism also must
be capable of grappling with ambiguity and the impact of a pluralistic and differentiated milieu on its character and fate. Further, rather than focusing on how
Americans disagree, Hofstadter thought it important to grasp how what they
share can limit, and thus make more vulnerable, the country's liberal regime.
Even reformers, he insisted, had been contained within a rather cramped set of
possibilities, especially with respect to property rights. Thus, writing about what
he called a "democracy of cupidity," he observed that the "fierceness of political
struggles has often been misleading; for the range of vision embraced by the primary contestants has always been bounded by the horizons of property and enterprise." No alternative conception existed, he worried, despite the need at a
time "the traditional ground is shifting under our feet."[47] "The highest pitch of
understanding," he cautioned, " . . . is not likely to emerge in a climate of opinion where intense self-examination has not yet begun."[48]

Hofstadter, whose historical contributions took an exploratory form, rich in
suggestive hypotheses, was particularly concerned to secure political liberalism
in circumstances where "pastoral legends" had been overcome by "the com-
plexities of modern American life." Like Hartz, he was especially keen to understand how the left could invigorate political debate and incorporate new
groups into the polity in a setting that had truncated its reach and imagination.
"The side of the left in American political history," he noted,[49]

> — that is, the side of popular causes and reform — had always been relatively
> free of the need or obligation to combat feudal traditions and entrenched
> aristocracies. It had neither revolutionary traditions, in the bourgeois sense
> . . . nor proletarianism and social democracy of the kind familiar in all the
> great countries of the West in the late nineteenth century. . . . Because it
> was always possible to assume a remarkable measure of social equality and
> a fair minimum of subsistence, the goal of revolt tended to be neither social
> democracy nor social equality, but greater opportunities.

---

47. Hofstadter, *Tradition*, p. viii. This challenge to the progressive view of history was not pressed
hard here by Hofstadter. Rather, as John Higham has observed, "He delivered it as a casual after-
thought to a narrative revealing a fascinating variety of political types" that, read together, underscored not so much the uniformity as the shortcomings of the American liberal political tradition.
John Higham, with Leonard Krieger and Felix Gilbert, *History: The Development of Historical
Studies in the United States* (Englewood Cliffs: Prentice-Hall, 1964), p. 213.

48. Richard Hofstadter, "Charles Beard and the Constitution," in Howard K. Beale, ed., *Charles
A. Beard: An Appraisal* (Lexington: University of Kentucky Press, 1954).

49. Hofstadter, *Reform*, p. 10.

Ascribing these limitations to "failings in the liberal tradition," he worried that they had produced "a certain proneness to fits of moral crusading" potentially harmful to the best features of the 'liberal' dimensions of the liberal state. Now, "having been at last torn from . . . habitual security," the country no longer can enjoy "an innocence and relaxation now that totalitarianism has emerged."[50]

Although this period is sometimes remembered for self-satisfied social science and well-pleased consensus history, neither Hofstadter nor Truman, nor, for that matter, any of their Seminar on the State colleagues, was a contented apologist.[51] "A democratic society," Hofstadter wrote, "can more safely be over-critical than over-indulgent of its institutions and leaders."[52] Rather, the members of this group and the larger political studies enlightenment soberly appreciated the American political system's positive attributes but they never produced unqualified endorsements. At the hub of their work lay the understanding that liberal democracies risk breakdown unless political participation is anchored by effective, legitimate institutions. Individuals and groups do not and should not meekly go away between elections. Rather, they should be expected to express their dissatisfactions and fight for their interests. But these efforts could come to threaten liberal values if political participation were not managed and canalized in the zone between the state and civil society by appropriate institutional arrangements. "Consensus," Hofstadter wrote, "to be effective,

---

50. Hofstadter, *Reform*, pp. 15, 328, 22.

51. "Hofstadter's writing never degenerated," his student, Eric Foner, observed, "into the uncritical celebration of the American experience that characterized much 'consensus' writing." Eric Foner, "The Education of Richard Hofstadter," *The Nation*, May 4, 1992, p. 601. Similarly, writing about *The American Political Tradition*, Richard Gillam observed that "in an unpublished portion of his introduction" Hofstadter observed that "the possibility of a split between 'officialdom' and 'the people' is 'particularly dangerous in the modern era of corporate capital, international tension, centralized communications, and skilled propaganda. Perhaps never in history has there been a more compelling need for constant critical evaluation of those who hold power. One of the best guides to such evaluation is a cold appraisal of those who have held power in the past'." Gillam, "Hofstadter," p. 76. For a critical, on target, discussion of consensus history, see John Higham, "The Cult of the 'American Consensus': Homogenizing Our History," *Commentary* 27 (February 1959). Describing how "classes have turned into myths, sections have lost their solidity, ideologies have vaporized into climates of opinion," and the "phrase '*the* American experience has become an incantation," he asked, pointedly, "How did this larcenous seizure of pragmatic attitudes for the sake of a conservative historiography come about?" (pp. 93, 95). Higham, though, wrongly herded Hofstadter, along with Daniel Boorstin and Clinton Rossiter, whom he rightly placed there, under this umbrella. A fine overview of Hofstadter's intellectual life is provided by Paula Fass, "Richard Hofstadter," *Dictionary of Literary Biography*, vol. 17 (Detroit: 1983).

52. Hofstadter, *Tradition*, p. xi.

must be a matter of behavior as well as thought, of institutions as well as theo-ries."[53] Specifically, he and his colleagues thought it critical to deploy political institutions to produce publics rather than masses, a theme that appeared with particular force in the work of C. Wright Mills.[54] "In the absence of standard-ized means of participation," Truman cautioned in the concluding chapter of *The Governmental Process*, "movements of the fascist type" threaten to develop, especially under conditions of significant inequality.[55]

For these reasons, the members of the Seminar on the State sought to con-nect the lineage of basic questions about governance to a new science of politi-cal behavior and institutional design. This would be theory about the modern state of a new kind, neither exclusively "ethical in character" or solely "an at-tempt to describe the actual world,"[56] but both. More than an epistemological location, the new political science thus would make a substantive commitment to liberal and democratic theory and to the value of a polity based on reason and plurality at the intersection of institutions and behavior. Focusing on *The Gov-ernmental Process*, Truman's classic study of interest groups, we can see how the near-absence of the term 'state' in his writing as well as in the work of his Semi-nar colleagues must not be allowed to mislead us, for the state was present as a constitutive element in their books and articles in four key dimensions.

First, the Seminar on the State grasped the task of liberal guardianship. Throughout, their work was charged by anxiety for the fate of enlightened liber-alism, not by complacency. Possessing few illusions about the irreducibly vio-lent core all modern states possess, they sought to defend both civil society and the liberal state against brutality-prone totalitarianism. They rightly understood, as had Hannah Arendt, that the liberalism of Locke, the liberalism they be-lieved to be at the heart of the American model's alternative to totalitarianism, is more statist in key respects than totalitarianism. At issue in the battle between liberalism and totalitarianism was not whether the modern sovereign state—a state jealous of its sovereign prerogatives, organized in a distinctive ensemble of institutions, inclusive and coercive in its reach, and differentiated from other in-stitutional sites—should exist as much as who would control or tame it and for what purposes. The political liberalism with which Truman, Hofstadter, and their colleagues identified sought to hedge and contain the sovereign state, not do away with it. Modern totalitarianism, these scholars knew, also aimed to hold

---

53. Hofstadter, *Progressive Historians*, p. 457.
54. C. Wright Mills, *White Collar: The American Middle Classes* (New York: Oxford University Press, 1951); C. Wright Mills, *The Power Elite* (New York: Oxford University Press, 1956).
55. Truman, *Governmental Process*, p. 522.
56. Dahl, *Preface*, p. 1.

the reins of the state, but differently, by using the instruments of antiliberal ideologies and mass movements.

"The great political task now as in the past," Truman concluded, "is to perpetuate a viable system." To this end, like Hofstadter who had focused on political leadership, he believed that a political class of politicians, leaders of interest groups, journalists, academics, and others engaged actively in political influence, were required to play a pivotal role. "In the future as in the past, they will provide the answer to the ancient question: *quis custodiet ipsos custodes?* Guardianship will emerge out of the affiliations of the guardians." This was a task of obligation and accountability.[57]

Second, as liberal democrats and as institutionalists, the members of the Seminar on the State also committed themselves to a particular kind and level of theory. Unlike their disciplinary antecedents in history and political science, they insisted on the requirement of theory. "The non-theoretical bias of the earlier agreement within the discipline," Truman observed, "thrust the study of political thought out of the mainstream and retained it largely as a gesture toward polite learning." This "philistinism" was worse than regrettable. It had narrowed the discipline and had cut it off from the succor work on political regimes from Aristotle through Locke and Mill could provide.[58]

More than an epistemological location, the approach to the state by the 'American' variant of the political studies enlightenment made a substantive commitment to liberal and democratic theory at the intersection of institutions and behavior. Taking the largest, constitutional regime rules for granted as stable givens, they sought to understand the systematic mutual impact of institutional arrangements on behavior and behavior on institutions in directing political participation and shaping political norms. Constitutional arrangements usher individuals and groups into the political process; once there, these patterning plans become permissive but are not determinative. Accordingly, political scientists must attend to the junction located between these grand regime features and political action, a space filled by institutions understood both as congeries of rules and as formal organizations.[59]

Third, their concern for the security and continuity of liberal political regimes and their assumption of a custodial role directed their work to the state as the site of political representation. The notion of representation, the political theorist Hannah Pitkin has pointed out, connotes making present inside the state the preferences, perspectives, and interests of members of civil society

57. Truman, *Governmental Process*, pp. 524, 535.
58. Truman, "Disillusion and Regeneration," p. 873.
59. Truman, *Governmental Process*, p. 522.

which otherwise would be absent.[60] It invites social and cultural plurality to come inside the confines of the state. It is oriented to securing the gains to liberty that come with the separation of the state from civil society without paying the price of a wholly autonomous state.

Rather than imagine a singular public or a fragmented mass, Truman insisted on the segmentation of the population into groups sharing similar views about specific matters under consideration. "The public is always specific to a particular situation or issue." Such publics seek influence through organization. The main vehicle is the interest group, which he understood not in terms of *a priori* categories such as those of class or gender but in terms of behavior and interaction. "An interest group," he wrote, "is a shared-attitude group that makes certain claims upon other groups in the society. If and when it makes its claims through or upon any of the institutions of government, it becomes a political interest group." Truman's liberal democracy is an arena for the competitive play of these groups, not for the discovery of a common public interest. What keeps this system stable is the mechanism of overlapping memberships. The population does not divide along fixed lines. The system comes to be moderated because individuals are not wholly absorbed into any specific group and because they usually belong to multiple groups. They have compound identities, a complex array of interests, and many pathways and different degrees of participation.[61]

This institutionalized competition of minorities, however, leaves the liberal regime vulnerable, Truman observed, because it is not self-equilibrating. Its stability requires two additional conditions: broadly shared values about the rules of the political game, especially civil liberties, and actors sufficiently committed to these values and the institutional arrangements which embed them. Legitimate norms and institutions are Truman's necessary conditions for a steadfast and legitimate polity. He insisted that the institutional mechanism of overlapping membership on which he relied cannot cushion the political order at times of crisis caused by "disturbance in established relationships" unless the liberal rules of the game are widely supported by the population as a whole.[62] But this condition, he cautioned, cannot be taken for granted. Mass support for the values of liberal democracy is not a given. The population may be mobilized by demagogues to become an illiberal mass; or it may withdraw its support from liberal norms at key moments of change and stress.

---

60. Hannah Fenichel Pitkin, *The Concept of Representation*. (Berkeley: University of California Press, 1967).

61. Truman, *Governmental Process*, pp. 219, 37.

62. Truman, *Governmental Process*, p. 511.

Fourth, this approach to the state might be called transactional because it is concerned with the institutions which pattern exchanges between the state and civil society in liberal regimes such as voting and elections, public opinion and interest group activity, journalism and communications, just the subjects the Seminar on the State regularly considered. Writing from this perspective, Truman made the ways in which interactive groups sharing political dispositions and interests intersected with the national state via public opinion, elections, and especially the legislative process the hub of his analysis of American democracy. "The activities of political interest groups," he noted, "imply controversy and conflict, the essence of politics," but inside a representative regime these conflicts can be contained because political institutions embody and operate by well-supported, legitimate, liberal rules of the game. By contrast to the constitutional democracies that had collapsed in interwar Europe, in the United States he expected "such changes as occur in the basic relationships that characterize the American governmental process will be gradual, slight, and almost imperceptible." As a result, "confidence in gradual adaptation assumes that the system will not so operate as to produce domestic or international disasters that will result in its being completely discredited." Still, he felt compelled to add, "Of this there can be no certainty."[63]

Quite clearly, the Seminar on the State did not abandon the state as its object. What its members did think, though, is that the liberal state is studied best in these distinct aspects rather than as a single, jumbo concept. Such a covering term—The State—they believed, is far too bulky as an instrument to parse and understand politics *inside* a liberal regime, like the American, marked by highly differentiated institutions and complex terms of transaction between the state and its citizens. By making the study of the state realistic and behavioral, inside an institutional frame, the Seminar helped demystify the state as an inclusive normative and metaphysical construct signifying common, collective interests transcending particularity. Its members pursued this task by showing how rules and institutions rather than unitary interests or a singular political culture could serve to integrate their diverse and fractious country.

IV.

The Columbia Seminar primarily probed two sets of questions: how liberal assumptions, institutions, and rules structure and limit the contours of American politics, and how citizens and their leaders shape the political process through their participation in interest groups, elections, political parties, and expressions

63. Truman, *Governmental Process*, pp. 502–503, 506, 512, 534, 535, 524.

of opinion. Lasswell, Dahl, and Lindblom undertook a complementary task, one that required the invention of a new historical, contextual, problem-solving, multi-method orientation to public policy that they wished to deploy to reinforce the soundness and steadiness of the country's liberal state. They understood that any simple model characterizing benevolent actors who search in disinterested fashion for effective policy instruments in order to govern in the public interest is hopelessly sanguine. Seeking to build bulwarks to counter illiberal alternatives via policy studies as part of the period's larger systematic effort to protect and defend the offspring of the Enlightenment, they treated the activities of government to regulate the economy and society as causes, not just as effects.

The scholarship they produced can be distinguished from prior efforts to analyze and recommend public policies by its broader scope and terms of reference, and by its more pointed motivation. When Lasswell retrospectively summed up "the policy orientation of political science" in 1967 at India's Patna University in 1967, he identified the two acts practiced by policy scientists—"understanding the policy process itself" and "locating and feeding knowledge . . . into the policy process"—as central aspects of what, referring to the Enlightenment, he called "the recovery of a great tradition rather than . . . a radical deviation from it." Policy studies, he continued, should advance the values of enlightened reason and secular control to defend liberal democracy against predacious adversaries. Public policy studies and liberal democracy, he stressed, are mutually dependent; for just as "the non-dogmatic, exploratory, systematic study of policy," he wrote, "evidently depends in our day on the continuation of a society whose structure is effectively pluralistic," so, he also believed, liberal democracy itself must be buttressed by systematic studies of public policy.[64] Likewise, Robert Dahl and Charles Lindblom insisted that the choice of particular social techniques to underpin rational social action to make policy to solve problems should be guided, and evaluated, by the contributions they make to the achievement of the key Enlightenment values they enumerated as "freedom, rationality, subjective equality, security, progress, and appropriate inclusion."[65]

The idea of a policy science, one reviewer of Lasswell's work observed, "is not a new one."[66] In part, of course, this suggestion is compelling. Policy is a congested term. Its etymology links it to civil administration and government, to

---

64. Harold Lasswell, *The Policy Orientation of Political Science* (Agra: Lakshmi Narain Agarwal), 1971, p. 7.

65. Robert A. Dahl and Charles E. Lindblom, *Politics, Economics, and Welfare: Planning and Politico-Economic Systems Resolved into Basic Social Processes* (New York: Harper, 1953), p. 28. In a footnote, they record that the values they enumerate are affiliated with "a list by Harold D. Lasswell, *Power and Personality*. W.W. Norton and Co., New York, 1948." (p. 28)

66. Paul Kecskemett, "The 'Policy Sciences': Aspiration and Outlook," *World Politics* 4 (July 1952): 520.

citizenship, to refinement and polish, to registers and record-keeping, to the regulation of internal order. In modern usage, public policy refers to the confluence of two elements: the 'policing' activities of governments and the creation of knowledge about these mechanisms of transaction.

The very existence of public policy in these modern senses can be traced to sixteenth- and seventeenth-century post-feudal Europe when the accumulation and concentration of sovereignty by national territorial states distinguished these forms of rule from their medieval predecessors by claiming unique authority within their borders and by recognizing boundaries demarcating other state units. This consolidation of sovereignty to particular kinds of increasingly centralized units produced a standardization of laws, coinage, taxation, language, and responsibility for security, all of which were requisites for systematic public policy. A corollary process was a growing set of structural separations within national boundaries distinguishing the realms of sovereignty, property, and civil society. With this unprecedented differentiation, states could not simply impose their will despotically. Instead, they had to create and deploy policies to transact and coordinate with other, 'private,' powerholders. State–society relations became more reciprocal, and public policy came to be synonymous with the outputs of governments seeking to act within and regulate this increasingly complex environment.

Producers of modern policy knowledge were those intellectuals who came to understand and manage these new sets of transaction. Such policy intellectuals, after Machiavelli, created a modern science of government with two main ends: to point rulers toward more effective transactions among the state, economy, and civil society, and to police, educate, and civilize the population in order to improve its character and render it more rational and governable.

The late-eighteenth-century democratic revolutions in Europe and North America, nineteenth-century industrialization under market capitalist auspices, and the creation of new institutions for the invention and dissemination of knowledge in the late nineteenth and early twentieth century, including the modern, discipline-based, research university, vastly altered the scale and complexity of policy activities by sovereign states as well as the provenance, scientific character, and organization of policy knowledge.

To be sure, there have been very different configurations of policy practices and ideas over the course of the past half-millennium, including, in the twentieth century, totalitarian ones. Lasswell and his colleagues sought to rescue and advance those policy options that value modernity's divisions among state, economy, and society as the first guarantor of liberty and rest on a bedrock of toleration and citizen rights which are not contingent on the give and take of day to day politics. Enlightened public policy they understood to be a distinctive subset of modern public policy.

Before the development of systematic social science, the pride of place in social analysis had belonged to the moral sciences entwined with classical political economy. Over the course of the nineteenth century, into the twentieth, this
integrated social knowledge was replaced by professionalized, discipline-based
attempts to grapple with the specific tensions inherent in the elaboration of
markets and citizenship in liberal societies. The central issue was how to shape
the state's interventions to make markets function effectively and to make their
distributional effects tolerable. From the perspective of transactions between
states and citizens, at issue was the balance between freedom and domination.

By the end of the nineteenth century, the gentlemen generalist historians
and lawyers who had produced policy knowledge had become archaic figures.
These "all-rounders" were steadily supplanted, on the one side, by academic
scholars in specialized social sciences, and, on the other side, by a growing body
of policy specialists who claimed knowledge that both drew upon and crossed
over the boundaries that divided the social sciences. Labor experts, social workers, organizers of social surveys, public administration specialists, reformers
concerned with social policy, and intellectuals within social movements and
political parties—both inside and outside the administrative apparatuses of
states—tried to come to grips with the intensification of the 'social problem' inherent in interactions among states, citizens, and markets. These policy intellectuals were a novel and distinctive breed. Their main orientation was not to
the social science disciplines as such; nor were they amateur seekers after a science of legislation in the manner of their mid-nineteenth-century predecessors.
Generalists continued to lead the civil service and go for careers in politics and
journalism; but increasingly, the choices they had to make were defined for
them by the specialist policy intellectuals who adopted the language of public
administration and social engineering. The central concern of these policy intellectuals was how to build a state capable of dealing with the unintegrated
poor and the challenges of increasingly assertive working classes both as economic actors and as weakly incorporated citizens. They sought to provide the
state not only with institutional prescriptions, but also with instrumental tools
such as labor statistics to contribute to the management of these tensions and
demands.

In the face of the thirty-year crisis confronting western civilization following
the outbreak of the First World War, this policy legacy, however powerful, Lasswell and his colleagues believed, had become woefully inadequate, for a radically new situation was at hand. We have already seen how, in 1941, Lasswell
had identified a new form of rule, the 'garrison state,' cutting across the liberal-
totalitarian antinomy. The maturation of total war as a concept after the First
World War, he feared, utterly had transformed not just the technology of war-

fare and the mobilization of production and propaganda, but the very character
of the state itself, even in liberal democracies. "With the socialization of danger
as a permanent characteristic of modern violence the nation becomes one uni-
fied technical enterprise." In such circumstances, he anguished, "what democratic values can be preserved, and how?"[67]

A year later, the lawyer and sociologist David Riesman took up this theme by
considering "civil liberties in a period of transition." The traditional distinction
between normal and special times had become obsolete. "It is unrealistic," he
cautioned, "to rely on sharp distinctions between war and peace to test the limits of civil liberty" for "today, it is 'peace' which is anomalous, not war." He presciently predicted "that after this war (which may last for many years), it is most
unlikely that we can, or even if we can that we will want to, return to 'normalcy'." Liberalism must be rethought in this context of permanent uncertainty
and mobilization to discover by way of "affirmative governmental action . . .
where an aggressive public policy might substitute new liberties for the vanish-
ing liberty of atomistic individuals." Like the Seminar scholars who, likewise,
were haunted by Weimar's collapse, Riesman concluded with a charged warning about fascism in America: "Like a flood, it begins in general erosions of traditional beliefs, in the ideological dust storms of long ago, in little rivulets of
lies, not caught by the authorized channels."[68]

Facing these pressures, the inventors of modern policy studies in the period
following the Second World War shared a keen sense of responsibility not only
for the fate of the United States, but for liberal democracy more generally. Concluding their extended consideration of the instruments of policymaking in liberal democracies, Robert Dahl and Charles Lindblom appended a postscript
that asserted the continuing appeal and viability of the faith of "Western man
. . . in his capacity for controlling his environment through observation and reason." Classical liberalism embracing the goals of "rational control over governments through democracy and rational control over 'economic' affairs through
capitalism," and classical socialism, holding "that man's rational control over
both government and 'economic' affairs could be vastly strengthened by gov-

67. Lasswell, "The Garrison State," pp. 459, 467. The applicability of Lasswell's model to the
American case has been controversial. There are important Lasswellian strands in the argument
developed by C. Wright Mills, *The Power Elite* (New York: Oxford University Press, 1956), which
places the military as one of three institutions whose leaders are at the pinnacle of American
power. For influential critiques of Lasswell and Mills, respectively, see Aaron Friedberg, "Why
Didn't the United States Become a Garrison State?," *International Security* 16 (Spring 1992); and
Daniel Bell, "Is There a Ruling Class in America? *The Power Elite* Reconsidered," in Bell, *The
End of Ideology.*
68. David Riesman, "Civil Liberties in a Period of Transition," in Carl J. Friedrich and Edward
S. Mason, eds., *Public Policy* 4 (1942): 47, 46, 45, 51, 93, 90, 96.

ernmentalizing economic affairs," had both been found wanting in the emergency decades since the Second World War. "But the core that is identical to both," which "seems to us to be a threefold belief in the desirability of extending freedom as far as it is possible to do so, in accepting the equal value of each individual in his claim to freedom, and in the possibility of achieving progress in extending freedom and equality through man's capacity for rational calculation and control," is still valid. Writing in italics, they underscored how "A central assumption of this book is that, despite all that has happened, the central core of belief is still viable."[69] In its service lie the means to make policy they sought to identify over the course of the prior 500 pages.

V.

They, and Lasswell, put particular emphasis on future policy ventures in the United States in pursuit of these ends because only there, at war's end, was there sufficient human capital and enough open political space to convene and advance the task of discovering policy instruments which could sustain a worthy political realm. "It will be recalled," Lasswell observed, "that so far as Europe was concerned the social sciences were among the casualties of the first World War, of the subsequent rise of Nazism in Germany and of the devastation wrought by World War II. The great French initiatives in the social sciences, associated with the name Durkheim, for instance, suffered gravely. The maturing social science of Germany, exemplified in the work of Max Weber . . . emigrated to the United States where a relatively open and productive society was able to provide a congenial environment."[70]

The kind of policy studies advocated by these scholars thus abjured a relativism of values. Grounded firmly in the Enlightenment, it sought to advance inquiry that could discover scientific means to promote desired ends. In the first period of his work in the 1930s at the University of Chicago devoted to advancing a new behavioral science of politics, Lasswell had distinguished radically between science and norms. Opening *Politics: Who Gets What, When, and How*, probably his best-known and widest-read book, he defined the "study of politics [as] the study of influence and the influential. The science of politics states conditions; the philosophy of politics justifies preferences. This book, restricted to political analysis, declares no preferences. It states conditions."[71]

---

69. Dahl and Lindblom, Politics, pp. 511–526.
70. Lasswell, *Policy Orientation*, p. 7.
71. Harold Lasswell, *Politics: Who Gets What, When How* (New York: McGraw Hill, 1936), p. 3.

In an insightful review of Lasswell's writing, David Easton took note of how, over time, and certainly by the late 1940s, Lasswell had relinquished this radical distinction between facts and norms. "In the first phase he was reluctant as a social scientist to state that he preferred one political system or set of goals to another. In the second phase, on the contrary, he believes passionately that the social sciences are doomed to sterility unless they accept the contemporary challenge and say something about our ultimate social objectives." In the first, prewar, period, Lasswell "was concerned solely with the development of a purely scientific, objective science of politics. Adhering to the Weberian tradition, he maintained that values lay beyond the margin of the social scientist *qua* scientist."[72] In his quest for a realistic political science during this term, Lasswell primarily focused on elites and power and directed his efforts to show how the marxist faith that class divisions could ultimately be transcended is an impossible utopia. Even more, basing his observations on Europe as well as the United States, he thought it to be the case that the imperative of elitist hierarchies ruled out the realistic possibility of democracy based on majority rule. Guided by the intellectual program of Pareto, he increasingly focused on studies of the composition and behavior of elites of various kinds. Indifferent to liberal and democratic values, he thus was able to ignore the tacit illiberal implications of his orientation and research designs which conceded as fact just that which Mannheim, Arendt, Polanyi most feared: a division of society into an effective governing elite and an atomized mass, often subject to the manipulation of symbols and mechanisms of persuasion.[73]

During and just after the Second World War, as he came to terms with the period's desolation, Lasswell's views underwent a sea change. His writing came to lose some of its detached, scientific aura. Now he was cautioning that it had become "painfully obvious that the whole trend of history can change and freedom and mobility can be wiped out," and "a vigorous reappraisal of . . . doctrine" was imperative. With a scarcity, under such conditions, of "intellectual resources of high quality," challenges to the liberal tradition had become especially pressing, and a new conscious organization of

---

72. Easton, "Lasswell," pp. 451, 459. In addition to Easton's fine overview, I also have been influenced in my reading of Lasswell by Richard M. Merelman, "Harold Lasswell's Political World: Weak Tea for Hard Times," British Journal of Political Science 11 (October 1981). The 'weak tea' in his title refers to Lasswell's policy science; with this characterization I disagree, as will be clear below.

73. This view can be found as early as Harold Lasswell, *Propaganda Technique in the World War* (New York: Knopf, 1927); and Harold Lasswell, *Psychopathology and Politics* (New York: Viking, 1960 [1930]).

inquiry to promote and protect liberal democracy had become the central project of the day.[74]

Writing in these charged circumstances, Lasswell's turn was marked by two simultaneous shifts. Rather than assume an elite-mass model as a given, he now understood that its very existence was what is most at stake in the study of power; hence he turned from the study of elites and their tools to the study of decisions, leaving open the nature and scope of the relevant participants. Liberal democracy now was put on an agenda of possibilities where, earlier, it had been set aside, at least implicitly, as hopelessly naïve. At issue was what Truman had called the governmental process: "It is evident," Lasswell now insisted, "that we cannot properly decide whether democratic government prevails in a given nation until we have examined the nature of the process by which the most influential decisions are made."[75] Later, of course, it was Dahl, in *Who Governs?*, who made just this focus on decisions the central hallmark of his study of power in New Haven.[76]

Concomitantly, Lasswell now was able to inquire not only about who ruled but also how citizens can come to control and limit what their rulers do, including the public policies they choose to adopt. If, in his early work, the people had been excluded *a priori* from power, now he celebrated democratic prospects, observing that "Democratic leadership is selected from a broad base and remains dependent upon the active support of the entire community. With few exceptions," he added, in a rather pollyanish turn, "every adult is eligible to have as much of a hand with the decision-making process as he wants and for which he is successful in winning the assent of his fellow citizens." In a stunning turnabout, he concluded that "the elite of democracy ('the ruling class') is society-wide."[77]

He then stated his values—"the progressive transformation of human society into a free man's commonwealth"—and oriented policy studies to achieve their realization by "providing a rational basis for the expansion of democratic science and policy," which he described "as part of the enlightenment process in society . . . designed to free mankind of suicidal illusions about the 'inevitability' of freedom by catastrophe."[78] By the late 1940s, Lasswell was counseling how a "developing science of democracy" must learn to "integrate science, morals, and politics," a far cry from his earlier value-free approach and one much closer to that of Karl Mannheim, who edited the series in England in which Lasswell

---

74. Harold D. Lasswell, " 'Inevitable' War: A Problem in the Control of Long-Range Expectations," World Politics 2 (October 1949): 29, 25.

75. Harold Lasswell, *Democracy Through Public Opinion* (Menasha, Wisconsin: George Banta Publishing, 1941), p. 11.

76. Robert A. Dahl, *Who Governs? Democracy and Power in an American City* (New Haven: Yale University Press), 1961.

77. Harold Lasswell, *Power and Personality* (New York: Norton, 1948), pp. 109–110.

78. Lasswell, *Power and Personality*, pp. 222, 221, 217.

published *The Analysis of Political Behaviour*.[79] "The developing science of democracy, within which he placed the study of public policy, he wrote,[80]

> is an arsenal of implements for the achievement of democratic ideals. . . .
> Without knowledge, democracy will surely fall. With knowledge, democracy may succeed. The significant advances of our time have not been in the discovery of new definitions of moral values or even in the skilful derivation of old definitions from more universal propositions. . . . The advances of our time have been in the technique of relating them to reality. In the process, science has clarified morals. This, indeed, is the distinctive contribution of science to morality. Science can ascertain the means appropriate to the completion of moral impulse — means at once consistent with the general definitions of morality and compatible with the fulfillment of moral purpose.

It was just this double-barreled substantive change and normative widening that underpinned Lasswell's turn to the policy sciences as instruments to guard and extend the tradition of enlightenment. His own shifts in attention and emphasis signified that he believed it was possible, indeed necessary, to simultaneously open new paths to the study of political behavior and to the study of policy, with both in service to enlightened liberal democracy.[81] Addressing the American Political Science Association as its President, in 1956, he would issue a call for his colleagues to reject "passivity" and "bear upon [their] puny shoulders the burden of culpability for the situation of the world today." The main tasks for political science could not escape the necessity of disciplined and engaged work on public policy to advance preferred values. Identifying the main job as that of clarifying those normative purposes and "originating policy alternatives by means of which goal values can be maximized," he called for studies of the liberal state to provide "a true center of integration where normative and descriptive frames of reference are simultaneously and continuously applied to the consideration of the policy issues confronting the body politic as a whole over the near, middle, and distant ranges of time."[82]

---

79. Harold Lasswell, The Analysis of Political Behavior: An WEmpirical Approach (London: Kegan Paul, Trench, Turbner, 1947), p. 1.
80. Lasswell, Political Behaviour, p. 1.
81. This "transformation in Lasswell's frame of reference," Easton has observed, "transcends in its significance the personal meaning it may have for him alone or even the importance it may have for contributing to a new approach to the empirical study of political power." Easton, "Lasswell," pp. 475–476.
82. Harold Lasswell, "The Political Science of Science: An Inquiry into the Possible Reconciliation of Mastery and Freedom," *American Political Science Review* 50 (December 1956): 968, 965, 972, 978, 979.

Across the divide between his work before and after the shocks of the Second World War, Lasswell was concerned with challenges to the survival of western constitutional democracy and liberal values, including defective personality structures, self-defeating symbolism, modern propaganda, and the rise of elites of skill, including elites expert in force. Well before his frontal engagement with desolation, he had been aware of the fragility of liberal states, having seen fascist movements and regimes first-hand in visits to Germany, Italy, and France in the 1920s, and never quite as confident as most of his American colleagues at the time in the future of liberal democracy. But now, in the late 1940s and early 1950s, these concerns had become preoccupations. If there were answers and remedies, he counseled, these must lie in powerful and reflexive studies of public policy.

In 1951, Lasswell and Daniel Lerner published the fruits of a major conference supported by the Carnegie Corporation that convened a who's who of American social science, including Kenneth Arrow, Edward Shils, Paul Lazarsfeld, Robert Merton, and Clyde Kluckhohn, to review and codify gains made by the policy sciences during and after the Second World War "in order to cope with the gigantic crises of our time."[83] Lasswell's agenda-setting essay, "The Policy Orientation," opened the collection these scholars produced. Situating the new challenges to policy squarely in the context of "the consequences of depression and war," and "the continuing crisis of national security," by which he meant far more than geopolitical conflict with the Soviet Union, Lasswell advanced the significance of a multidisciplinary effort based in the social sciences to advance rationality and improve human choice. Substantively, he promoted a problem-centered focus on "fundamental problems," located on a higher and more demanding plane than mere technical adjustments to social insurance, health policy, and the like. Normatively, he endeavored to advance liberal democracy's prospects by making the clarification of value goals central to policy analysis, citing as a central instance "the mistreatment of Negroes and other colored peoples" and, citing Myrdal's *American Dilemma*, also supported by the Carnegie Foundation, as exemplary. Analytically, he sought to join two levels of analysis: methods focusing on choice, especially decision-theory drawn both from micro-economics and cognitive psychology, deployed in tandem with an appreciation and deep concern for history, context, and "the institutional pattern *from* which we are moving and the pattern *toward* which we are going," in order to advance speculative and probabilistic models, a goal he herded under the umbrella he called "developmental constructs." Policy sciences braiding these elements, Lasswell argued, could improve "the rationality of the policy

---

83. Harold Dwight Lasswell and Daniel Lerner, eds., *The Policy Sciences: Recent Developments in Scope and Methods* (Stanford: Stanford University Press, 1951), p. 7.

process" and become "relevant to the policy problems of a given period." He defined these quandaries as issues on the scale of depression, war, and America's racial divide, problems more fundamental than mere "topical issues of the moment."[84] All in all, he counseled, we should "think of the policy sciences as the disciplines concerned with explaining the policy-making and policy-executing process, and with locating data and providing interpretations which are relevant to the policy problems of a given period."[85]

These issues, he understood, could not be confined inside the welfare state narrowly conceived or limited to domestic policy questions. National security and individual freedom, the title he had used for a book published the prior year during some of the hottest moments of the Cold War, now were inextricably entwined, like it or not. Modern liberalism and socialism, each of which Lasswell considered aspects of what he called "a vast struggle to unfetter the individual from the bonds of preceding status forms of society," had become vulnerable to the globe's dramatic escalation of violence, brutality, and insecurity. "As matters stand today," he wrote,[86]

the continuing crisis of insecurity may bring disaster to both conceptions. For the most drastic fate that could befall mankind, aside from physical annihilation, is the turning of the clock back from the hour of freedom and the forging anew of the chains of caste in the heat of chronic crisis. This is the true measure of the peril represented by the garrison-police state, which has already emerged in the Soviet Union, and which it is the aim of sound policy to prevent in the United States and elsewhere on the globe.

Commissioned by the Committee for Economic Development, a relatively progressive think-tank venture founded in 1942 by leading figures in business concerned about levels of employment after the war, the book defined its "central problem" as "how to maintain a proper balance between national security and individual freedom in a continuing crisis of national defense." Asking how the crisis could be endured "with the least loss of fundamental freedoms," Lasswell identified civilian supremacy, freedom of information, civil liberties, and a free economy as the principles of national security he wished to secure in the face of atomic weapons, higher defense spending, more centralized and secretive government, a growing atmosphere of suspicion, and a decline in the ca-

84. Harold Lasswell, "The Policy Orientation," in Lasswell and Lerner, pp. 3–15.
85. Lasswell, "Policy Orientation," p. 14.
86. Harold Dwight Lasswell, *National Security and Individual Freedom* (New York: McGraw Hill, 1950), p. 49.

pacity of the press, public opinion, political parties, courts, civilian agencies, and especially Congress.[87] "Our aim, he insisted, must be "to prevent successful aggression by a totalitarian dictatorship without becoming transformed in the process into a garrison prison."[88]

A very similar set of concerns helped bring Robert Dahl to the arena of policy studies. His early work, including a wry consideration of the choices taken to operationalize democratic socialism by the postwar Labour Party government in Britain and a tough-minded contrast between the requirements of democratic and Marxist conceptions of political parties, probed, in effect, whether the liberal and socialist traditions could be compatible.[89] But his first papers also included a review of two decades of prior work in public administration where, sounding much like Lasswell, Dahl averred that a pure science of administration is not possible in human affairs because "science as such is not concerned with the discovery or elucidation of normative values," nor can science "construct a bridge across the great gap from 'is' to 'ought'."[90]

Soon, in his first book, he turned, again much like Lasswell, to the problem of the public control of foreign affairs at a time when "crisis is normal." More particularly, he wished to know whether Congress, the most important liberal democratic institution in American public life, possessed adequate and appropriate abilities to govern and make thoughtful policy, quickly when needed, as an effective partner for the executive branch. Guided explicitly by the values of rational decisionmaking and responsiveness to public wishes, he focused on the forces that affected the opinion of influential members of Congress, the competence members possess, and their role in making foreign and defense policy. The most basic changes he advocated were aimed at equipping Congress to be an effective and representative policymaking body when dealing with subjects where the President and executive branch controlled key information and expertise. "In an age of total war," he concluded only three options were possible: "a frank dictatorship of the modern type" on the Politburo model, extensive executive discretion, thus putting 'democracy' in inverted commas, or a genuinely collaborative arrangement. If this option cannot be achieved, he cautioned, Congress "must inescapably become more and more the democratic shadow of

---

87. Lasswell, *National Security*, pp. 23–49.

88. Lasswell, *National Security*, p. 49.

89. Robert A. Dahl, "Workers' Control of Industry and the British Labour Party," *American Political Science Review* 41 (October 1947); Robert A. Dahl, "Marxism and Free Parties," *Journal of Politics* 10 (November 1948).

90. Robert A. Dahl, "The Science of Public Administration: Three Problems," *Public Administration Review* 7 (Winter 1947): 2, 4. Much the same point was made by Herbert Simon, *Administrative Behavior* (New York: Macmillan, 1947), chapter 2.

the first alternative."[91] Shortly thereafter, Dahl was the senior author of a report on the domestic control of atomic energy, urgently calling for more attention to this question by fellow social scientists, who had ceded the relevant ground to the scientific community and governmental decisions, often cloaked in undue secrecy.[92]

In this period, Charles Lindblom, a young Yale economist soon to be his co-author, was grappling, skeptically, with the implications of the market-disturbing qualities of trade unions for the efficient operation of markets, thus threatening to disturb effective policymaking regarding the tradeoff of inflation and unemployment because their monopolistic capacities implied a distortion of market allocations. Sounding not a little like Polanyi in assessing how social democratic interventions, of which he broadly approved, had been destructive to European economic systems in the 1920s, Lindblom calculated that union power after the Second World War, if not effectively controlled either by unions themselves or by others, could impede the ability of modern capitalism to generate jobs and growth.[93] Presenting this argument as a "diagnosis" rather than a preference, he opened with a Preface in which he not only declared himself a liberal rather than a conservative, but also implied that his findings had more radical implications. "I am not pamphleteering that a 'bad' unionism is destroying a 'good' competitive system," he wrote. "The obvious virtues of unionism and the equally obvious deficiencies of competition preclude so naïve an interpretation of the conflict."[94] Precisely because unionism is a form of (largely desirable) power, it should not be confused with an instrument that directly produces the public interest of social betterment. "Its usefulness," he concluded, "depends upon public policy," yet, as he cautioned, "intelligent public policy is immensely more difficult to achieve in the face of this conflict than otherwise."[95]

---

91. Robert A. Dahl, *Congress and Foreign Policy* (New York: Norton, 1950), pp. 241, 263, 264.

92. Robert A. Dahl and Ralph S. Brown, Jr., *Domestic Control of Atomic Energy* (New York: Social Science Research Council, Bulletin Number 8, 1951).

93. Lindblom, *Unions*. Earlier versions of the argument appeared as Charles E. Lindblom, " 'Bargaining Power' in Price and Wage Determination," *The Quarterly Journal of Economics* 62 (May 1948), and Charles E. Lindblom, "The Union as a Monopoly," *The Quarterly Journal of Economics* 62 (November 1948).

94. Lindblom, *Unions*, p. v.

95. Lindblom, *Unions*, vi. Just as his own book was coming into print, Lindblom wrote a largely laudatory review of C. Wright Mills, *The New Men of Power: America's Labor Leaders* (New York: Harcourt, Brace, 1948) for the *American Sociological Review* 14 (June 1949). Mills, while writing what might be thought of as a collective biography of the new generation of labor leaders, had announced that they "are now the strategic elite in American society." (Mills, p. 391) Lindblom thought this book "should receive the great public attention given to Hayek's *Road to Serfdom*, a less scholarly and less original work." (p. 432) Unlike most economists who thought they were in

"Depends on public policy" is a phrase that Lasswell, Dahl, and Lindblom all had come to endorse. Such a view, though, invited many more questions than, perforce, could be answered at the time. Dahl and Lindblom's immense collaborative work, *Politics, Economics, and Welfare*, published in 1953, was the period's most systematic search for answers. The anxieties and goals both Dahl and Lindblom brought to this search for a new way to study public policy thus was grounded in their apprehensive, normatively oriented, social science and the puzzles it had revealed. Though much Lasswell's junior, their concern for the fate of the liberal political tradition and torment about how a liberal regime can best respond to totalitarian challenges also underlay their sense of the exigency for policy studies that could deploy an arsenal of effective techniques to advance desired values.

This program, Dahl and Lindblom advised, required a self-conscious enhancement of "social techniques and rational social action" *within* the liberal polity with which to effectively confront the "grand alternatives and the 'ism's."[96] Liberal democracy currently lacked such a body of knowledge, and thus was unduly vulnerable and restricted in its scope of effective action. Dahl had underscored just this absence when, in 1950, he reviewed Karl Mannheim's posthumously published essays on democratic planning.[97] Though he shared Mannheim's "sympathy for democratic politics," "tolerance for the pluralism of democratic societies," and his "humanistic faith in the possibilities of democratic control over social development," Dahl thought Mannheim's strong preference for effective public capacity to shape socially important outcomes could not possibly be realized by exhortation and unsystematic flashes of insight unless some key problems he had considered only insufficiently were addressed.

The first was too high a level of generality. Mannheim had stated that he offered "no blueprints," only a "general vision." Not enough, said Dahl. Neither statements of goals nor loose descriptions of techniques bordering on truisms are sufficient. Nor, for that matter, was Mannheim's call for interdisciplinary collaboration. By whom, Dahl wanted to know, and for what ends? A second problem was even more basic. Statements of value, Dahl insisted, invited, but could not substitute for, the contribution of systematic social science. Goals and tech-

---

possession of far superior tools than political scientists, Lindblom based his collaboration with Dahl not only on mutual personal regard but also on a balanced view of their two disciplines. Writing four years after the publication of their book, he expressed a belief "that political scientists would more accurately value their own discipline if they better understood what little reason economists had for self-satisfaction." Charles E. Lindblom, "In Praise of Political Science," *World Politics* 9 (January 1957): 252.

96. Dahl and Lindblom, *Politics*, p. 3.

97. Karl Mannheim, *Freedom, Power, and Democratic Planning* (New York: Oxford University Press, 1950). Dahl's review appeared in the *American Sociological Review* 15 (December 1950).

niques cannot be reduced one to the other; neither should one be substituted for the other. Policy studies must be both normative and scientific, he agreed, but not by eliding their differences or the field of tension they define together.

Growing out of a course Dahl and Lindblom had taught about 'planning' at Yale over a six year period, *Politics, Economics, and Welfare* represented a systematic effort to address these issues and thus move well beyond Mannheim to construct a genuine policy science that could protect the Enlightenment and guard liberal democracy. Their treatise pressed the development of a theoretically driven marriage between economics and politics to produce a fresh, policy-capable, political economy to guide choice in vexing and complex circumstances by connecting particular social techniques and organizational forms to "possibilities for rational action, for planning, for reform—in short, for solving problems." This mid-level site of action they thought to be superior either to simple individual-level studies of rationality or to grand ideological discourses that they considered too abstract and permissive to serve as useful guides to practical policy decisions. Like other liberals, they were suspicious of grand narratives. Unlike other liberals, they did not think liberalism on its own, without elaboration, could possess sufficient resources to guide key decisions about public policy.

Seeking to know the impact of utilizing alternative instruments to rationally plan and direct public policy, they sought to accomplish two large goals: first, to show in detail how policy techniques are vital for the achievement of cherished values like freedom, democracy, and equality, and, second, to get inside major institutional sites, including the price system and contemporary democracy, and inside basic social processes, including organizational hierarchy and bargaining, in order to be able to elaborate their significance for these values. Put differently, they sought to develop and place a combination of ethical and positive theory within the space of governance.

This orientation to policy, especially its famous emphasis on incrementalism and learning, has been understood by followers and critics alike who stress that it represented an effort to replace politics by technique and ideology by method. This is a serious misreading. Dahl and Lindblom intended no substitution. Quite the reverse. They projected a focus on means rather than ideology or content to strengthen the institutions and deepen the capacities of decisionmakers within liberal democracies in order to underwrite "still viable" Enlightenment values. They grasped that this body of commitments "is a kind of act of faith" under difficult circumstances; but they also affirmed that a realistic analysis of social processes in western liberal democracies lent support to their belief these values in fact still could be secured.[98]

---

98. Dahl and Lindblom, *Politics*, pp. 516–517.

The view that there is a tradeoff between policy studies focusing on nitty gritty processes and substance and large normative goals is as false as the common understanding that David Truman and the other members of the Seminar on the State had replaced the state by attention to the political process. Like these colleagues, Dahl and Lindblom sought to thicken liberalism and *its* state. Rather than treat the liberal state whole, as a single macrostructure, they were concerned to attend to its interior content, its organization, and its processes in order to make it viable, effective, and worthy of legitimate mass support. Their policy theory thus was geared to provide underpinnings in the political process both for the Enlightenment commitments they cherished and for the type of political regime they believed to be best-equipped to advance them. Discerningly, C. Wright Mills understood both that *Politics, Economics, and Welfare* had "gone considerably beyond" Mannheim's writing on planning and that its attempt to ask how the society's most important values "that derive from the humanist strain of the Western society" could be made "widely and securely available" had produced "in fact, an insurgent's book, a technical handbook for latter-day reformers."[99]

VI.

The Brookings Lectures of 1955 were devoted to 'research frontiers in politics and government.' Herbert Simon addressed recent advances in organization theory; Richard Snyder spoke about the impact and potential of game theory; Paul David considered electoral realignments. David Truman chose to review 'the impact on political science of the revolution in the behavioral sciences,' while Robert Dahl, focusing on public policy, examined 'hierarchy, democracy, and bargaining in politics and economics.'[100]

Truman's text is most noteworthy not for its genuine appreciation of the contributions made to political studies by important advances in research techniques, especially the maturation of the sample survey, lab and field experimen-

---

99. C. Wright Mills' review appeared in the *American Sociological Review*, 4 (August 1954): 495, 496. Although Mills announced the book had produced "better sociology than is generally available nowadays," some economists were less sure about the contributions to their discipline. William Baumol, for example, criticized its taxonomic bent, and its failure to systematically utilize social choice theory or his own work on public goods. William J. Baumol, "Economic Theory and the Political Scientist," *World Politics* 6 (January 1954).

100. Bailey, et al., *Research Frontiers*. The remaining three lectures were by Stephen Bailey on legislative studies, Alfred de Grazia on electoral behavior, and Malcolm Moos on the nominating process.

tation, and content analysis, but for its cautionary stance about the importation from other disciplines of theory based on empirical verification. Most theory in the behavioral sciences either had been "concerned with individual behavior or with action in small, face-to-face groups" or with "explanation of a wide range of not specifically relevant to any particular institutional context," whether in organization theory, communication theory, or in high-level systems of abstract formulations, most notably the then regnant effort by Talcott Parsons to produce a general theory of action.

Though not without impact in his discipline, such approaches, Truman cautioned, cannot simply be imported or projected into the sphere of political science. The political institutions of the modern state, including the institutions that link the state to its citizens in a broadly liberal polity, cannot, indeed must not, lose their specificity to a quest for more general theory, like that of Parsons. Further, since much that goes on in the behavioral sciences is "individual or at least non-institutional" in character, acts of importation risk losing the specificity of the subject matter that gives life to the study of politics and the state, so much so that "one risks ceasing to be a political scientist" unless the scholar remembers to take "into account the factors peculiar to the institution that he is studying." Warning against "an incautious attempt merely to project" the new behavioral techniques of research "into the realm of governmental institutions," he concluded with a strong plea to build a political science that refuses to choose between political behavior and state-oriented institutional analysis, all the while insisting that technique not overwhelm the selection of political issues to study and the theory to be developed or applied. "It would be a pity if political science were to adopt the position of the inebriated gentleman who, having lost his watch in a dark alley while making his way home in the small hours of the night, insisted on searching for it near the lamp post on the main street because there was more light there."[101]

In a complementary lecture, Dahl recalled his listeners to the urgent tasks of policy studies. While stressing the importance of simplified models, conceptual abstractions, and analytically guided applications of such processes as bargaining and hierarchical relations, he insisted that we not lose sight of the purposes underpinning the systematic study of public policy. Focusing on problems of power and participation for liberal democracy, he called for better, more realistic understanding of how relatively modest levels of political participation could be made both effective and consistent with real checks on what political elites are free to do. He insisted that the time horizons of students of policy be stretched, and that, most important, the scholarship of social scientists and his-

---

101. Truman,"Behavioral Sciences," In Bailey, et al., *Frontiers*, pp. 223, 224, 230, 227.

torians engaged with policy be made to confront "the great gap between the actual policy choices made in Western societies over the past century and a body
of social theory that sought to analyze these choices in terms of mutually exclusive grand alternatives." If liberal polities were to prosper, this space had to be
filled with guided social knowledge tempered by moral purpose, not just by policy analysts but by students of politics more generally. He closed the lecture
with a homily. "This task is, at base, a moral task, for it is founded, ultimately on
some belief, incoherent as it may be, that certain ends are preferable to other
ends, at least in that time and that place and that situation."[102]

Three years later, Dahl, who by then had published his landmark *Preface to
Democratic Theory*,[103] enunciated what may be read as an epigraph for the sensibilities of his period's extended seminar on the state, insisting on the value of a
charged relationship between political thought and empirical research, between state-centered macroscopic inquiry and realistic studies of political behavior, and between facts and norms. "It would be easy to kill off political theory altogether in the name of empiricism and rigor," he commented. "But to do
so would be of no service to the intellectual community." Referring to the big issues of statebuilding, political regimes, and statecraft of the kind that occupied
not only Arendt and Polanyi but also many of his colleagues in the academic
mainstream in the postwar years, Dahl noted that while "political macroanalysis
suffers from certain inherent difficulties . . . we cannot afford to abandon it."
Without embedding systematic studies of process, behavior, power, and decision within this level of analysis, that of the state, he warned, "the social sciences
will move haltingly on, concerned often with a meticulous observation of the
trivial, and political theory will take up permanent cohabitation with literary
criticism."[104]

---

102. Robert A. Dahl, "Hierarchy, Democracy, and Bargaining in Politics and Economics," in Bailey, et al., *Frontiers*, pp. 67, 69.
103. Dahl, *Preface*. "Democratic theory," he wrote, "is concerned with processes by which ordinary citizens exert a relatively high degree of control over leaders." (p. 3)
104. Robert A. Dahl, "Political Theory: Truth and Consequences," *World Politics*, 11 (October
1958): 102, 98.

Four

A NEW OBJECTIVITY

The cosmography of Israel identifies a passageway beneath the Holy of Holies at Jerusalem's First and Second Temples. It led to the *Tehom*, the fathomless deep of darkness, chaos, disorder.[1] The priestly stratum, the *Cohanim*, was charged to block this passageway. I have understood the purpose of this book to ask whether, today, when we have no Temple, no priestly caste, no fixed validity, and no revealed truth, an extended and fortified Enlightenment, rooted in its original values of toleration, reason, rule of law, free inquiry, and opposition to despotism, might successfully guard the passageway to the *Tehom*.

My intellectual history of the political studies enlightenment has approached this question obliquely by revisiting the charged moment when these scholars who sought to understand the sources of their insulted expectations

---

1. A concern with chaos recurs in this tradition. Accounting for the title of his study of Nazi Germany, Franz Neumann explained, "In the Jewish eschatology of Babylonian origin—Behemoth and Leviathan designate two monsters, Behemoth ruling the land (the desert), Leviathan the sea, the first male, the second female. The land animals venerate Behemoth, the sea animals Leviathan, as their masters. Both are monsters of the Chaos." In this *mythos*, which recurs in Jewish writings, Behemoth and Leviathan either will be destroyed by God or by each other. By contrast, the Temple's priests were human, and it fell to their responsibility to construct barriers to chaos. Franz Neumann, *Behemoth: The Structure and Practice of National Socialism* (London: Victor Gollancz, 1942), p. 5.

and develop a fresh approach to the liberal state grappled with the shocking constellation of total war, totalitarianism, and holocaust. "Where are the limits of Enlightenment?," the German novelist and satirist Christoph Martin Wieland had inquired in April 1789. "Where," he replied, "with all the light possible, there is nothing more to see." When the political studies enlightenment set to work, they understood they had to pierce their period's darkness or humankind would be unable to escape the prospect of becoming "night birds. . . . who screech most shrilly when the sun pricks them in their eyes."[2]

I.

As I compose this coda, yet another stack of books is piled high on my desk. Indicative of how the Enlightenment and its legacies have come under assault in the humanities, the social sciences, and the wider culture, they announce, among other subjects, a 'postmodernist critique of the project of enlightenment'; a 're-quiem for modern politics,' the result of 'the tragedy of enlightenment'; 'contra-dictions of modernity' in a study of 'enlightenment and genocide'; 'the politics of enlightenment in the aftermath of modernity'; even 'remnants of the Enlighten-ment in National Socialism.'[3] Their authors tend to see a singular 'project': ratio-nalist, godless, scientific, cool, Eurocentric, regulatory, patriarchal, racist, impe-rial, and lawful.[4] To be sure, the various analysts do not pick the same descriptors, but irrespective of whether they fault the Enlightenment for its disastrous attempts to dominate nature, its amoral pluralism and absence of virtue, or its biased uni-tary ontology which they believe makes room only for a narrow band of humanity, thought, and value, they tend to see a coherent, well-bounded, Enlightenment which they treat as the reflection, emblem, and cause of modernity's ailments and upheavals.

---

2. Christoph Martin Wieland, "A Couple of Gold Nuggets, from the . . . Wastepaper, or Six An-swers to Six Questions," in James Schmidt, ed., *What is Enlightenment? Eighteenth-Century An-swers and Twentieth-Century Questions* (Berkeley: University of California Press, 1996), pp. 80. 82.
3. Sven-Eric Liedman, *The Postmodernist Critique of the Project of Enlightenment* (Amsterdam: Rodopi, 1994); William Ophuls, *Requiem for Modern Politics.* (Boulder: Westview Press, 1997); James Kaye and Bo Stråth, *Enlightenment and Genocide, Contradictions of Modernity* (Brussels: Peter Lang, 2000); George Trey, *Solidarity and Difference: The Politics of Enlightenment in the Af-termath of Modernity* (Albany: SUNY Press, 1998); and Lawrence Birkin, *Hitler as Philosophe: Remnants of the Enlightenment in National Socialism* (Westport, Connecticut: Praeger, 1995).
4. "Indeed, sometimes it appears that the only commentators who pronounce on what '*the* En-lightenment' stood for are those who are in the process of dismissing it." In James Schmidt, "Lib-eralism and Enlightenment in Eighteenth Century Germany," *Critical Review* 13 (Winter/Spring 1999): 46.

Current critics can be grouped in two distinctive if internally diverse clusters. For the first, who might loosely be grouped as premodern, the Enlightenment is too thin, besotted by relativism, and incapable of searching and finding the good; a betrayal of traditional philosophy and theology. Aristotle, after all, thought moral conflict a badge of ignorance and Aquinas believed the moral virtues composed a beneficent unity. On this reading, the Enlightenment (as a capstone of Cartesian realism) substituted logic for content, method for virtue, and agnosticism for belief, producing a fateful loss of bearings and a reduction both to human thought and ambition. By contrast, for the second set, who loosely may be grouped as postmodern, the Enlightenment and its legacy is too thick, characterized by the *hubris* of imposing a master narrative which artificially values only particular and limited aspects of human capacities and sensations and is marked by stereotypes and prejudices that remain unexamined. In this accounting, its universalism is a pretense and its ideas are instruments of power and domination. Its tolerant glove masks the repressive fist of national-state concentrations of military, organizational, fiscal, and knowledge-based endowments as well as nimble fingers that regulate the micro-dynamics of daily life, including those in the zone of personal intimacy.

Polanyi, Arendt, Hofstadter, Truman, Lasswell, Dahl, and the other scholars of the political studies enlightenment would have sought to parry both sets of these imputations, I believe, in much the same manner that they resisted the assaults mounted by the critics of their time.[5] They understood, just as the detractors of the 1940s did, that the Enlightenment's version of modernity, despite its ambiguities and heterogeneity, did embrace pluralism, human reason and autonomy, science and technology as the mastery of nature, and the goal of social control.[6] But they drew contrary lessons about the relationship of desolation and

---

5. In dealing with the pre-modern strain, mounting a rejoinder to it, see Robert C. Bartlett, *The Idea of Enlightenment: A Post-Mortem Study* (Toronto: University of Toronto Press, 2001). Bartlett's aim is "to shake the conviction that the idea of enlightenment is necessarily and obviously dead [and] to encourage a re-examination of the limits and possibilities of reason." (ix) A thoughtful consideration of the post-modern strain, with an effort to fashion a fresh enlightenment for post-modern times is Keith Michael Baker and Peter Hans Reill, eds., *What's Left of Enlightenment? A Postmodern Question* (Stanford: Stanford University Press, 2001). For a subtle treatment of the Counter-Enlightenment, see Darrin M. McMahon, *Enemies of the Enlightenment: The French Counter-Enlightenment and the Making of Modernity* (Oxford: Oxford University Press, 2001).

6. These commitments, of course, were charged with contradictory meanings and possibilities. "On the one hand," Ernest Gellner noted, "by eroding and deriding all the old transcendental bases of certainty and hierarchy, [the Enlightenment] undermined the authority of the self-appointed agents of the Higher Order, and the residual legatee of sovereignty was man himself and his mundane interests. In this sense, the Enlightenment was on the side of liberty and equality.

enlightenment. The Enlightenment's search for control, they grasped, had been animated from the start by anxiety in situations where neither the thought of the ancients nor medieval religious doctrine any longer could speak effectively. In this context—which broadly remains our own, if in vastly expanded and distended fashion—the aspects of Enlightenment thought which some contemporary critics see as too thin and others as too thick are better appraised as appealing attributes. The absence of a search for a unitary good; the inclination to find room for diversity of thought tempered by common standards of discourse;[7] and the emplacement of instruments of social control are indispensable checks on organized evil and authorizations essential to the toleration of difference. For without a standpoint conferring a sense of location appropriate to the variety of modern conditions, they understood, we lack the capacity not just for analysis but for judgment.

This view defining the proper perspective and orientation to knowledge of a free intelligentsia was embraced by leading figures in the political studies enlightenment of the 1940s and early 1950s. This multifaceted group, I have argued, originated a coherent design and conceived a program for the study of matters political more appealing than either of the stark choices we have been offered in the so-called culture wars.[8] We have been confronted, on the one side, in a kind of throwback to the pre-Socratics, by the assertion that reason alone can discover truth based on an uncritical embrace of a particular (and partial) reading of Kant's ambitions for the Enlightenment as a progressive, trans-local, disinterested, culturally disembedded civilizing project. This account, implanted on a self-congratulatory hegemony for modern reason, reasserts with confidence that just the right methods and procedures can, indeed will, yield truth. On the other side stands a disenchantment of truth, an excessive relativity of values risking nihilism, jettisoning the possibility of distinguishing systematic accounts of reality from mere interest or opinion, and often insisting on the unmediated linkage of sensation and knowledge. This sharp rebuff to the European Enlightenment, rejecting causality and rationality, effectively aestheticizes politics by treating its aspirations and standards merely as

---

On the other hand, the rationality it commended required the authority or experts and the implementation of their plans," thus introducing a "technicist-authoritarian element." Ernest Gellner, "The Struggle to Catch Up," *Times Literary Supplement*, December 9, 1994, p. 14.

7. Of course, there were Enlightenment figures who did seek after a unitary good and who rejected diversity in the name of reason. This point is made forcefully by Isaiah Berlin, in *The Crooked Timber of Humanity: Chapters in the History of Ideas* (New York: Knopf, 1991); and by Jacob Talmon in *The Origins of Totalitarian Democracy* (London: Secker and Warburg, 1952)

8. Though most frequently a series of battles in the humanities, these extend, of course, to history and the social sciences, and to broader cultural trends.

an ideological discourse entwined in a metanarrative of truth-seeking masking privilege and power.

In these ways, an inculpable worship of reason has confronted a sustained revulsion from rationalism in our universities and in the public realm. The political studies enlightenment fashioned a distinctive, cogent, and resonant alternative to these two positions. The body of work its members produced in the face of desolation, especially its more empirical, even behavioral, aspects, often has been understood by defenders and detractors alike as simply having reproduced a trustful and aseptic Enlightenment vision. This, it has been my burden to show, is not correct. They scorned the simple, the thin, and the disposition to believe too readily. They also thought humankind had nothing to put in the place of Enlightenment. Hence their act of rescue by coming to terms with radical evil and by using systematic knowledge to learn how to construct institutional and policy arrangements to confine its ugly endowments.

By reflecting on this effort to hold fast by revising and extending the Enlightenment's legacies at a desperate time, perhaps we can come to think more clearly about our own conundrums as scholars and as citizens. As the Enlightenment question has been pressed by advocates of tradition, such as the political philosophers Alisdair MacIntyre and Allan Bloom, and by postmodern, postcolonial critics of its bounded hypocrisy, sustained by partial readings of Derrida and Foucault,[9] those of us unhappy with these options might well still discover useful guideposts in the work of scholars who produced political knowledge some five and six decades ago in the midst of a moment stamped by the greatest shocks and stresses the Enlightenment tradition ever had faced both objectively and self-consciously on its own ground. At that wretched moment, the American political studies enlightenment advanced more than a series of normative or philosophical positions. Most important, they advanced the junction of history and social

---

9. Alisdair MacIntyre, *After Virtue: A Study in Moral Theory* (Notre Dame, Indiana: Notre Dame University Press, 1984); Allan Bloom, *The Closing of the American Mind* (New York: Simon and Schuster, 1987); Richard Rorty, *Philosophy and the Mirror of Nature* (Princeton: Princeton University Press, 1979); John McCarthy, ed., *Modern Enlightenment and the Rule of Reason* (Washington, D.C.: The Catholic University of America Press, 1998); Hugo A. Meynell, *Postmodernism and the New Enlightenment* (Washington, D.C.: The Catholic University of America Press, 1999); Piet Strydom, *Discourse and Knowledge: The Making of Enlightenment Sociology* (Liverpool: Liverpool University Press, 2000); Karlis Racevskis, *Postmodernism and the Search for Enlightenment* (Charlottesville: University of Virginia Press, 1993); and Padmini Mongia, ed., *Contemporary Postcolonial Theory: A Reader* (New Delhi: Oxford University Press, 1997). For a thoughtful review of books concerned with the darker side of the earlier Renaissance, the Enlightenment's precursor, see Anthony Grafton, "The West vs. The Rest," *New York Review of Books*, April 10, 1997.

science as their preferred site for the discovery of answers, thus continuing and revivifying one of the most important offspring of Enlightenment. Not any social science selected from the cacophony of competing rational projects, to be sure, but an analytical, historically informed social science to serve as a guardian of decency[10] in an era when humankind, hardened and embittered by experience, no longer could call on traditional mores, practices, institutions, and restraints, or familiar combinations of ideology and utopia, to perform this role.

Motivated by a sense of outrage, scandal, and surprise, the political studies enlightenment produced a political science marked by sorrow and charged by anxiety inside the field of tension defined by the general promise of enlightenment and the particularities of Europe's age of barbarism. One only has to read John Locke's *Letter Concerning Toleration* to understand how realistic dread — in his case anxiety about religious warfare — can motivate thinking combining sociological and political realism, institutional creativity, and normative purpose without lapsing into irrationalism or hysteria. Even before the Second World War and its murderous camps, Gilbert Murray submitted, "The world is dominated by fear — fear created by the Great War and perpetuated by its consequences and memories."[11] By the new war's end, social scientists and historians were left with a deep, persisting fear-inducing uncertainty. They did not

---

10. This choice is worth considering. Most reflections on this century's intense brutality have taken literary form, combining tropes of realism, irony, and fantasy. It is arguable that reality becomes more actual, as it were, when transmuted by literary form capable of conveying detail. The members of the political studies enlightenment were convinced, however, at minimum that such representations had to be accompanied not only by sober, detailed historical accounts but also by systematic social inquiry capable of a more powerful understanding at the levels of ideas and institutions of how the descent to barbarism had happened and how its consequences might be grappled with to make a more decent future.

11. Gilbert Murray, *Liberality and Civilization: Lectures Given at the Invitation of the Hibbert Trustees in the Universities of Bristol, Glasgow, and Birmingham in October and November 1937* (London: George Allen and Unwin, 1938), p. 89. The broad orientation to recent and current events by the political studies enlightenment was much like that announced by Karl Popper in the second edition to *The Open Society and its Enemies*: "Although much of what is contained in this book took shape at an earlier date, the final decision to write it was made in March 1938, on the day I received the news of the invasion of Austria. The writing extended into 1943; and the fact that most of the book was written during the grave years when the outcome of the war was uncertain may help to explain why some of its criticism strikes me to-day as more emotional and harsher in tone than I could wish. But it was not the time to mince words — or at least, this was what I then felt. Neither war nor any other contemporary event was explicitly mentioned in the book; but it was an attempt to understand those events and their background, and some of the issues which were likely to arise after the war was won." Karl Popper, *The Open Society and its Enemies*, 2nd ed. (London: Routledge and Kegan Paul, 1952).

cower. Instead, they confronted this new normative condition of humankind to produce a body of work in the spirit of what the late Judith Shklar, synthesizing her European and American experiences, resonantly called a liberalism of fear (which she opposed to a more aseptic, and, in her view, more naïve liberalism of rights), a melancholic dystopian liberalism without illusions and stripped of fantasy that stares hard at cruelty, coercion, and protean, unjust abuses of power; a liberalism seeking, above all, to defend humankind against public cruelty and oppression in full knowledge of the nonrational and irrational capacities people possess to do great harm. This kind of liberalism was grounded in a tragic, but not fatalistic, perspective, in a frank acknowledgment, as Arendt put it, of the "darkness of the human heart."[12] This "liberalism," Shklar wrote "is, in fact, extremely difficult and constraining, far too much so for those who cannot endure contradiction, diversity, and the risks of freedom."[13] As her fellow political theorist, John Dunn, has noted, though "driven by an awareness of the overwhelming grimness of much of human political life, its saturation with suffering and evil, the liberalism of fear is in no way an excuse for passivity, still less a counsel of despair."[14]

Whether in Shklar's hands or those of members of the earlier political studies enlightenment, it is, rather, a call to purposeful clarity, crisp understanding, and institutional defense equipped to advance the best values of the Enlightenment by "emancipating American liberalism from naïveté. . . . without obstructing potential moral progress" by steering a course between ingenuousness and cynicism, and by incorporating, as Lionel Trilling famously put it, "the emotions and the imagination . . . into its essence and existence—in the interests, that is, of its vision of a general enlargement and freedom and rational direction of human life." A key task, especially in the United States where liberalism and its Enlightenment premises have been dominant for so long, is to

---

12. Hannah Arendt, *On Revolution* (London: Faber & Faber, 1963), pp. 92–93.

13. Judith N. Shklar, "The Liberalism of Fear," in Nancy Rosenblum, ed., *Liberalism and the Moral Life* (Cambridge: Harvard University Press, 1989). The term 'liberalism of fear' in the sense of political theory geared to defend against public cruelty in the situation posed by modernity's pluralism in which there always are minorities first was introduced in Judith N. Shklar, *Ordinary Vices* (Cambridge, Harvard University Press, 1984), p. 5. For a fine, appreciative volume considering Shklar's distinctive liberal theory, see Bernard Yack, ed., *Liberalism Without Illusions: Essays on Liberal Theory and the Political Vision of Judith N. Shklar* (Chicago: University of Chicago Press, 1996).

14. John Dunn, "Hope over Fear: Judith Shklar as Political Educator," in Yack, ed., *Liberalism*, p. 53. Shklar wrote appreciatively about Arendt more than once. See her essays, "Hannah Arendt's Triumph," *The New Republic*, December 27, 1975, pp. 8–10; "Rethinking the Past," *Social Research* 44 (1977): 80–90; and "Hannah Arendt as Pariah," *Partisan Review*, 50 (1983): 64–77.

"approach liberalism in a critical spirit," leaning against its inclination to "ideas of a certain kind and a certain simplicity."[15]

Before total war, totalitarianism, and the holocaust, liberalism's premises and commitments had been so tacit inside American political studies they often were not noticed. In the aftermath of the pervasive and prominent disasters of the Second World War, however, liberal values and institutions, ideas and methods, orientations and practices, could not remain unexpressed or unobserved. At this moment, liberalism, recently reincarnated in a New Deal version with a social democratic tinge, became a fighting doctrine, literally so, with two clear foes, condensed, despite the differences between bolshevism and fascism, into totalitarianism as a single category. If still hegemonic in America, political liberalism—the doctrine first fashioned in early modern Europe before the Enlightenment to advance religious toleration, defend members of civil society against tyrannical regimes, and guide the construction of political orders respectful of human autonomy—was forced to confront its vulnerabilities and the exposed position of the Enlightenment tradition in which it now nestled, and to do so inside the deep cold of unprecedented desolation.

The mind concentrated. The political studies enlightenment confronted the wreckage not just of their times but the dashed hopes of reason and knowledge. There was no gainsaying the hideousness revealed to be located at the very center of western modernity or the requirement that such dark places be probed. They recognized that western scholarship's vast achievements in banishing ignorance and darkness had fastened a high degree of *hubris* about the power of secularized light and reason to an unwarranted optimism about human nature. Nonetheless, these postwar scholars did not renounce this vision's core commitment to reason's powers but attached it to a darker and greater range of sensibility about the compass of human capacities as they shifted their orientation from

---

15. Benjamin DeMott, "Rediscovering Complexity," *The Atlantic Monthly*, September 1988, pp. 68, 69. Lionel Trilling, "Preface," *The Liberal Imagination: Essays on Literature and Society* (New York: Harcourt, Brace, 1950), pp. xi, xii. I thank Robert Merton, who, along with his Columbia colleagues Richard Hoftstadter and Lionel Trilling is one of its three subjects, for directing me to DeMott's article whose principal purpose was to rescue the combination of liberality and intricacy in the sober thought and measured tones of the postwar generation from the simplified and mythical remembrance of their neoconservative students and successors. Of the studies I know about scholars and intellectuals in this postwar period, DeMott's brief piece comes closest to apprehending the themes I am addressing in this volume. Yet, to my preference, his compass is somewhat narrow, restricted to American liberalism and not the larger fate of the Enlightenment within which it is embedded; to native-born scholars exclusively; to national concerns with race and class but not the greater context of total war, totalitarianism, and holocaust in the era of crisis dating from the First World War.

unreflective sanguinity to reflective alarm. In so doing, they did not put aside the Enlightenment's faith in reason or the liberal political project. They recast these legacies in more astute and knowing ways. Tethering desolation and enlightenment, each aspired, like Tocqueville, to become a "liberal of a new kind"[16] to fortify prospects for a worthy politics.

Political science, history, and sociology are more accomplished today than the work of the forties generation in at least two respects. The subjects we now consider are more extensive. Neglected features of the human experience have been moved from a zone of ignorance to a zone of inquiry; think, for example, of the gains accomplished by women's studies or area studies. Further, the tools and technologies we possess to probe our subjects and test our ideas have become much more capable. The 'science' in social science really has advanced quite a lot both in terms of how research designs are organized and in the range of methods available to parse tough questions and identify causal mechanisms. Despite these radical gains, there also have been radical losses. Today's social, historical, and policy sciences have confirmed the undesired worries of Truman, Dahl, and others as they have come increasingly to detach subjects from methods, and purposes from instruments. Reading most issues of the *American Political Science Review*, the discipline's flagship journal, offers an exercise in applied schizophrenia, the result of the stark disjuncture dividing description and analysis from judgment and normative purpose, thus also mirroring Strauss's and Horkheimer and Adorno's laments about the divided character of Enlightenment thought.

For all their considerable differences, the scholars to whom I have attended considered this bipolarity to be arbitrary. The continuing appeal of their work in part is a consequence of the connections they fastened between the realist, behavioral, and pragmatist tendencies that had been dominant in the interwar academy and their own deeper, heavier, more brooding, sometimes semiphilosophical reflections on dark times. Refusing to separate facticity and norms, they sought both to thicken political theory and to delineate specific institutional situations, past and present, and their social actors, processes, and choices, each in tandem with the other. The products of this conjoining, we have seen, made considerable, and insufficiently appreciated, contributions both to empirical social science, analytical history, and political theory, "beside

---

16. This is Tocqueville's self-description in a letter of July 24, 1836. Gustave de Beaumont, *Memoirs, Letters, and Remains of Alexis de Tocqueville* (Boston: Tickenor and Fields, 1862, volume 1), p. 382; cited in Margie Lloyd, "In Tocqueville's Shadow: Hannah Arendt's Liberal Republicanism," *The Review of Politics* 57 (Winter 1995): 37.

which the current preoccupations of liberal thought may come to seem pretty trivial."[17]

II.

This program of research is best understood, I believe, as a deepening and fulfillment of the ambition Karl Mannheim sought to achieve in *Ideology and Utopia*, published in 1929 in a setting of weakening constitutional democracy and a cacophony of conflicting movements, parties, and world-views. Identifying a special role for scholars and intellectuals "who might play the part of watchmen in what otherwise would be a pitch-black night," he had sought to reconcile the deep pluralism of incommensurable political perspectives with a functioning liberal political order under increasingly difficult, soon to be impossible, circumstances. In tethering a darker view of the Enlightenment's patrimony to systematic history and social science, the political studies enlightenment undertook to achieve what Mannheim called "a new type of objectivity in the social sciences," a set of standards "attainable not through the exclusion of evaluations but through the critical awareness and control of them." This 'new objectivity' was to be situated not outside the clash of modernity's ideologies, political estimations, and diverse ways of life, but inside its irreducible heterogeneity; a situation Mannheim believed that need not convey us into the morass of relativism.[18]

Composed inside late Weimar's combination of creativity and putrescence, *Ideology and Utopia* was the first milestone twentieth-century book within the ambit of Enlightenment to call into question the *Britannica* version of unfolding disciplinary reason based on the assumption of a single, universal, standard of objectivity. Though a fierce partisan of reason and liberal values, Mannheim judged it necessary when faced with the legacies of total war and the prospects of totalitarianism to elucidate a sense of objectivity obtained "not through the exclusion of evaluations but through the critical awareness and control of them." This project, he believed, had been made necessary by "the contempo-

---

17. David Miller, "The Nagging Glory: Hannah Arendt and the Greek Polis," *Times Literary Supplement*, July 9, 1993, p. 7. Critical overviews, not entirely in harmony with my own views, include James Farr, John S. Dryzek, and Stephen T. Leonard, eds., *Political Science in History: Research Programs and Political Traditions* (New York: Cambridge University Press, 1995); Peter Novick, *That Noble Dream: The 'Objectivity Question' and the American Historical Profession* (New York: Cambridge University Press, 1988); and Tom Bottomore and Robert Nisbet, eds., *A History of Sociological Analysis* (New York: Basic Books, 1987).

18. Karl Mannheim, *Ideology and Utopia* (London: Routledge, 1936 [1929]), pp. 143, 5, 44.

rary predicament of thought" in which "the continuous elaboration of concepts concerning things and situations has collapsed in the face of a multiplicity of fundamentally divergent definitions." Even on the eve of the Depression and well before the Second World War, he noted the collapse of the singular, universal framework the *Britannica* had affirmed. Now, he argued, western intellectuals were confronted, like it or not, with "the irreconcilability of the conflicting conceptions of the world."[19]

Having not erased, but having "shattered to a large extent" the hegemony of religion, the Enlightenment, Mannheim perceived, had opened the way to a fusion of politics as a struggle for power combined with competing political conceptions of the world. "First liberalism, then haltingly following its example conservatism, and finally socialism made of its political aims a philosophical credo, a world-view with well-established methods of thought and prescribed conclusions." The result was an "amalgamation" of politics and scientific discourse and a new form of diversity, as "to the split in the religious world-view was added the fractionalization of political outlooks."[20]

These developments mandated political discussion as the very substance of liberal and democratic politics while amplifying it as a source of danger. In

---

19. Mannheim, *Ideology*, p. 7. Mannheim's thematic and personal links to the émigré members of the American political studies enlightenment were close, if complicated. No European scholar in this period could avoid engagement with this controversial figure who had achieved high visibility and standing at an early point in his career. A young Hannah Arendt reviewed the text shortly after it appeared. More broadly, all the members of the political studies enlightenment were deeply familiar with Mannheim's work. Received visibly if unevenly by the American academy after the publication of the English edition in 1936, Mannheim's scholarship on ideas and ideology was a major influence on Richard Hofstadter in the period between *The American Political Tradition* and *The Age of Reform*, just as his later work on planning oriented Robert Dahl to the subject. Irrespective of such direct influence, the program undertaken by the political studies Enlightenment in the United States can be grasped through the prism of Mannheim's work in the late 1920s. Like the scholars I treat in this text, Mannheim, as he put it, sought "to learn as a sociologist by close observation the secret (even if it is infernal) of these new times," and "to carry liberal values forward." His biographers comment, "His problem remains irresistible to reflective people at the end of the twentieth century. Mannheim's project was to link thinking to emancipation despite strong evidence against the connection." David Kettler and Volker Meja, *Karl Mannheim and the Crisis of Liberalism: The Secret of These New Times* (New Brunswick: Transaction Publishers, 1995), p. 1. For an extended discussion of Mannheim's reception in the United States, see David Kettler and Volker Meja, " 'That typically German kind of sociology which verges toward philosophy': The Dispute about *Ideology and Utopia* in the United States," *Sociological Theory* 12 (November 1994). Hannah Arendt's "Philosophie und Soziologie" appeared in *Die Gesellschaft* 7, no. 2 (1930). Robert Dahl's review of Mannheim, *Freedom, Power, and Democratic Planning* appeared in the *American Sociological Review*, 15 (December 1950).

20. Mannheim, *Ideology*, p. 33.

these conditions, politics is concerned with objects and materials of real consequence, but, concomitantly, politics also can "become a life-and-death struggle" gripped by "emotional undercurrents" that crystallize both in ideologies "so intensively interest-bound to a situation that they are simply no longer able to see certain facts which would undermine their sense of domination," and utopias possessed by "certain oppressed groups so strongly interested in the destruction and transformation of a given condition of society that they unwittingly see only those elements in the situation which tend to negate it." Within such a politics "in a world of upheaval," conflict can go beyond defeating antagonistic views to attempts to "annihilate . . . the intellectual foundations upon which these beliefs and attitudes rest."[21]

Social science had new responsibilities in this situation charged with an "uncertainty which had become an ever more unbearable grief in public life."[22] A thin behaviorism,[23] concentrating on the externally perceivable and "content to attribute importance to what is measurable merely because it happens to be measurable," had to be replaced, he counseled, not by a flight to the higher reaches of political philosophy, but to a new and deeper set of systematic studies suspended between empiricism and 'truth.' The details of his sociology of knowledge, crafted in this spirit, are far less significant, I believe, than Mannheim's "*systematization* of the doubt which is to be found in social life as a vague insecurity and uncertainty," and his "relational as distinct from the merely relative" approach to knowledge that abjures the search for absolute values while holding on to "a quest for reality." In this way, he counsels, "to see more clearly the confusion into which our social and intellectual life has fallen represents an enrichment rather than a loss."[24] Throughout, as David Kettler, Volker Meja, and Nico Stehr insightfully note, "his rationalism always points to the method and achievements of the Enlightenment," while leaving open "the boundaries of the Enlightenment," especially as Mannheim sought to take "the irrational seriously while preserving reason."[25]

---

21. Mannheim, *Ideology*, pp. 34, 36, 57.

22. Mannheim, *Ideology*, p. 45.

23. Mannheim wrote a critique of American behavioral social science in an extensive consideration of the state of the art review found in Stuart A. Rice, ed., *Methods in Social Science* (Chicago: University of Chicago Press, 1931). Mannheim's book review appeared in the *American Journal of Sociology*, 38 (September 1932).

24. Mannheim, *Ideology*, pp. 45, 70, 87, 94.

25. David Kettler, Volker Meja, and Nico Stehr, "Rationalizing the Irrational: Karl Mannheim and the Besetting Sin of German Intellectuals," *American Journal of Sociology*, 95 (May 1990), pp. 1452, 1453.

After a brief period in which he was able to advance this project from his academic chair in Frankfurt and his leadership, with Paul Tillich and Adolph Löwe of a 'Liberalism Seminar,' Mannheim's world collapsed. "Deprived of his language and culture" his attempt in an English exile "to uphold his Enlightenment cultural-sociological program," marked by a turn away from the sociology of knowledge to planning and, later, under the influence of T.S. Eliot and his circle, to religion in High Anglican form, "cannot be judged a success."[26] But sustained by American patrons who inserted *Ideology and Utopia* into their New Deal milieu, Mannheim's work helped define the country's political studies enlightenment. The preface written by Louis Wirth, the noted University of Chicago sociologist and a pioneer figure in urban studies who, with Edward Shils, had translated *Ideology* to introduce Mannheim to American scholarship, underscored the relevance, even urgency, of this work for American scholars at a time when "What was once regarded as the esoteric concern of a few intellectuals in a single country has become the common plight of the modern man." Weimar's troubles had intensified and diffused. "It may seem like grim humor to speak of the beneficent influences arising out of an upheaval that has shaken the foundations of our social and intellectual order," Wirth wryly observed, but

---

26. Claudia Honegger, "The Disappearance of the Sociology of Knowledge and *Kultursoziologie* after 1933," in David Kettler, ed., "Contested Legacies," a preparatory document for a conference on "The German-Speaking Intellectual and Cultural Emigration to the United States and United Kingdom, 1933–1945," Bard College, August 13–15, 2002. For a powerful discussion of how "Mannheim's promising theoretical beginnings were disrupted by the brute facts of his generation's biography," see Kettler, Meja, and Stehr, "Rationalizing the Irrational." They acutely take note of how he "veered abruptly from the inside to the outside of the talk about the crisis of rationality," observing how throughout the 1920s Mannheim's theme was "the need to find ways of thinking capable of meeting fundamental objections to liberal rationalism without abandoning the needs of 'modern man' in favor of some disruptive celebration of the irrational, or, indeed, abandoning the ideal of genuine knowledge for guiding human conduct." But when in "English exile after 1933, Mannheim turned to a militant rationalist counterattack, disavowing much he himself once admired and done. . . . Mannheim abandoned his highest hopes for the sociology of knowledge when confronted by fascism. . . . The emancipation from Weimar culture turned into a barren exile." (pp. 1451, 1452, 1459, 1467) There is a parallel discussion in John Herman Randall's review of Mannheim's *Man and Society in an Age of Reconstruction* (New York: Harcourt Brace, 1940), where he observes that "his more recent English experience has altered the whole temper of this thought, and brought him close to the Anglo-American philosophy of social control and intelligent reconstruction of society." *Journal of the History of Ideas*, 2 (June 1941), p. 373. Reviewing the same book, C. Wright Mills observed how Mannheim had turned back to "the comprehensive themes of the Enlightenment" rather than the more differentiated, contested, and wry reflections he had offered earlier. The Mills review is in the *American Sociological Review*, 6 (December 1940).

"it must be asserted that the spectacle of change and confusion, which confronts social science, presents it at the same time with unprecedented opportunities for fruitful new development." Now that the "partial victory . . . of enlightened minds" over unreason that had been achieved "for a brief interlude between the eras of medieval spiritualized darkness and the rise of modern secular dictatorships" had been "chastened," an "intellectual world . . . [that] had at least a common frame of reference which offered a measure of certainty to the participants in that world and gave them a sense of mutual respect and trust" had transmuted into "the spectacle of a battlefield of warring parties and conflicting doctrines." A unitary belief in Enlightenment, "irretrievably lost," now faced "the threat to exterminate what rationality and objectivity has been won in human affairs." He urged that *Ideology and Utopia*, a book that offered a guide to issues that "could only be raised in a society and in an epoch marked by profound social and intellectual upheaval" as a "product of this period of chaos and unsettlement," be utilized as a charter document both for social inquiry and for the deployment of social knowledge under these new, deeply threatening, conditions of uncertainty.[27]

Wirth's understanding of the significance of *Ideology and Utopia* (though often obscured by Mannheim's frequently murky and elusive formulations), I believe, defines quite precisely the motivation and character of the program the political studies enlightenment later developed. Faced with the collapse of the rational synthesis so visibly represented by the pre-First World War *Britannica*, the loss of a situation in which it seemed that ideals and reality could be homogeneous and reason faced no ineluctable barriers, the advancement of deeply conflicting ideological and material interests, the rise of nihilistic activism privileging deeds, the diminution of idealism to naïveté, and the vague, diffuse, unconfident qualities of enlightened political thought,[28] its affiliates sought to build a zone for situated inquiry in a space designated by the poles of philosophy and ethics, history and systematic social science, and epistemology, and by letting go of a sanitary neo-Kantian view of social science without giving up on claims to rationality.[29] Rejecting the stark distinction between politics and sci-

---

27. Louis Wirth, "Preface," in Mannheim, *Ideology*, pp. xii, xiv, xv, xxvi, xxvii.
28. These traits are noted in Leonard Krieger, "The Intellectuals and European Society," *Political Science Quarterly*, 67 (June 1952).
29. This search is nicely framed and summarized in Richard Ashcraft, "Political Theory and Political Action in Karl Mannheim's Thought: Reflections upon *Ideology and Utopia* and its Critics," *Comparative Studies in Society and History*, 23 (January 1981), and in Dick Perls, "Karl Mannheim and the Sociology of Scientific Knowledge: Toward a New Agenda," *Sociological Theory*, 14 (March 1996).

ence that Max Weber had advanced,[30] transcending Karl Marx's overly constrained world of class struggle, and going beyond classical liberalism's penchant
for methodological individualism, like Mannheim they demanded that the liberal political process be capable of giving expression to, while containing, the
widest spectrum of ideological and utopian views. New empirical conditions
made this quest especially difficult, thus defining a role for intellectuals who
could stand at least partially outside the ordinary fray of political contest to lend
transparency and critical reflection to the terms of collision within political life.[31]

In this, Mannheim was the most influential precursor to the effort by the political studies enlightenment to repair the weaknesses that had left the Enlightenment and the liberal tradition, to which he had been fiercely committed, so
vulnerable.[32] Working without guarantees, Mannheim had not only wrestled
with how to map the sociological distribution of beliefs along lines of stratification and ideas, but also had tried to navigate within such a map to place 'objectivity' within realistic presuppositions.[33] This was a map of 'in-betweens': between Marxism and anti-Marxism, metaphysics and science, individualism and
collectivism, consensus and conflict, theory and empiricism, rationality and irrationality, dialogue and discord. It also was situated in a space between traditional philosophy and its search for sure value and modern political theory cog-
nizant of deep human differences.

Famously, Mannheim identified a special role for intellectuals, controver-
sially asserting their standing outside the order of social stratification, thus offering them at least partial independence from conflicting positions in the public

---

30. In his famous lectures at the University of Munich in 1918 on "Politics as a Vocation" and
"Science as a Vocation," translated and published in Hans Gerth and C. Wright Mills, eds., *From
Max Weber: Essays in Sociology* (New York: Oxford University Press, 1946). Also see, Ahmad
Sadri, *Max Weber's Sociology of Intellectuals* (New York: Oxford University Press, 1992).

31. Given the 'in-between' character and placement of Mannheim's ideas in *Ideology and
Utopia*, his work was subjected to various sharp critiques: ranging from Marxists, including those
of the Frankfurt School, who found fault in his abandonment of their preferred versions of class
analysis to critics of what looked like his abandonment of a search for truth based on firm philosophical foundations. The former line of emphasis was expressed in a 1929 review by Herbert
Marcuse, "Zur Wahrheitsproblematik der soziologischen Methode," reprinted in Volker Meja
and Nico Stehr, eds., *Der Streit um die Wissenssoziologie* (Frankfurt: Suhrkamp, 1982). The latter
can be found in the two reviews published in the *American Sociological Review*: by Alexander von
Schelting, 4 (August 1936) and by Hans Speier 43 (July 1937).

32. "In my understanding," Mannheim wrote in an unpublished manuscript near the publication of *Ideology and Utopia*, I have discerned that liberalism is obsolete, but my attitudes are still
at a liberal level." Cited in Ashcraft, "Mannheim," p. 48.

33. For a discussion along such lines, see Willard A. Mullins, "Truth and Ideology: Reflections
on Mannheim's Paradox," *History and Theory*, 18 (May 1979).

sphere. Challenging intellectuals to an awareness of their potential role in producing a framework within which divergent views could contend without eradicating reason, Mannheim cautioned against a foundationless relativism despite the irretrievable loss of the vision of a unitary Enlightenment. The understanding "that all historical knowledge is relational knowledge, and can only be formulated with reference to the position of the observer,"[34] does not, he declared firmly, insinuate a lapse into relativism, a term that only can have meaning when juxtaposed to just the static and absolute notion of truth he rejected.[35]

Though Mannheim influenced some individual members of the political studies enlightenment, I underscore his themes and enjoinings in *Ideology and Utopia* less because he indirectly, and in some instances directly, shaped the work of Polanyi, Arendt, Truman, Hofstadter, Dahl, Lindblom, or Lasswell, but because this book quite precisely renders the conditions, program, challenges, difficulties, and potential pitfalls of the program they, too, advanced. If, under conditions of anxiety, disorganization, disappointment, institutional detachment, and uncertainty, as Mannheim then understood in 1929, intellectuals had both a special responsibility and an uncommon freedom, how much more true this was after 1945, especially in privileged American surroundings, where the First World War, but not the Second, had appeared as a mere pause on the pathway of enlightened, liberal optimism.[36] There, the political studies enlightenment powerfully elaborated Mannheim's revisionist social studies on a large scale.

III.

I have mentioned pitfalls, and there were more than a few. As a source of political knowledge, anxiety is two-edged. I have stressed its creative powers, but it carries more than a few dangers and distorting effects. These, alas, were espe-

---

34. Mannheim, *Ideology*, p. 71.

35. I have been guided in my understanding of Mannheim on these points by Harvey Goldman, "From Sociological Theory to Sociology of Knowledge and Back: Karl Mannheim and the Sociology of Intellectual Knowledge Production," *Sociological Theory*, 12 (November 1994).

36. By the conclusion of the period I am examining, American political knowledge had bifurcated between those who continued to see reason for anxiety and alarm and those who did not. Writing in 1956, Wishy contrasted the work of Arthur Schlesinger, Jr., Peter Viereck, David Riesman, John Kenneth Galbraith, and others whose "more open optimism is proclaimed . . . about the new promise of American life with others, including C. Wright Mills, Lewis Mumford, and Hannah Arendt who "are more stirred by the possibilities of the collapse and destruction of liberal-bourgeois democracy." Wishy, "Revolt," p. 243.

cially apparent when members of the political studies enlightenment engaged with social movements, with the national security state in an age of Cold War, and with deep-seated structural inequalities, especially those based on race. In the United States, collision with these uncomfortable realities often produced a combination of evasion about unappealing features of America's state, economy, and society and excessive alarm about mass political participation.

Of course, when Robert Dahl wrote in 1956 that "the full assimilation of Negroes into the normal system already has occurred in many northern states and now seems to be slowly to be taking place even in the South,"[37] putting a remarkably optimistic spin on the developments immediately following *Brown v. Board of Education*, he certainly was aware that Jim Crow and racism more generally were alive and well; and when Truman's long treatise wholly ignored the role of the military in American life, he knew a great deal about NSC-68 and the issues C. Wright Mills soon was to make so central to his spirited analysis of the role of the armed forces in American life.[38] It was not, I think, mainly the ideological or the ethical proclivities of this generation that pushed such key subjects into a zone of silence, although this did play a part, but the very character of some features of the liberal political theory they sought to develop to secure a vibrant nontotalitarian politics.

Some aspects of these theoretical limitations were noted effectively some time ago in a large and impressive body of critical literature. By focusing on actual behavior and decisions, the political scientists of this generation underestimated the system's skewed capacity to set agendas. Nor did they fully appreciate the biased qualities of actual participation along class lines.[39] But I think there is a deeper problem, whose roots can be found in Joseph Schumpeter's influential effort, which most of the American wing of the political studies enlightenment emulated, to find alternatives to the period's objectivist approaches, Marxist and otherwise, to stratification and hierarchy.[40]

---

37. Dahl, *A Preface to Democratic Theory* (Chicago: University of Chicago Press, 1956), vol. 1, pp. 138–139.

38. Mills, *The Power Elite*.

39. The relevant literature is massive. For pioneering work along these lines see E. E. Schattschneider, *The Semi-Sovereign People* (New York: Holt, 1960); Peter Bachrach and Morton S. Baratz, "The Two Faces of Power," *American Political Science Review*, 57 (December 1962); Grant McConnell, *Private Power and American Democracy* (New York: Knopf, 1966); and Theodore J. Lowi, *The End of Liberalism* (New York: Norton, 1969).

40. Joseph A. Schumpeter, *Capitalism, Socialism, and Democracy* (New York: Harper, 1942). Schumpeter devoted the first section of his book to a critical, but not wholly unsympathetic, account of Marx's writings, announcing, in effect, that he wished his book to be understood as an attempt to develop a surrogate at the same level of analysis.

Schumpeter's discussion of democracy proved particularly influential because it provided the postwar generation with unsentimental and hardheaded political foundations. At the height of the Second World War, he had agonized over the diminishing prospects of capitalism. Melancholic over what he thought was its inevitable dislocation by bureaucratic socialism, he had sought to salvage the prospect at least of a democratic socialism; but democracy of what kind? Not, he argued, the democracy of the classical doctrine grounded in the idea that the people decide on behalf of the realization of a common good. Government neither is premised on nor is a search for such a public interest. None exists. Rule by the people, moreover, is dangerous, because there is massive evidence against the rational capacity of the masses. "The typical citizen drops down to a lower level of mental performance as soon as he enters the political field. . . . He becomes a primitive again. His thinking becomes associative and affective."[41] Without the props of a common good or a rational public, Schumpeter proposed the role of the people be limited to the act of selecting a government every four or five years. Then they should get out of the way to let informed elites rule.

It was this highly elitist vision that Robert Dahl thought "excellent."[42] Its key elements, including a special role for elites, distrust of the mass, stress on procedures, and a rejection of simple notions of the public interest, trace unifying threads across many key texts about American politics in the postwar period. Truman and Dahl, however, were not pure Schumpeterians. They were committed not just to an elitist version of political liberalism, but to democracy including its participatory elements. "At minimum," Dahl wrote, as I have noted, "it seems to me, democratic theory is concerned with processes by which ordinary citizens exert a high degree of control over leaders"; and Truman focused on the play and conflict of interests in-between elections and outside of the electoral process.[43]

In spite of diverse points of entry and emphasis, not one member of the political studies enlightenment, to my knowledge, dissented from Schumpeter's search for a realistic alternative to the classical utopian theory of democracy, entailing a rejection of 'the people' as a meaningful category, not only because, empirically, no such singular entity sharing common interests actually can exist under modern conditions, but because a populist orientation risks making the people available for anti-liberal forms of political mobilization. Dahl's *A Preface*

---

41. Schumpeter, *Capitalism*, p. 262.
42. With the caveat that he disagreed with the notion, as an empirical matter, that elections and party activity are of little consequence in determining public policy. Dahl, *Preface*, p. 131.
43. Dahl, *Preface*, p. 3.

to Democratic Theory turned on just these points. He situated his preferred regime type of polyarchical democracy as a more desirable and hardheaded alternative to two other democratic models. The first he described as Madison's system, an orientation so concerned with the dangers of political participation and so distrustful of the people that it tilted too far in the direction of preserving "the liberties of certain minorities whose advantages of status, power, and wealth, he thought, probably would not be tolerated indefinitely by a constitutionally untrammeled minority." Madisonian democracy, he concluded, "goes about as far as it is possible to go while still remaining within the rubric of democracy." The second view Dahl labeled populistic democracy. Stressing the sovereignty of the majority, this model, he argued, runs afoul of the fact that citizens do not care intensely and equally about different issues. Nor does this approach sufficiently take into account goals that might compete with political equality and popular sovereignty. These two purposes, he argued, "are not absolute goals; we must ask ourselves how much leisure, privacy, consensus, stability, income, security, progress, status, and probably many other goals we are prepared to forego for an additional increment of political equality."[44]

Dahl crafted an alternative by transcending the antinomy of the majority versus the minority. In seeking a balance between normative maximization and empirical description, he insisted that in a diverse and complex world of multiple interests and identities there are no majorities, only many minorities, even minorities within minorities. "Hence we cannot correctly describe the actual operations of democratic societies in terms of the contrasts between majorities and minorities. We can only distinguish groups of various types and sizes, all seeking in various ways to advance their goals, usually at the expense, at least in part, of others."[45] This central feature of America's regime is what makes it normatively attractive and different from illiberal competitors. It also is the mainspring of stability.

Dahl's goal thus was not abstract equality or the sovereignty of the majority, but an attainable and desirable "political system in which all the active and legitimate groups in the population can make themselves heard at some crucial

---

44. For Dahl, populistic democracy is flawed for more than this set of ethical reasons. Unlike Madisonianism, it violates the requisite that liberal democratic theory be empirical as well as normative. As a set of aspirations which cannot be operationalized, "it tells us nothing about the real world" or about political behavior. It also is naive. It fails to define membership in the political system (who will be admitted and under what terms) or to recognize that "every society develops a ruling class." Even more important, it is insensitive to the fact that political preferences develop over time within the political process or that majorities are not fixed entities. Dahl, *Preface*, pp. 31, 32, 51, 54.
45. Dahl, *Preface*, p. 131.

stage in the process of decision." This, he hastened to add in his realist voice, does not mean "that every group has equal control over the outcome." Dahl's democracy is a system of endless bargaining in which "the making of governmental decisions is not a majestic march of great majorities united upon certain matters of basic policy. It is the steady appeasement of relatively small groups."[46] Dahl designed his next book, *Who Governs?*, to be an empirical investigation of just this system at work. In his community study site of New Haven, he found that inequalities were dispersed; majorities and coalitions were situational; intensities varied from issue to issue and from group to group; and the system contained enough slack so that those who wished to have influence could prove influential even under conditions of inequality in wealth, social position, and knowledge.[47] Later, he came to realize this, at best, was a partial view.[48]

Looking back in 1971, just three years after his response as provost to Columbia's upheavals effectively had cost him the university's presidency, first Truman elaborated on how he had closed his book with a paragraph concerning liberal democracy's "guardians and their affiliations" under conditions "of dissensus on the rules": "Neither the closing sentence of *The Governmental Process*," he wrote,[49]

> nor the pages that precede it assert that the system is self-corrective. On the contrary, the book contends that the essentials of the system are peculiarly in the custody of those in key governmental positions and those who occupy leading positions within the groups that make up the structure intervening between the government and the ordinary citizen. Such people are, in the technical and neutral sense of the term, elites. Given the ambiguity and dissensus on the rules, elite understanding and constructive action are essential to the continued vitality of the rules and to the survival of the system.

Truman then appended a remarkable statement. "In the subtle politics of developing emergency," he wrote, "the elites are, for all practical purposes, the people."

46. Dahl, *Preface*, pp. 137, 145, 146.
47. Robert A. Dahl, *Who Governs? Democracy and Power in an American City* (New Haven: Yale University Press, 1961). Most treatments of this book have debated its empirical and pluralist portrait of New Haven without sufficient attention to its tight linkage with the political theory of *A Preface to Democratic Theory*, nor to its realization of the larger anxious project of his generation of political scientists.
48. See Robert A. Dahl, *Dilemmas of Pluralist Democracy: Autonomy vs. Control* (New Haven: Yale University Press, 1982).
49. Truman, "Introduction to the Second Edition," *The Governmental Process* (New York: Knopf), p. xliv.

When Truman had turned in the conclusion to *The Governmental Process* to his fear of an American version of a politics of decay and revolution, he had focused on the problem posed by deep differences in values and political orientations which obtain when specific groups "arrive at interpretations of the 'rules of the game' that are at great variance with those held by most of the civilian population."[50] This unhappy circumstance is unlikely to arise, he observed, when citizens actually hold overlapping memberships in interest groups. After all, that is the purpose of this mechanism. He was forced to concede, however, that many Americans, especially at the bottom of the social hierarchies of class and race, do not possess such group memberships since, in fact, political participation is closely tied to social and economic inequality. As a result, many Americans, he conceded, are not integrated into the group system he so painstakingly had described. These unanchored, unincorporated citizens worried him a great deal. They are the most vulnerable, he hypothesized, to the appeals of anti-democratic ideologies and movements. Incredibly, Truman considered America's racial order, after virtually 520 pages of near-total silence on the subject, exclusively through the prism of these fears. His prose was tortured:[51]

> The appearance of groups representing Negroes, especially in the South, groups whose interpretations of the 'rules of the game' are divergent from those of the previously organized and privileged segments of the community, are a case in point. Caste and class interpretations of widespread unorganized interests may be at least a ready source of instability as conflicts between more restricted organized groups.

The problem with the emergent civil rights movement (this, in 1951!) was that it threatened the political stability of the system because it challenged the existing rules of the game. The value consensus required to keep the system on an even keel is "not threatened by the existence of a multiplicity of organized groups so long as the 'rules of the game' remain meaningful guides to action." But, of course, when excluded groups challenge their exclusion there can be no ready agreement on the status of the rules. "In the loss of such meanings," Truman cautioned with foreboding, "lie the seeds of the whirlwind."[52]

Two decades later, Truman did not back away from this passage. To the contrary, he celebrated it for having heralded "the complex and swiftly moving politics of the Northern ghettos: the scorn of the black militant for the apparent vagueness and even hypocrisy of the white liberal, the appeal of the Black Pan-

---

50. Truman, *Governmental Process*, p. 521.
51. Truman, *Governmental Process*, p. 523.
52. Truman, *Governmental Process*, p. 524.

thers, the discarding of black leaders without whose ability to work within the system the court decisions of the past two decades and the civil rights legislation of the 1960s would not have appeared, and the ugly shadow of the backlash." Blacks had dismissed the rules of the game "as 'whitey's' rules."[53] The whirlwind had come. In the aftermath of these developments in black America, but also in the aftermath of the New Left and the student movement, Truman insisted that "were I rewriting the book today I would give [the theme of elite responsibility in the face of the collapse of common meanings] considerably more prominence."[54]

Truman thus implied in 1951 and again in 1971 that it would be far better for the excluded to remain apolitical than challenge the dirty secrets of the country's liberal regime.[55] His fear of mass politics and political disorder contorted liberal democracy itself by treating disruption and protest under virtually all conditions, even those of the racially segregated South, as if they must stand outside the normal process of legitimate political participation. As a result, Truman found it difficult to distinguish movements he hated, such as the anti-communism of the radical right, from movements whose goals he admired, such as the struggle for civil rights, because he thought that collective action itself, as a form of politics, challenging the fairness of the rules of the game constituted a keen threat to political stability and the viability of liberal democracy.[56] Anxiety, it is all too clear, can conduce paralysis or worse.

IV.

If it is wrong to celebrate the political studies enlightenment while forgetting its lapses and silences about subjects like race,[57] so we should also remember that

---

53. Truman, "Introduction to the Second Edition," pp. xliii, xliv.
54. Truman, "Introduction to the Second Edition," pp. xliii, xliv.
55. I hasten, from personal interactions when he was Dean of Columbia College, where I was a student and he was my teacher, to add that I can attest that Truman held strong pro-civil rights views in the 1960s. He took positive note of the participation of students in civil rights protests in an address to alumni on 'Dean's Day,' February 5, 1966. David B. Truman, "The Causes and Nature of Student Unrest," in David B. Truman and Fritz Stern, "The Background of Student Unrest," pamphlet distributed by the Association of Alumni of Columbia College, 1966, pp. 26–27.
56. As David Greenstone demonstrated in his incisive, though not unsympathetic, reexamination of Dahl's New Haven cases, this orientation hardly was unique to Truman. J. David Greenstone, "Group Theories," in Fred Greenstein and Nelson Polsby, *Handbook of Political Science* (New York: Addison-Wesley, 1965).
57. I also have in mind Hannah Arendt's remarkably jarring disagreement with federal enforcement of the *Brown v. Board* program of racial desegregation in her "Reflections on Little Rock," *Dissent* 6 (Winter 1959) that found "discrimination" to be "as indispensable a social right as equality

with respect to some of the same issues its frames of reference permitted, even facilitated, rather different responses. The period's producers of political knowledge had choices to make. And they did choose. The year before Truman published his retrospective consideration on *The Governmental Process* refracted through the experiences of the civil rights and student movements of the 1960s, movements that transformed the United States vastly for the better, Richard Hoftstadter joined his New Left graduate student Michael Wallace to publish an incisive essay on 'Violence in America,' underscoring how "one is impressed that most American violence—and this also illuminates its relationship to state power—has been initiated with a 'conservative' bias. It has been unleashed against abolitionists, Catholics, radicals, workers, and labor organizers, Negroes, Orientals, and other ethnic or racial or ideological minorities. . . . A high proportion of our violent actions has thus come from the top dogs or the middle dogs."[58]

It is, of course, possible to include Arendt's consideration of Africa, particularly her silences about African history and agency, in a reasonable reckoning with the shortcomings of the postwar reconstruction of the tradition of Enlightenment, drawing, as she does at times, on the placement of Africa and its people in the "dark background of mere givenness."[59] But I am more impressed by the singular achievement for her time, albeit on terms now dated, that anticipated the new global history by incorporating colonialism and racism into the heart of European history. In so doing, "Imperialism," the central section of *The Origins of Totalitarianism*, heralded the most forceful and persuasive aspects of today's assault on simple, indefensible, Eurocentric versions of modernism. But rather than turn the dark side of Europe upside down as some postcolonial critics have been wont to do, as if it is remotely possible for anticolonial, antiracist projects to divorce themselves entirely from Europe in a global age, Arendt affirmed the assets of an enlightened and liberal Europe purged of exclusiveness, essentialism, and racism. At once analytical and literary, systematic and speculative, *Origins* still offers not only a model of how to look backwards without worshipping

---

is a political right.". Like Truman, Arendt supported civil rights, making this clear in 'preliminary remarks' to her article, stating, "I should make it clear that as a Jew I take my sympathy for the cause of the Negroes as for all oppressed and under-privileged peoples for granted and should appreciate it if the reader did likewise."

58. Richard Hofstadter and Michael Wallace, "Reflections on Violence in the United States," in Richard Hofstadter and Michael Wallace, eds., *American Violence: A Documentary History* (New York: Knopf, 1970), p. 11.

59. Hannah Arendt, *The Origins of Totalitarianism* (London: George Allen and Unwin, 1951), p. 301. A sharply critical assessment of Arendt's work along these lines is Anne Norton, "Heart of Darkness: Africa and African Americans in the Writings of Hannah Arendt, in Bonnie Honig, ed., *Feminist Interpretations of Hannah Arendt* (University Park: The Pennsylvania State University Press, 1995).

"the idol of origins," but also how to look forward, even in the face of desolation, crossing boundaries usually not traversed.[60]

Especially at moments when members of the political studies enlightenment found a critical voice in the manner of Arendt and Hofstadter, refusing to confuse fear for liberalism's fate with excuses for Europe or America's least attractive features, they defined a perspective that remains, today, an appealing, powerful, even indispensable guide. For this tradition reminds us that the darkest aspects of the human condition cannot be wished away, and that we must learn to fight, using all the normative and analytical tools at our command, for the kind of decent Enlightenment we should wish to have. At its best, too, the political studies enlightenment advised against too narrow a construction of democracy and against a self-complacent liberalism. More than a decade after the collapse of the last great totalitarian antagonist, and at a time of fresh desolation and often surprising threats to the best aspects of the West's enlightened patrimony, this counsel is especially germane.

---

60. I am struck by how some of the most thoughtful postcolonial voices are now reconsidering an engagement with the Enlightenment on terms that understand that the provenance of an idea does not necessarily dictate its worth. See, for rich examples, Nicholas B. Dirks, "Postcolonialism and its Discontents: History, Anthropology, and Postcolonial Critique," in Joan Scott and Debra Keates, eds., *Schools of Thought: Twenty-Five Years of Interpretive Social Science* (Princeton: Princeton University Press, 2001); David Scott, *Refashioning Futures: Criticism after Postcoloniality* (Princeton: Princeton University Press, 1999); Uday Singh Mehta, *Liberalism and Empire: A Study in Nineteenth-Century British Liberal Thought* (Chicago: University of Chicago Press, 1999); and Dipesh Chakrabarty, *Provincializing Europe: Postcolonial Thought and Historical Difference.* (Princeton: Princeton University Press, 2000).

INDEX